THE UNIVERSITY OF ARIZONA

GREGORY MCNAMEE

THE UNIVERSITY OF
ARIZONA

A History in 100 Stories

SENTINEL
PEAK

SENTINEL PEAK
An imprint of The University of Arizona Press
www.uapress.arizona.edu

We respectfully acknowledge the University of Arizona is on the land and territories of Indigenous peoples. Today, Arizona is home to twenty-two federally recognized tribes, with Tucson being home to the O'odham and the Yaqui. Committed to diversity and inclusion, the University strives to build sustainable relationships with sovereign Native Nations and Indigenous communities through education offerings, partnerships, and community service.

ISBN-13: 978-1-941451-14-4 (paperback)
ISBN-13: 978-1-941451-13-7 (ebook)

Cover design by Leigh McDonald
Cover photograph by Antonio Villagomez
Designed and typeset by Leigh McDonald in Garamond Premiere Pro 11/15 and Proxima Nova (display)

Library of Congress Cataloging-in-Publication Data
Names: McNamee, Gregory, author.
Title: The University of Arizona : a history in 100 stories / Gregory McNamee.
Description: Tucson : Sentinel Peak, an imprint of the University of Arizona Press, 2024. | Includes index.
Identifiers: LCCN 2024005294 (print) | LCCN 2024005295 (ebook) | ISBN 9781941451144 (paperback) | ISBN 9781941451137 (ebook)
Subjects: LCSH: University of Arizona—History.
Classification: LCC LD193 .M36 2024 (print) | LCC LD193 (ebook) | DDC 378.791/776—dc23/eng/20240619
LC record available at https://lccn.loc.gov/2024005294
LC ebook record available at https://lccn.loc.gov/2024005295

Printed in the United States of America
♾ This paper meets the requirements of ANSI/NISO Z39.48-1992 (Permanence of Paper).

CONTENTS

THE UNIVERSITY OF ARIZONA

The Turtle Pond on the northwest edge of campus. Photograph by David Olsen.

INTRODUCTION

O N A quiet corner of the campus of the University of Arizona, in one of the oldest sections of its thirty-three-acre Historic District, stands a small oasis, always a welcome thing in the desert. At its center is a shallow pond, a hundred or so feet in circumference, populated by koi and red-eared turtles, the latter of which are fond of clambering up and down the pond's gabbro walls. Surrounded by palm trees and stands of native grass, the Turtle Pond is a lure for herons, cardinals, owls, all sorts of bird life. For humans, it is a place of solace and reflection that hides in plain sight: many pass by, but fewer stop, a solitude that I welcomed when I sat alongside the pond almost daily to read Dostoyevsky, Aeschylus, Lévi-Strauss—and especially when I took comfort there in the jittery hours after an air force jet crashed on the corner of Highland Avenue and Sixth Street on October 26, 1978.

Renovated in 2023, the Turtle Pond seems as if it has been there since time immemorial, but that's not quite so. The land on which it stands was once on the grounds of the home built for the first president of the University, Theodore B. Comstock, in 1893. The pond, facing out on a then-dirt Park Avenue, was not added until 1933, only three years before the President's House—a handsome two-story Victorian structure—was demolished to make room for the Gila Hall undergraduate dormitory. Fortunately, the Turtle Pond, also known as the President's Pond, survived the transformation, having already become a favorite retreat for students.

Wander through that old campus, and you'll find hidden arbors, narrow passageways, secret tunnels, and buildings from the first years of the University. At the heart of that wonderland is Old Main, graced with another water feature, a fountain inaugurated in 1920 to honor thirteen students who gave their lives on the battlefields of World War I. Old Main is the oldest surviving building on campus, and it is there that our story begins.

But not quite yet, not before a touch of backstory. When Abraham Lincoln signed the Morrill Land-Grant Act into law in 1862, Arizona was too wild and woolly yet to harbor even the idea of a university. The question of where to establish such an institution did not enter into wide discussion until the site of the territorial capital was settled: first Prescott, then Tucson, then Prescott again, and finally Phoenix, which claimed both the capital and the territorial insane asylum, leaving Tucson with something of a consolation prize, a university that had yet to be funded or have a single brick laid.

That was all to Tucson's gain in time, although some of the inhabitants didn't quite see it that way—local boosters still smarted at the loss of the legislature to the much younger upstart cow town to the north and made their displeasure known. For its part, the legislature was immediately tightfisted when it came to funding the new school. (A miserly attitude toward higher education is, in Arizona as elsewhere, a frequent legislative leitmotif.) Building local financial and political support for the University was a matter of sometimes delicate negotiation, but the effort quickly took, thanks in large measure to Jacob S. Mansfeld, Selim M. Franklin, Mose Drachman, and other persuasive and generous residents of Tucson.

Selim Franklin, Tucson attorney, politician, and one of the founders of the University of Arizona.

The months and years passed after the University was officially founded on March 12, 1885, and funds were secured. Preceded by a boiler house and a barn, Old Main was built and dedicated in 1891, and after it, one by one, came greenhouses, a couple of cottages, the aforementioned President's House, more greenhouses, an aviary, and other structures. Only Old Main stands to bear testimony to that time, when the University settled into its mission and opened its doors to students.

The first class of three students, graduating in 1895, was much younger on average than the student body today. Charles Oma Rouse, for instance, was just fourteen and a half when he enrolled. After earning his law degree, he served as the school superintendent for Pima County until his untimely death at twenty-nine. Mercedes A. Shibell was fifteen, and on leaving school she worked as an expert in food management and logistics, advising the U.S. military in France during World War I. Happily, she lived to be ninety, long enough to be honored at the University's seventy-fifth anniversary. Born in Scotland and the daughter of the University's groundskeeper, Mary F. Walker was seventeen. She also participated in that anniversary celebration.

There were fewer students in that first graduating class than there were members of the Arizona Board of Regents and the faculty, by one and two, respectively. It wasn't long before the imbalance was remedied with the recruitment of more students. More than half of them were women, for in those progressive days, the framers of Arizona's constitution specified that women were to be admitted to the University from the start. (By contrast, Yale University admitted women as undergraduates only in 1969.) The women students were exempted from the mandatory military drills and courses in tactics, but otherwise the curriculum was narrowly defined, with nothing in the way of electives. In the agriculture course of study, for instance, all students took algebra, geometry, trigonometry, and chemistry—and, for reasons that seem a touch obscure, both French and German. In their senior year, they even took a course in canning and otherwise preserving fruits, along with a trimester of veterinary science. Students of engineering were required to take the same course in agricultural law as their agriculture-destined peers, while the mining course of study added mechanics, surveying, geology, and metallurgy to the mix. All students took periodic classes in what the 1891 catalog calls "English studies," but it was expected that they had a handle already on subjects such as history, arithmetic, writing (that is, the ability "to write legibly and spell simple common words correctly"), and drawing; students who lacked that formal education, many from rural communities and ranches, were offered a yearlong "preparatory course" to address any shortcomings. Oddly, perhaps, the University now specified that enrollees had to be at least sixteen years old, despite the academic success of that first class.

The University's first presidents concerned themselves with the literal business of institution building: constructing classrooms, dormitories, offices, laboratories, a library, and the like, and then filling them with growing numbers of students and teachers. While the University followed the German model that assumed professors would conduct research in their respective fields, the emphasis was on teaching—mostly at the undergraduate level for

Tucson in 1909. If you look closely, you can find Old Main in the middle of the image.

the first few decades, with graduate courses added as various departments grew into schools and colleges.

So it continued for decades. Then, with the dawn of the space race, two things converged that would transform the University of Arizona from a teaching school to a world-class research institution. One was a massive influx of federal funds into research of practically every variety, especially anything remotely connected to space sciences. The other was a far-seeing president named Richard A. Harvill, a brilliant and popular professor of economics here until being named to head the University in 1951. Harvill was an institution builder par excellence, and he seemingly had no off button: wherever a person turned around, there was an academic department being shored up, a new doctoral program being established, a new building rising. In his two decades as president, in fact, nearly four dozen buildings went up, including the Lunar and Planetary Laboratory, augmenting Arizona's long standing as a powerhouse of astronomical research. In Harvill's time as president, the University of Arizona Press (UA Press) was created, KUAT-TV went online, and millions on millions of dollars in grants came flowing in. The result was the remaking of the entire university, hitherto strong in anthropology, agriculture, geology, and space sciences but with otherwise mostly middling departments not widely known to the rest of the scholarly world—a very far cry from the excellence of nearly every academic unit today. Librarian Phyllis Ball did some back-of-the-envelope calculations, and the Harvill-era numbers are striking: the student population when he began as president in 1951 was 5,700, a figure that nearly quintupled to 26,500 in 1971, his last year. Harvill closed out his career by awarding diplomas to the first graduating class of the College of Medicine, created through his efforts over many years.

Richard Harvill's program of growth was continued—and at an even more productive pace—by his successor, John P. Schaefer, a professor of chemistry who, at just thirty-six years of age, was appointed to the presidency in 1971 after serving as dean of the College of Liberal Arts. Schaefer's hand was in dozens of major improvements, from buildings such as the Main Library and the Flandrau Science Center & Planetarium to hiring first-rate faculty members and leveraging existing strengths, such as emphasizing cancer and heart disease research at the University. (It's no coincidence that the world's first artificial heart came about during his tenure at the University, for Schaefer saw to it that the funding was available for it and made sure that the inventor, Dr. Jack Copeland, had the support he needed.) Schaefer also approved the building of what is now called the McKale Memorial Center, for many years the largest indoor collegiate arena in the country, and helped secure funding for the new Southwest Institute for Research on Women, both featured in the pages that follow. His name turns up often in the narrative, and for very good reason: if Jacob Mansfeld was the University's founding father, and attorney and territorial legislator Selim Franklin its godfather, John Schaefer is the visionary chief architect of the University of Arizona that we know today. Honoring both his skill at the art form and his creation of the entity, as we will also see, the Center for Creative Photography on campus bears his name.

It's always tempting to think that the golden age has just missed us today, and certainly John Schaefer's successor, Henry Koffler, might have felt that. Koffler came to the presidency in 1982, the first full year in which the federal government, with Ronald Reagan—always mistrustful of higher education—at its helm, began to slash university-bound funding. The state legislature, only rarely generous to begin with, tightened its fist. Even with that limited support, however, Koffler grew undergraduate enrollment by a full third, established support units to help ensure the retention and academic success of minority students, and oversaw the expansion of the main campus and satellite campuses and the construction of such iconic structures as the Gould-Simpson Building and, yes, the John P. Schaefer Center for Creative Photography in its present home in the Fine Arts Complex.

John Schaefer credits the creation, under Richard Harvill's presidency, of the Institute of Atmospheric Physics (IAP) as the spark—or perhaps lightning bolt—that fired the University's evolution into a research powerhouse. It's worth noting that while the chief work of that unit was carried out by physicists and meteorologists, as the name suggests, many of its contributions have drawn on the insights of hydrologists, geologists, climatologists, plant scientists, geographers, historians, and ethnographers. The IAP was made possible through federal funds from the forerunner of the National Science Foundation (NSF). Federal grants being once mysterious things in the world of land-grant colleges, Schaefer draws a moral of sorts over Harvill's vigorous championing, writing, "Federal resources available to the sciences offered the University of Arizona an opportunity to develop far beyond the potential means that the State could or would provide." Leading that charge with Harvill was A. Richard (Dick) Kassander Jr., a physicist who was both a gifted scholar and a skillful administrator. Dick Kassander, first as the IAP's head and, in 1972, as the university's first vice president for research, helped oversee the expansion of the school's programs in scientific areas such as planetary sciences and hydrology. As John Schaefer would later remark, "Dick was the kind of visionary we needed at that time. He appreciated what research was all about and why it was important for the University to make its mark there." Joining the effort with tireless enthusiasm was Albert B. Weaver, provost for academic affairs, who was committed to hiring the very best faculty across the board and building outstanding programs. Fittingly, the University's Albert B. Weaver Science-Engineering Library is named in his honor.

That collective impetus, then, led to the spectacular growth of the sciences at the University—though Harvill, Schaefer, and Koffler worked diligently to send funds toward the arts, social sciences, and humanities as well. But something else happened in the process:

scholars discovered that their work benefited from collaboration across disciplines, as evidenced by IAP. In the last half century, indeed, many of the most extraordinary intellectual developments on campus have been interdisciplinary in origin and nature, as when chemists, engineers, and physicians collaborate to develop implantable heart tissue, and philosophers, neurologists, and biologists work together to discern the innermost workings of the human mind. It's worth noting that John Schaefer, though trained in the sciences, taught humanities courses during his time as dean. In that interdisciplinary spirit, the current College of Humanities leads the way in "digital humanities," the application of the most modern technology to ancient questions of what makes us human. And the Confluencenter for Creative Inquiry, founded in 2010, provides a home for interdisciplinary collaboration in the arts, humanities, and social sciences, funding projects that, for example, join multimedia art with the study of climate change and that examine how borders and divisions separate people—but sometimes bring them together as well, as viewed through the lenses of art, history, geography, law, and language.

Diversity of intellect thrives on diversity of people. Just as two of the first three graduates of the University were women, so too are women are contributing to and leading every discipline, every department, every unit. There is work yet to do there, particularly in recruitment and retention and the ever-pressing problem of equal pay. The University has also led the way in building academic programs and faculties, as well as a student body, that well represents Native American communities. The noted Lakota attorney and writer Vine Deloria Jr. founded the first master's degree program in American Indian studies in 1982. The first Native American to be tenured in anthropology, the first Native American to receive a master of fine arts degree, the first Native American judge—all these firsts occurred at the University of Arizona. The first Black head coach in university-level college basketball, Fred Snowden, began the process of turning the Wildcats into a national contender. The first major contingent of students from the newly independent nation of Kazakhstan studied here in the early 1990s, while the faculty and student body alike represent every continent and most of the countries of the world.

Diversity of intellect, diversity of people—all require financial generosity. As I said, our state's legislators have often been less than free spending when it comes to higher education, rejecting, for instance, a recommendation in 2023 by a committee of leading businesspeople to raise taxes to support the state's universities and community colleges. The costs these days are staggering—though, we might note, the University of Arizona is less expensive than most land-grant institutions and has been vigorous in extending scholarships and financial aid to students, including tuition waivers for Native American students enrolled in any of the state's twenty-two tribes. Yet, owing to the now apparently forgotten requirement of article

II, section 6 of Arizona's constitution that "the instruction furnished shall be as nearly free as possible," tuition was for a long while even less expensive by far: during my undergraduate years, I paid the modern equivalent of $1,310 a semester for a full course load, about one-sixth of the annual cost in-state students pay today. At the risk of mooning nostalgically for that aforementioned golden age, let me add only that with a part-time job I could pay for tuition, books, off-campus housing (albeit on the rough-and-tumble side), and gas, and without taking out a single loan. We owe the students of today the same opportunity, and it would be a fine thing if our alumni could build consensus on the point and get some legislative weight behind it.

But that's a matter for the future, and in many ways the future appears to be bright—at least as bright as it can be in a time of political turmoil and a rapidly changing climate. (University of Arizona researchers, of course, are working on solutions to both problems even as I write.) Made up of forty-four colleges and schools, the University ranks among the top twenty research institutions in the United States. A biosciences innovation hub is rising in downtown Phoenix, which can be only improved with a Wildcat presence. Inventions are flowing from the UA Tech Park, which has recently been graced with several start-up firms from Ukraine, one of which is developing batteries from renewable materials. In 2023, the University was named the number-one school in the United States for producing Fulbright Scholars, carrying the name of the University around the world. A tribal microcampus, the first of many to come, opened that year to serve the Pascua Yaqui community. In 2022, the University's first-year class was the most ethnically diverse in the school's history, including a Lati-

A red-eared turtle surveys the domain of the Turtle Pond. Photograph by David Olsen.

na/o population of nearly 25 percent of the total student enrollment of 45,000, and with the highest average GPA ever at 3.67. They deserve every bit of support, material and intellectual, that we can give them, for, though it's a truism, it's an important one: they are our future. I wish them all, and those who come after them, nothing but success and happiness—and plenty of visits to the Turtle Pond.

For the time being, let us embark on a meandering and, I hope, pleasant journey across time and space. This book is a celebration of scholarly accomplishments, student excellence, contributions to the knowledge and well-being of the world, and the broad range of people who made them all possible—a rich combination that has held true since the very beginning of the school's history, a history that, in the pages that follow, will take us from a small brick-and-stone building in a sea of dust to an intellectual center of worldwide importance.

Our tour of the University of Arizona begins with its setting, cultural, natural, and historical. It then turns to the four disciplines (interdisciplinary disciplines at that) that formed the earliest intellectual pillars of the University: agriculture, earth sciences, astronomy, and anthropology. Some of our later stops will be thematic, calling on medicine, the humanities, languages, athletics, and many of the other sciences in which Arizona excels—a host of topics that together provide a wealth of knowledge on every conceivable subject, the universe hidden within the word "university," so vitally present at every turn and corner of our campus and our desert heartland. And some of our stops will be to visit favorite places and moments, whether the University's ever-growing libraries or thrilling moments on the playing field. Onward!

"Let us establish an institution of learning, where for all time to come the youth of the land may learn to become better citizens than we are, and all our shortcomings will be forgotten in a misty past and we will be remembered for this one great achievement."

—SELIM FRANKLIN

Old Main, the oldest building on campus. Photograph by David Olsen.

THE SETTING

If you look out from a western window of the University's tallest buildings, you'll see, just a couple of miles distant, the serpentine Santa Cruz River, the reason for Tucson's very being. Since time immemorial, the river has supported the O'odham people, whose forerunners were growing maize under the shadow of "A" Mountain five thousand and more years ago and who gave Tucson its name: "black base," referring to the peak's dark basalt. Part of the Spanish Empire and then Mexico, Tucson was long an entrepôt of trade and local culture—and, thanks to a small group of visionary citizens in the late nineteenth century, the home of what would become a great university. The natural setting of the University of Arizona is just one of its treasures—and once the desert gets into your blood, as many Wildcats have discovered, it never leaves.

ON NATIVE GROUND

The Native American Land Acknowledgment

T HAS been the work of generations of anthropologists, archaeologists, geneticists, linguists, and paleontologists to establish the fact that the human settlement of the Americas has a very long history, a history that University of Arizona scholars have long taken the lead in developing. And while the chronology of settlement is constantly being extended and reframed—it was once received wisdom that humans arrived here ten thousand years ago, but the timeline now stands at twenty-five thousand years and will doubtless be pushed further back in time—it is a matter of record that the first humans to arrive were the ancestors of today's Native American peoples.

The University of Arizona honors that long history with a sixty-one-word affirmation:

> We respectfully acknowledge the University of Arizona is on the land and territories of Indigenous peoples. Today, Arizona is home to 22 federally recognized tribes, with Tucson being home to the O'odham and the Yaqui. Committed to diversity and inclusion, the University strives to build sustainable relationships with sovereign Native Nations and Indigenous communities through education offerings, partnerships, and community service.

The principal homeland on which the University of Arizona stands is that of the Desert People, the Tohono O'odham, who have been here for millennia. Tucson is also home to the Pascua Yaqui Tribe, established after Yaqui people from Sonora fled genocide during the years preceding the Mexican Revolution, while the University medical complex in Phoenix stands on lands historically belonging to the Akimel O'odham, the People of the Flowing Water. But recognition of the other nineteen entities goes beyond a mere formality: it commemorates both the fact that the University is active everywhere in the state, on lands belonging to those many groups, and that people from all of them are members of the University's faculty, staff, student body, and alumni.

Formalized in 2021 with the participation of many Indigenous scholars and leaders, the land acknowledgment takes the idea of our University's origins as a land-grant institution and, in just a few words, deepens the idea of what a land grant has truly meant in Arizona history. A permanent exhibit of tribal flags in the University of Arizona BookStore gives further expression to our debt, impossible to repay fully, to those who came before.

Tribal flags at the Student Union Bookstore. The twenty-two flags on display honor Arizona's Native nations. Photograph by David Olsen.

IN THE BEGINNING

Old Main

"WHAT DO we want with a university? What good will it do us? Who in hell ever heard of a university professor buying a drink?" So, reported early settler Mose Drachman, was the sentiment of Tucsonans when, having lost their bid to relocate the capital here, the city was awarded the University of Arizona and a $25,000 appropriation for it, thanks in large part to the efforts of a twenty-five-year-old Tucsonan in the territorial legislature, Selim Franklin. It took a while for the animosity to die down, by which time the first regent, Jacob Mansfeld, had convinced three landowners to donate forty acres as the site of the school. On October 27, 1887, ground was broken for its first building. Four years later, construction had yet to be completed, for the $25,000 was exhausted, and the regents had to ask the state legislature for another appropriation that allowed them to put a roof on the building and install windows. Thus, five years after the original appropriation, was the first home of the School of Mines created, and with the hiring of a professor of agriculture, Frank A. Gulley, and a dean of mining, Theodore Comstock, the University of Arizona opened its doors on October 1, 1891.

For several years, Old Main—a name that became official only in 1927—was the sole building on campus, serving as a combination of classrooms, auditorium, dining hall, laboratory, library, student dorm, and faculty housing. Designed by a Canadian architect named James Miller Creighton, who built the rococo Pinal County Courthouse in Florence and numerous hotels in Phoenix, Old Main was done in a kind of style that architectural historians call a "territorial hybrid," with a wraparound porch. Unusually for Tucson, given its

Jacob S. Mansfeld, the principal founder of the University of Arizona.

hardpan soil, the building had a basement. Recalled Creighton, "We had to cut corners in those days. We sank the structure six feet below the surface so the ground itself would help support the building."

In 1895, the University's first graduating class, made up of three students who had entered as early as the age of fourteen, marched out of Old Main. Soon other buildings began to pop up on campus, including Herring Hall and two extensive greenhouses. As the campus grew, Old Main slowly fell into disrepair, so much so that it was condemned and slated for demolition in 1938. The onset of World War II, though, meant an expanded need for officer training, and the building was spared to house the candidates. It was long after associated with the Reserve Officers' Training Corps (ROTC), whose offices were located there, with Old Main serving as the site of a good-natured snowball fight between future military leaders and antiwar protestors in December 1971.

Upkeep of the building scarcely improved until, in April 1972, it was listed in the National Register of Historic Places. Soon after, the second floor was extensively remodeled and became the longtime domain of the dean of students, while ROTC retained its offices in the basement. In the half century since, the building has undergone several upgrades, with the most extensive of them completed in 2014 under the direction of Tucson architecture firm Poster Frost Mirto, one of whose consultants rightly called the building "the heart and soul of the University." Fittingly, the historic building now houses the office of the University's president.

Old Main did not please every viewer, even when it was new. Rosemary Taylor, the daughter of Mose and Ethel Drachman, recounts in her 1943 memoir, *Chicken Every Sunday*, that when she was very young, "Tucson's university consisted of one extremely ugly brick building and two stone dormitories, set down in the midst of the mesquite and cactus about two miles from the center of town." When Mose Drachman bought land at $4 an acre adjacent to the campus, Ethel asked why on earth he would want property "way out there in the country." Mose replied that he'd carved up the property into lots, forming the basis of the historic West University neighborhood and making a handsome profit in the bargain. Rosemary went on to attend the University, and the Drachman name has long figured prominently in the history of town and gown alike.

A TUCSON LANDMARK

"A" Mountain

FOR EONS, a craggy black peak has stood on the western end of Tucson's present-day downtown, looming above the site of an ancient O'odham village and the site of the first Spanish settlement. (The mountain used to perch atop the Santa Catalinas, many miles distant, but that's another story, one puzzled out by University of Arizona geologists back in the 1970s.) When Americans arrived in number in the 1860s, the mountain did service as a heliograph station, a technology with which soldiers sent signals from mountaintop to mountaintop using sunlight, mirrors, and secret codes. For that reason, the low mountain was called Sentinel Peak.

That changed in 1914, when an undergraduate civil engineering student and varsity football player, Albert H. Condron, suggested to a professor that as a class project Sentinel Peak be surveyed in order to find a location for a giant "A"—to celebrate a gridiron victory over Pomona College on Thanksgiving Day of that year. The professor approved the project, and Condron, now president of the student body, set about collecting donations from students and alumni, an effort helped along by a generous stake from the noted Tucson portrait photographer Al Buehman.

Over fourteen Saturdays in the winter and early spring of 1915 and 1916, University students laid out an outline for an "A" that would extend 160 feet up and down the slope and 70 feet across, dug a deep trench, filled it with heavy volcanic rocks that they cleared from the mountainside, and then hauled cement and water up the steep rise by means of horses and buckboard wagons. On the final Saturday, March 4, 1916, President Rufus B. von KleinSmid canceled all classes (there were Saturday classes until John Schaefer became president in 1971) and encouraged every student to pitch in on the final work of building a two-foot-tall concrete frame for the "A" and then whitewashing the completed structure—which, the *Arizona Wildcat* proudly reported, could be seen from the far side of the Tucson valley thirty miles away. The "A" has been well tended ever since, and it's still a hallmark of our city.

The total cost of building "A" Mountain, the name by which the former Sentinel Peak has been known ever since, was reported to be $397, or about $11,330 today—quite the bargain, considering all the work involved. For his part, Albert Condron, a native of Los Angeles, went on to have a distinguished career as a developer and planner. A few years after graduating in 1916, he was appointed Tucson's city manager, and while in office he planned and built Tucson's first airport and many arterial streets still in use today. He also dreamed up La Fiesta de Vaqueros and its motorless Rodeo Day parade, inaugurated in 1925, which Tucsonans still celebrate every February—and which until recently earned University students a day off.

HOME IS THE DESERT

The Joseph Wood Krutch Garden

E VERYTHING IN the desert bites. If it does not bite, it stings. Or it stinks, or stabs, or
stains—or stalks away. The desert, dry, austere, full of strange-shaped plants like the
chain cholla and the boojum tree, seems singularly uninviting, as if to say, well, you've
seen quite enough of me, now go away.

This is what so many visitors to the desert have thought, anyway, gazing out train and
car and plane windows on the way to the green climes of either coast. It took an East Coast
bookworm to change their minds, a man who, without ever having really planned it that
way, transformed himself into a preeminent desert rat and a great defender of a Tucson that
has mostly since disappeared.

Joseph Wood Krutch (his last name rhymes with *pooch*) was born in 1898 in Knoxville,
Tennessee. After teaching English in high school and serving in World War I, he began
writing, and eventually he became the drama critic for the *Nation*, one of the country's most
important cultural magazines. In 1950, though long identified with the cultural life of New
York City, Krutch packed up his books and made off for the improbable locale of Tucson,
where he and his wife, Marcelle, bought a five-acre parcel of land surrounded by a thick
saguaro forest. On that then-remote property, now on the campus of Tucson Medical Center, Krutch cultivated a delightful garden made up of native and exotic cacti and succulents,
as well as trees and flowers from the surrounding Sonoran Desert.

Joseph Wood Krutch spent the last two decades of his life in that desert home near the
Rillito at a time when the population of Tucson was a sixth of what it is today. He kept pretty

Saguaro blossoms in the Joseph Wood Krutch Memorial Garden. Photograph by Gregory McNamee.

much to himself, but he did turn up from time to time as a speaker at local business lunches and the like, where, anticipating Edward Abbey and the environmentalists who followed, he shocked boosters by urging that they stop promoting Tucson and instead work on keeping the town small. They didn't comply.

Joseph Wood Krutch died in 1970. His desert home stood intact for a few years, and then the bulldozers arrived. It's small consolation to desert lovers, perhaps, but one of the prettiest gardens in Tucson, a small but diverse collection of desert plants at the University of Arizona, commemorates him. It contains trees and cacti that have been growing there for more than a century, well before Krutch arrived here, but somehow it seems fitting that he should be a tutelary spirit for them.

Named in the writer's honor in 1980, the Joseph Wood Krutch Garden is far older than its name. One of the first features on the campus at its founding was a small cactus garden, which once stood in front of Old Main, planted by a professor of botany named James W. Toumey. He moved on to Yale University, where he founded its famous School of Forestry, and his garden was tended by volunteers and students, as well as University groundskeepers. In 1929, the garden was moved from the west side of Old Main to the east side, and the following year the noted biologist and explorer Godfrey Sykes planted boojum trees that he had brought up from Baja California, Mexico. Over the years, the garden grew larger and larger to the east, taking up what is now the Mall all the way to the present-day Albert B. Weaver Science-Engineering Library.

In 1950—the year Krutch moved to Tucson—construction began on the Student Union, and the cactus garden was scaled far back, with a few specimens moved to an area in front of Bear Down Gym. By 1967, only a patch of the Mall was still planted with cacti, populated by a few survivors from the original cactus garden after the Mall was seeded with grass. The present garden, located on the Mall directly south of the Alumni Plaza, contains numerous Sonoran Desert plants, including saguaros, organ-pipe cactus, agaves, acacias, night-blooming cereus, and mesquite trees, making it an island honoring the natural beauty of our arid home.

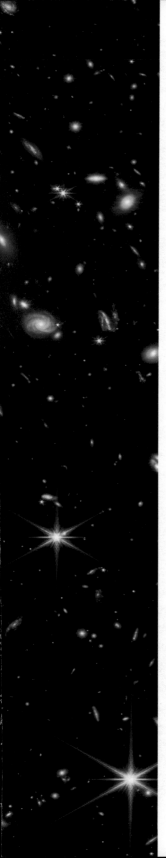

THE FOUR PILLARS

Like that of Tucson, its desert home, the story of the University of Arizona begins with agriculture. To that discipline, geology and mining were immediately added, speaking to the fact that Arizona's economy was historically long dependent on extracting minerals and ores from the earth. Both agriculture, a gathering of disciplines that embrace everything from economics to plant pathology, and those earth sciences remain central to the University today. Along with them, the University has excelled in two other foundational disciplines: astronomy and anthropology, both of which are definitively interdisciplinary—and both of which have spread the University's name out into the world and the universe. Think of these four as the pillars on which the University of Arizona has so carefully been built over fifteen decades.

RAISING ARIZONA

The College of Agriculture, Life & Environmental Sciences

FOUR OF the five vaunted Cs that underlie Arizona's traditional economy—copper, cotton, cattle, citrus, and climate—have to do with agriculture. It's no surprise, then, that the state's premier and oldest land-grant institution should have its deepest roots, beg pardon, in farming and livestock growing. For generations, the University of Arizona has trained farmers, livestock growers, agronomists, food scientists, analysts, soil scientists, agricultural economists, and other workers in every aspect of the business of bringing food and other agricultural products to market and table.

Neither is it a surprise, given all this, that the very first permanent faculty member hired by the University of Arizona, way back in 1890, was a Michigan transplant named Frank Gulley, who succeeded the temporarily appointed Selim Franklin, an attorney with no relevant experience but whose presence qualified the University to apply for federal grants. Named professor of agriculture by the Board of Regents at an annual salary of $3,300 (about $140,000 today), Gulley was charged not only with establishing a curriculum in agriculture but also with heading the University's experimental farm. Gulley worked alone for a year, energetically throwing himself into the construction of what would become Old Main and a couple of outbuildings while sketching out a program of instruction, writing bulletins for distribution to farmers, securing funds for research projects, and establishing experimental farms in Phoenix, Tempe, and Yuma.

In 1891, Gulley wrote to an acquaintance in Texas to ask if he might recommend someone to head the newly established School of Mines. That acquaintance, Theodore Comstock, nominated himself, and Gulley arranged for him to be hired as a colleague with equal power as professor and dean, even granting Comstock a higher salary than his own on the rationale that mining engineers earned more than farmers on the open market.

Alas, Comstock repaid the favor by lobbying the Board of Regents to name him president, a title Gulley had refused as being too grandiose for a school that barely existed except on paper. The board acceded, and Comstock immediately set about easing Gulley out of his position. (No one ever said that academic politics was nice.) Gulley left to become an executive for a succession of agricultural firms, finally ending up as the head of a chicken farm across the Mississippi River from Saint Louis. He died in 1939, barely remembered. Comstock's tenure as president lasted only a year, when he, too, left Tucson for a business position in Los Angeles, dying there in 1915.

Before leaving, Gulley had sunk a couple of deep wells and established gardens around Old Main, and in 1895, the year after he left, an eighty-foot-long greenhouse rose to join a couple of smaller ones. Botany students helped put in a cactus garden on the other side of the main building. Meanwhile, agriculture classes were taught wherever there were available spaces. Complained a professor named William Stowe Devol, "There has been but little addition to the facilities for instruction during the past year. . . . The department is very much hampered in its work because of some very urgent needs which it is not able to supply." After channeling federal funds earmarked for research to pay for some basic costs for the college, Devol lost his job by order of Arizona's governor.

The classroom situation was remedied in 1915, when, following two years of construction, a home was built for the College of Agriculture, due south of Old Main. Later named for the first dean of the college, Robert H. Forbes, the building is still in use, emblazoned from the start with the legend "Research—Education—Extension." That mission was well served by a growing faculty, notable among its early members a botanist named John James (J. J.) Thornber, who taught for half a century while riding the ranges and farms and cataloging native grasses, plants that were dangerous to cattle, and other useful subjects. So solid was the early faculty, in fact, that other agricultural schools, including Stanford University and the University of Iowa, regularly lured Arizona professors away, as did the U.S. Department of Agriculture (USDA). The college also had to fend off forays from the school to the north, for Tempe Normal School, later Arizona State University, made several efforts through the legislature to move it to Tempe. And so important was agriculture to the state and the University that it was no mere symbolism that the office of the president was for many years located inside the College of Agriculture.

A grain field flourishes in Maricopa, Arizona, site of one of the UA's experimental farms.
Photograph by Gregory McNamee.

The college had brought its tripartite mission to its hometown in 1909, when it purchased an eighty-acre parcel about four miles north of campus near the Rillito River. The Campbell Avenue Farm, as it's known today, was originally devoted to dairy production, and it retains that function while serving as a laboratory for livestock research. It even hosts a store where one can buy meat and other goods produced on the property. The Campbell Avenue Farm is but one of the dozen-odd college farms around the state at sites selected for climate, growing conditions, and specialized studies, such as the ongoing research in drought-resistant plants being conducted at the research farm in Maricopa. (See the entry for the TERRA project.) One of those facilities is just across the street from the Campbell Avenue Farm, called Tucson Village Farm, where young people learn how to grow organic produce in an urban setting.

The College of Agriculture spawned several other institutions as it grew. One was the Department of Home Economics, which calved off on its own in 1959. It is now called the Department of Nutritional Sciences. The college also added graduate programs over the years, with a master's degree course of study established in 1940. Now called the College of Agriculture, Life & Environmental Sciences, the school continues to develop its mission.

Incidentally, one of the great contributions of the college's extension and research functions was the development of so-called Pima cotton, a plant that yields a high-quality, strong fiber used in the manufacture of clothing and other goods. Early strains of drought-tolerant, fine cotton were first grown at the Salt River Valley Experimental Farm near

Mesa, Arizona, in the 1920s. In the 1970s, plots all along the Salt and Gila River Valleys were producing hybrid strains, improved in the 1990s with the addition of genetic lines from as far away as Egypt and the Caribbean islands of Saint Vincent and Barbados. Upland and Pima cotton hybrids were further improved at University farms at Buckeye, Goodyear, Stanfield, and Marana. The next time you're wearing a well-made cotton garment, chances are good that it came into being thanks to the efforts of University of Arizona agricultural researchers.

A FISH STORY

The Environmental Research Laboratory

THE GULF Coast of Louisiana. The Gulf of California. The Gulf of Siam. Conjure up images of where shrimp come from, and they're likely to be places at some distance from landlocked Arizona. It might therefore come as a surprise that we have a source of the tasty crustaceans close to home: in the entirely unlikely confines of Gila Bend, Arizona, a small, hot town on the southwestern edge of Maricopa County, where hundreds of thousands of pounds of shrimp are grown, along with tilapia, trout, bass, and other aquatic foods.

The story begins in the early 1970s with a professor in the College of Agriculture named Merle Jensen, then the associate head of the college's network of experimental stations. A visionary advocate of what he called "tomorrow's agriculture today," Jensen foresaw a time when food production would be ever more critical with demographic and environmental changes. Although he was a trained horticulturalist—he designed the Walt Disney World EPCOT Center's terrestrial landscaping—Jensen pushed for hydroponics gardening, for the development of drought-tolerant citrus and lettuce breeds, and especially for aquaculture. The latter, its programs headquartered at the college's Environmental Research Laboratory, was born from the insight that fishery water could be used to irrigate plants. For their part, Arizona farmers had long since introduced fish to irrigation canals to keep the canals clean. "We put it all together," he remarked. "While irrigation water is moving towards fields, use that water and energy—it's already paid for—to grow another cash crop, a food crop, before sending it on its way."

The Environmental Research Laboratory boosted aquaculture for years while engaging in other agriculture-related projects. About the time Jensen retired in 2003, much of its work came under the purview of the new Department of Environmental Science within the College of Agriculture and Life Sciences. Local aquaculture remains a topic on the agenda, but researchers are also working on broader-scale projects. For instance, Jean McLain, a professor and microbiologist, has been using the Tucson-area Sweetwater Wetlands, which uses reclaimed wastewater to nurture an oasis along the Santa Cruz River, to study the mechanisms behind algal blooms and how to prevent them. Given the increasing presence of potentially deadly algal blooms in fisheries around the world as a consequence of climate change, this is work of the utmost importance. So, too, is an ongoing project to make the agricultural use of groundwater more efficient by rotating crops and planting cover crops to increase the retention of rainwater. That project is one of the largest ever funded by the USDA, and it may make all the difference to desert agriculture in a time of water scarcity.

TERRA

Feeding the Future World

I N THE year 2100, by most estimates, the human population of the world will stand at nearly 11 billion people, about a third more people than are alive today. At the same time, world cropland and agricultural yields are decreasing thanks to a warming climate and disruptions in rainfall and snow patterns. Energy will be at a premium, especially if the world is slow to shed its reliance on fossil fuels. And food demand around the world is projected to double between 2020 and 2050.

All this portends a dark and hungry future for millions and even billions of people.

Scientists at the University of Arizona are working in collaboration with researchers at the Donald Danforth Plant Science Center, Kansas State University, the USDA, and other institutions and companies to address this looming problem. One approach is visible from miles away in the flat farmland south of the Gila River, where the University maintains an agricultural research farm near the town of Maricopa. You might think of it as the world's largest scanner, some fifty feet high, that weighs thirty tons and moves along steel rails over crop rows the length of four football fields.

Watching this giant contraption go up, local farmers asked whether the University was going to be looking for extraterrestrials or if the scanner was some sort of spying device planted by the National Security Agency. It's not. Instead, backed by the U.S. Department of Energy, TERRA (Transportation Energy Resources from Renewable Agriculture) bombards a 1.25-acre field studded with thousands of sensors, reading data from forty-two thousand plants below. The data that are returned to the scanner, at a rate of about five terabytes a

The **TERRA** scanner at the University's experimental farm in Maricopa, Arizona.
Photograph by Gregory McNamee.

day, are then reviewed to determine which plants are thriving under experimental conditions that are expected to resemble the future climate. Those that produce good yields are then selected for breeding, while those that fail are pulled.

This regime of measurement, called "high throughput phenotyping," allows scientists to look at individual plants a couple of times a day with an eye to determining which plants are the most drought tolerant, what genetic characteristics they share with other successful plants, and which hold greatest promise for longevity. Of particular interest is developing hybrid plant varieties that can extend their root systems deeper or wider below the surface than existing ones, maximizing available water resources.

The earliest measurements were taken of sorghum, which is an important animal food crop and source of biofuel in southern Africa, whose present climatic conditions resemble those of central Arizona. Future experiments will center on crops of leafy plants, grains, and trees, with seeds and data that will then be released to the public. It's all literally a matter of life and death, and the University of Arizona is leading the way toward a brighter future.

A CAMPUS GEM

The Alfie Norville Gem & Mineral Museum

ACCORDING TO the latest edition of *Mineralogy of Arizona*, an industry-standard reference work first published by UA Press in 1977, there are 986 known minerals in Arizona. When the University was founded as a school of mines and agriculture, the number of known minerals was a fraction of that count. What the first students of geology here knew was that it took lots of hard work to get at almost all of them, and that some were very rare indeed.

That fact gave impetus to the foundation, as long ago as 1893, of what the University register called a museum that would give "an adequate representative of the ores and minerals of Arizona, as well as a place for the deposit of everything illustrative of the practical workings of the mines, mills, and furnaces." Theodore Comstock, director of the School of Mines, was to be the first curator of that museum, even though it was originally intended to find a home alongside the territorial capitol in Phoenix. When it turned out that there was no room available for it there, the legislature decreed that the museum be housed in Tucson, and so it was, crammed into every unused corner of Old Main.

In 1905, the museum moved across the way to the Douglass Building, sharing space with the geology faculty and its classrooms—as well as the math, history, and English departments, making for a tight fit, especially when mixed in with the university's burgeoning collection of Native American artifacts. In 1915, the Arizona State Museum was founded, with Byron Cummings as its director, and the anthropological artifacts went to what is now the Forbes Building, leaving the mineral collection to languish in boxes and scattered bookcases on the second floor of the Mines and Engineering Building. In 1958, when a new building went up for the Geology Department just a couple of hundred feet away, the Mineral Museum went there, and in 1993, when that building became too crowded, the collection was transferred to the basement of the Flandrau Science Center.

Enter entrepreneur Alfena Norville (1925–2015), widely known in the community as Alfie. Illinois-born Alfie was the first woman in Tucson to be a licensed stockbroker. She was also a philanthropist of boundless energy, serving on the university's board of directors, active among campus groups and agencies ranging from astronomy to religion and, yes, geology. A Wildcat fan of every sport who turned up at nearly every home game, Alfie also founded the Gem and Jewelry Exchange, a central part of Tucson's larger Gem and Mineral Show held across the city each winter. She and her husband, Allan Norville, funded an endowed professorship in the Sarver Heart Center at the University Medical Center, and she steered plenty of donations of both minerals and money to the Mineral Museum.

Thanks to a generous gift from Allan Norville in honor of Alfie, the museum began its long move downtown to the restored Pima County Courthouse in 2017. Containing a goodly number of those known 986 minerals, as well as specimens from all over the world, the Alfie Norville Gem & Mineral Museum—at once the oldest and newest of the University of Arizona's Museums—celebrated its grand opening in its new home in February 2022.

Some of the minerals on display, incidentally, were provided by another University angel, J. David Lowell (1928–2020). A Wildcat football player who earned a bachelor's degree in mining engineering in 1949, Lowell enjoyed a long career as an exploration geologist and discovered not only the world's largest concentration of copper, in Chile, but also more copper deposits worldwide than any other geologist, yielding billions of dollars' worth of copper ore. He also funded the University's Institute of Mineral Resources, as well as the addition at the north end of the football stadium called the Lowell-Stevens Football Facility. The University awarded Lowell an honorary doctorate in 2000.

LIVING ON EARTH

The Critical Zone

W E LIVE on a ball of rock. Atop much of it is water. Surrounding it is water and gas. In a small region just above, at, and just below Earth's land surface, rock, water, gases, and other components have combined over billions of years to make life possible—and that life is what makes Earth a very rare place indeed.

In broad terms, the critical zone, that region, extends from the tops of the tallest trees to the impermeable layer of bedrock that lies below our planet's surface. That is a small distance, ranging in most places from a few dozen to a few thousand feet. Within this thin veneer, life exists and does its work to make further life possible. The critical zone is the permeable skin of Earth, which supports all life here, for which reason it well deserves the *critical* part of its name.

Scientists who study the critical zone work in a variety of disciplines, bringing different insights and tools to a complex subject that demands many approaches. At the heart of that study are the disciplines that make up earth science. Critical zone researchers include geologists and geophysicists, soil scientists, atmospheric scientists, and hydrologists. Because the critical zone is the region of life, ecologists, microbiologists, entomologists, and many other kinds of life scientists play a part. Chemists and biochemists are essential to our understanding of interactions in the critical zone, while engineers and computer scientists provide sensor networks and other instruments to support the acquisition and interpretation of the data collected by the researchers.

In short, the critical zone is a common meeting ground for scholars and researchers in a broad range of scientific disciplines, all focusing their efforts on the same geographic location, and each part essential to the whole. These scientists bring exhaustive knowledge of their home disciplines—a geologist, for example, will typically hold a doctorate and have extensive experience in studying specific geological problems, while an atmospheric scientist will have an exhaustive knowledge of how our planet's climate works. Yet they also understand that, in order to understand how Earth works as a complex system, they need to fit their work into a larger picture of multidisciplinary and interdisciplinary cooperation.

Dozens of scientists, researchers, and staff members at the University of Arizona work on matters related to the critical zone. Among them are Jon Chorover, professor and head of the Department of Environmental Science, who studies the biogeochemistry of soil, sediment, and water, with special attention to how pollutants affect their interactions. Additionally, he is the principal investigator at two critical zone observatories, one in the Santa Catalina Mountains north of Tucson, the other in the Jemez Mountains near Santa Fe, New Mexico, that track such things as how rainwater moves from the sky into aquifers far below. Professor Karletta Chief, Diné (Navajo) from Black Mesa, Arizona, studies ways to improve our understanding of watershed hydrology and how natural and human disturbances affect it, particularly in thinking about the long-term health of water resources in a time of climate change and increasing drought. Mónica Ramírez-Andreotta, an associate professor, studies food production, environmental justice, and communicating research to nonspecialist audiences. Assistant professor Joseph Blankinship investigates the roles of soil microorganisms in controlling ecosystem services, including the "glues" they produce that help prevent wind and water erosion, enzymes that release plant nutrients, residues that sequester carbon, and metabolic activities that both produce and consume atmospheric greenhouse gases, studies that range across the disciplines of biology, chemistry, physics, and engineering with the aim of improving soil and plant health and sustaining agriculture in arid lands.

Critical zone research is, well, critically important in a rapidly changing world, and the University of Arizona has emerged as a world leader in this multifaceted field.

EXPLORING THE WORLD

Laurence McKinley Gould, George Gaylord Simpson, and the Gould-Simpson Building

I F YOU'VE been in the Sonoran Desert for any length of time, you'll appreciate the old adage that there are five seasons here, four of them hot and one of them less hot. That's the—beg pardon—polar opposite of Antarctica, where, early in the history of the continent's exploration, a distinguished University of Arizona scientist made great contributions.

That scientist was the geologist Laurence McKinley Gould (1896–1995), who accompanied aviator Richard E. Byrd on his first expedition to Antarctica in 1928. As chief scientist, Gould struck out on a dogsled and described much of the continent's central coast, so much that other explorers named several features, including Gould Bay and Mount Gould, for him. He mapped hundreds of miles on the Antarctic ice, traveling by sled into the remote, rugged Queen Maud Mountains, among other forbidding destinations. After climbing 13,350-foot-tall Mount Fridtjof Nansen, near the South Pole, he determined from its sedimentary history that Antarctica—which he called "a veritable paradise for a geologist"—was once connected to the ancient southern supercontinent of Gondwana.

On returning from Antarctica, Gould served as a professor of geology at Carleton College. In 1945, he was named the school's president, a position he held until retiring in 1962. He didn't stay retired for long, though, for his geologist colleagues at the University of Arizona convinced him that the sunny Sonoran Desert was also a paradise, and he taught courses in quaternary geology and other geoscientific topics to Arizona students until finally retiring for good in 1979.

Gould's colleague George Gaylord Simpson (1902–84) was similarly footloose. A professor of zoology at Columbia University and, later, head curator for geology of both the American Museum of Natural History in New York and Harvard University's Museum of Comparative Zoology, Simpson thought he was retired too, until those same geologists lured him to Tucson to teach paleontology. He was only too glad to make the move, working with the University's extensive collection of fossils. Famed for his travels in the remote barrancas of southernmost South America—not quite within hailing distance of Antarctica but, as he recounted in his 1934 memoir *Attending Marvels*, subject to the same awful weather—Simpson made important discoveries over a long career about animal evolution and the migration of ancient animals from continent to continent. A popular professor at Arizona, he finally retired in 1982.

The Gould-Simpson Building, which houses the Department of Geosciences, bears the names of those two great scholars. Completed in 1985, the ten-story-tall structure was once among the tallest buildings in Tucson, and many visitors come to it just to make their way to the top floors, now housing the Department of Computer Science, to take in the best views of campus. Today several Arizona researchers work in Antarctica, most in environmental sciences and geosciences, many housed, when they are on campus, in the building named for their distinguished predecessors. Antarctica and Patagonia are far from the Sonoran Desert, but that aptly illustrates a central fact: there's not a corner of the globe that some University of Arizona scholar has not studied, visited, described, and made known to the rest of us.

CIRCLES OF LIFE

The Laboratory of Tree-Ring Research

BORN IN Windsor, Vermont, Andrew Ellicott (A. E.) Douglass (1867–1962) received a bachelor's degree in astronomy from Trinity College in Hartford, Connecticut. To pay for graduate work, he took a position at the Harvard College Observatory as an assistant while joining a mission to establish an observatory in Peru. Along the way, he met a wealthy financier named Percival Lowell, who recruited the young scientist to find a site for an astronomical observatory, astronomy being one of his many pastimes. In 1894, Douglass located the site for the Lowell Observatory in Flagstaff, Arizona, and worked there until 1901, when, after a run-in with Lowell, he lost his position.

Douglass was both resourceful and well rounded, and he made ends meet by teaching Spanish and geography at what is now Northern Arizona University while serving as a probate judge in Flagstaff. There, among the tall ponderosa pines of campus and city, he divined, using his training in physics as much as his interest in natural history, that tree rings were records of solar cycles of growth: the wide rings of certain species of trees recorded wet years, narrow rings dry years. Each year, a tree adds a new layer of wood, a ring that can be counted. From this observation, Douglass conjectured that by studying the climatological record of a region such as the Colorado Plateau, predictions could be made about future weather cycles.

Douglass moved south to Tucson in 1906 to teach at the University of Arizona, rising to the rank of professor and teaching both physics and astronomy. There Douglass elaborated the science of dendrochronology, which uses those tree rings to determine the age of a particular piece of wood. He developed a ponderosa pine chronology dating back hundreds of years, which enabled archaeologists to use timber taken from sites such as Mesa Verde to date their construction, an important window on prehistory. The noted archaeologist Emil Haury helped fine-tune his chronology with the discovery of a site that filled in a gap that extended the record to the eighth century CE. At present, the chronology—established mostly from ponderosa and bristlecone pines—had been pushed far back, extending nearly to the end of the last ice age.

From his vantage point as a professor and, in time, director of the Steward Observatory on campus, Douglass lobbied for the creation for a laboratory in which he and his assistants could conduct dendrochronological research. In 1935, funding was approved, and in 1937 the Laboratory for Tree-Ring Research was established, allowing the University of Arizona to amass the world's most comprehensive collection of dendrochronological material and data, a distinction it still enjoys.

A. E. Douglass with the core of a giant sequoia, one of the earliest specimens in the Laboratory of Tree-Ring Research. Photograph courtesy of Arizona State Museum.

Though bombarded by submissions of tree cores from scholars all over the world, the Laboratory was something of an afterthought, with parts of its collection stored in various locations around campus—including, for a time, the football stadium, where the laboratory was also housed under supposedly temporary conditions that lasted for seventy years. In 2011, however, thanks to a generous donation by Agnese Nelms Haury and other patrons, ground was broken for a new building across the street from the Math East building, where some of the laboratory's collection had been stored. In March 2013, the Laboratory for Tree-Ring Research, with a brilliant design that suggests both a forest and something from the distant future, was dedicated and named in honor of former director Bryant Bannister.

Among the most prized of the materials housed in the new laboratory comes with a rather tangled story. In 1964, a graduate student in geography scaled 13,065-foot-tall Wheeler Peak in what is now Nevada's Great Basin National Park in order to take core samples from a stand of bristlecone pines. His drill bit, technically called a Swedish increment borer, snapped, and he had no spare for the expensive part. With the permission of the National Park Service, he instead cut an ancient tree down, spelling an end to its life. (The borer, by contrast, has been likened to a needle delivering a flu shot.) He did so, only to realize, as he counted its rings, that the tree was 4,844 years old, then the oldest living tree that had ever been recorded. Later, a second graduate student was dispatched to the same location to gather more slices of the tree that has since been called Prometheus, a segment of which is on exhibit at the laboratory. Later still, to atone for his error, the chagrined first graduate student, who went on to become a professor of geography at the University of Utah, devoted considerable effort to securing national park status for the site of the tree.

Prometheus is not the oldest bristlecone pine: a core sample of another tree turned up a date of 5,062 years. But the laboratory does much more than simply tabulate the ages of trees. Among its research programs are measures of how air pollution affects the growth of urban trees, the incidence of wildfires over the course of centuries, and the relative strengths of seasonal monsoon as a record of climate variations in the past.

A. E. Douglass lived a good long life, dying in 1962 at the age of ninety-four. Among the many roles he filled at the University of Arizona was a three-month stint as interim president (1910–11), during which time he wrote numerous proposals for curriculum reform and physical plant improvements. A brilliant and energetic scholar, he was one of the early architects of the University's rise to scientific preeminence.

A CENTURY AND MORE IN THE HEAVENS

Astronomy at the University

THE UNIVERSITY of Arizona had barely opened its doors when a visiting lecturer suggested that, with the desert's clear skies and the campus's remoteness from town, it would be fitting to set up a telescope and teach introductory courses in astronomy. Given the tiny faculty and crowded facilities, the administration was not quick to act, and it took a couple of decades for the University to hire A. E. Douglass, late of the Lowell Observatory in Flagstaff. Douglass immediately set about raising funds to build an observatory, a successful project about which we'll shortly see more.

Douglass was an energetic promoter of science, and in 1922 he inaugurated a public outreach program involving a lecture followed by outdoor telescope viewing. That proved a great lure for students, and in 1929 the University awarded the first bachelor's degree in astronomy, to a young man named Philip C. Keenan, who went on to develop a star classification system based on luminosity. It would be another thirty years before a new master's program produced its first graduate, Michael Chriss, who taught courses in the history of astronomy, while the year 1965 saw the first doctorates, awarded to five students.

That crop of PhDs was the outcome of the hard work of a Dutch-born astronomer named Gerard P. Kuiper (1905–73), who founded the Lunar and Planetary Laboratory (LPL) in 1960, lured by President Richard Harvill and, from his post at the University of Chicago, Kitt Peak National Observatory director Aden Meinel. A dogged fundraiser, Kuiper drummed up $1.2 million (about $11.6 million today) from NASA to build a home for LPL and the Department of Astronomy, generously sharing space with the physics and mechanical engineering departments until they acquired their own buildings. Inaugurated in 1965, the Space Sciences Building, now the Kuiper Space Sciences Building, became a hive of activity that has not slowed in more than half a century, so much so that LPL now occupies three buildings in the astronomy complex on the east end of the Mall. In 2007, for instance, LPL became the first public-university institution to head a NASA planetary mission, the *Phoenix* Mars lander. Four years later, LPL headed OSIRIS-REx (more about which follows). Besides a building, Kuiper's name is enshrined in the Kuiper belt, a circumstellar disc beyond Neptune that contains what might be thought of as the scrap material left over after the solar system was formed, including miniature planets such as Pluto and Orcus.

In 1973, perhaps sensing his impending death, Kuiper recruited astronomer Charles P. Sonett (1924–2011) to succeed him as director of LPL, as well as to head a new interdisciplinary department of planetary sciences. With funding flowing in from federal grants and an uncharacteristi-

Astronomer Gerard P. Kuiper in 1964. Photograph courtesy of NASA.

cally generous legislature, to say nothing of the tireless advocacy of President John Schaefer, the new department embarked on dozens of significant programs. Sonett also headed the Ames Magnetic Fields Explorer program, which analyzed, among other things, how the moon holds up to the rigors of the solar wind. Presciently, too, Sonett studied how Earth's climate is conditioned by solar cycles. An expert in rocketry and nuclear physics, Sonett played an outsize role in bring NASA projects to the University.

Another significant figure in the development of planetary sciences at Arizona was Anton M. J. (Tom) Gehrels (1925–2011), known to one and all as Tom. A hero of the Dutch resistance during World War II, Gehrels became an expert in asteroid formation and cataloged thousands of them, including many near-Earth specimens. He also initiated the ongoing Space Science Series published by UA Press, editing or co-editing several volumes himself. A University professor for fifty years and, beg pardon, a pioneering scientist in the Pioneer programs that preceded the moon landing of 1969, Tom Gehrels is honored in the name of a large planetoid in the asteroid belt, 1777 Gehrels.

Just so, the asteroid (75562) Wilkening honors Laurel L. Wilkening (1944–2019), the first woman to head LPL and the first woman to hold the post of dean of sciences. She arrived in Tucson as an assistant professor in 1973 and proved herself a leading authority on comets and meteorites, quickly rising to the rank of full professor. On the side, she also strongly advocated, successfully, for the creation of the Department of Women's Studies (now the Department of Gender & Women's Studies) at the University and later was one of the chief donors to the Women's Plaza of Honor on the west end of campus. Renowned not only for her scholarship but also for her encouragement of students and colleagues, Wilkening stood out as an administrator—too well, we might say, since she was hired away to become the first woman provost of the University of Washington and then chancellor of the University of California, Irvine.

Nearly every NASA mission since 1960 has involved Arizona scientists. Today the University of Arizona, with a body of faculty and staff numbering in the hundreds, is an international leader in planetary sciences and astronomy, contributing more than $560 million to the local economy each year. Its scientists, among them such world-class scholars as Peter Strittmatter and J. Roger Angel, are involved in countless projects. One recent study concerns the analysis of the brightest gamma rays ever recorded, evidence that somewhere a star has collapsed, leaving a solar system without its sun—an event that occurred at least 1.9 billion years ago. The study makes use of a variety of telescopes here, and soon the James Webb Space Telescope and Hubble Space Telescope will be put to work. Another study involves locating human-made objects in space, which principal investigator Vishnu Reddy likens to "tracking a firefly that's flying around a searchlight." Future astronauts will be thankful for the work, which reduces the chances of an inadvertent collision in Earth's orbit. Still other researchers in astrobiology and other disciplines scan the heavens for habitable planets. Dark matter, black holes, the origins of the universe, the search for intelligent life on other planets—whatever it is, if it has to do with the study of space, a University of Arizona scholar is leading the way.

SEEING STARS

The Steward Observatory

T MAY be hard to picture now, but there was a time, in the early twentieth century, when what is now Cherry Avenue—roughly the midway dividing line of the present Mall—was far enough from the main University campus that it was the site of a privately owned ostrich farm.

Long before he began to work to build the Laboratory of Tree-Ring Research, A. E. Douglass, who arrived on campus in 1906, was engrossed in the work of building a new Department of Astronomy. Meanwhile, President Rufus von KleinSmid was occupied in constructing a new home for the College of Agriculture, a task that was completed in 1915. That done, the president returned to fundraising to expand the campus even further. Douglass had made a pitch for an astronomical observatory to house a "large telescope," but the funds were nowhere to be had—until that is, small-town Tucson and its network of warm personal connections eased the way.

The connector was Clara Fish Roberts (1876–1965), the first student to enroll in the University's inaugural class. After earning her BS in mining in 1897, Roberts worked as a schoolteacher, and in 1917, she was the first woman elected to the Tucson School Board. Along the way, Roberts befriended Lavinia Steward (1870–1957), whose husband had earned a substantial sum of money by selling his Illinois mill to the company that would soon become Quaker Oats. Steward and her husband settled in a large house in Oracle, northeast of Tucson, where he died in 1902 of heart disease. Steward continued to live in Oracle but often visited Tucson, meeting Roberts by way of a nephew in the banking business. Roberts,

The Steward Observatory in 1920, at the far eastern edge of campus at the time.

always active on campus, introduced Steward to von KleinSmid and Douglass. In October 1916, Steward, an astronomy enthusiast, donated $60,000 (about $1.7 million today) to endow what was immediately called the Steward Observatory.

Lavinia Steward died in 1917. Construction of the observatory continued apace, but World War I interrupted the manufacture of its 36-inch telescope, which was supposed to be made in France but was finally made by several American firms. The telescope, very nearly state of the art in its time, was finally mounted on July 10, 1922, and Douglass happily went to work observing the planet Venus as his first sustained project.

Unhappily, however, the once-remote ostrich farm on which the observatory was sited was no longer remote. New houses had risen along Cherry Avenue, and the University's new tennis courts stood just across the street from the Steward Observatory. When the University authorized the addition of lights to the tennis courts to permit night play, the dark sky around the observatory brightened annoyingly. Astronomers at the observatory labored on nonetheless until 1963, when Kitt Peak National Observatory began operations and the 36-inch telescope was moved to the distant site and its dark skies. The telescope is still in use as part of the battery of instruments employed by the Spacewatch Project, which keeps an eye out on asteroids, comets, and other small objects in the near solar system.

A smaller, 20-inch telescope was installed in the Steward Observatory after the larger one was removed, mostly for the use of students. The domed building itself, now on the National Register of Historic Places, contains a visitor center with displays of equipment of the vintage that Douglass would have used in his explorations of the heavens.

TEACHING THE STARS

Bringing Astronomy to the Public

A YOUNG GRADUATE student, Kate Dibiasky, scans the skies. She discovers an asteroid hurtling toward Earth—directly toward Earth, with inevitably catastrophic consequences. The president of the United States can scarcely be bothered when she receives the bad news, and the NASA director—a friend of the president's and a major donor, without an ounce of scientific training—tells the world not to worry. When it turns out that the asteroid, perhaps like the real-life Bennu (about which more soon), contains a huge store of rare-earth elements worth trillions of dollars, then ears begin to perk up—but most people, without a direct claim to that fortune, go about their daily business, ignoring the threat even as they ignore the dangers of pandemics, climate change, the seventh extinction, and anything else that might trouble their sleep.

It's an all-too-plausible scenario. Fortunately, it's that of a film, *Don't Look Up*, first aired on Netflix on Christmas Eve 2021. The science in the film is certainly plausible, too, and that's thanks to University of Arizona professor of planetary sciences Amy Mainzer, a technical advisor to the production from the time when it was first being scripted. Indeed, scientists lauded it, most seeing it as an allegory for, yes, climate change. Said renowned researcher Peter Kalmus, "speaking as a climate scientist doing everything I can to wake people up and avoid planetary destruction, it's . . . the most accurate film about society's terrifying nonresponse to climate breakdown I've seen."

Mainzer, an internationally recognized authority on planetary defense and asteroid detection, directs NASA's Near-Earth Object Wide-Field Infrared Survey Explorer at the

University of Arizona, billed as "the largest space-based asteroid-hunting project in history." Her extracurricular work on the film, in which she gave a realistic account of what would happen if a comet did collide with Earth—nothing good, to be sure—is what is known as outreach, an aspect of academic life that our astronomers take very seriously.

Astrophysicist Erika Hamden, for example, does most of her teaching inside the classroom—but she also takes part in the popular public forum provided by the vehicle of TED Talks, speaking on such things as the study of distant galaxies and the origin of hydrogen. Chris Impey, a distinguished professor of astronomy and pioneer of online instruction, has delivered lectures to more than 350,000 delighted audience members and has written many popular books on astronomy, including *Worlds Without End: Exoplanets, Habitability, and the Future of Humanity*. "It is astonishingly likely that we are not the only time and place that an advanced civilization has evolved," Impey writes—though if they're smart, those other civilizations won't have destroyed their homes and thus won't need to seek homes on other planets.

If they do, then there's the work of William K. Hartmann to turn to. A student of meteor impacts, among many other subjects, and one of the founders of the Planetary Science Institute after earning his PhD in astronomy here, Bill Hartmann has written popular books about Mars and other planets, illustrated with his own paintings, which are so accomplished that many of them hang in the halls of NASA headquarters, the Smithsonian's National Air and Space Museum, and other important venues.

Outreach through popular media is but one aspect of astronomical education. The University of Arizona is a world leader in the area thanks to its NASA Center for Astronomy Education, which, combining science and pedagogical techniques, produces instructors able to teach introductory astronomy at many levels of education, including the undergraduate staple Astronomy 101. If you'd like to brush up on your knowledge of the Doppler shift, Hubble's law, star formation, and other topics—and space collisions, too, if on a galactic scale—then have a look at the topflight body of instructional materials at www.as.arizona.edu.

MINING OTHER WORLDS

OSIRIS-REx

ASTEROIDS ARE mysterious objects. We usually hear about them only when they pass by close to Earth—news that arrives with understandable worry, since asteroids sometimes collide with the planets in our solar system. Indeed, it's believed that the impact of an asteroid about six miles in diameter caused a chain of events that led to the extinction of dinosaurs and many other species sixty-five million years ago.

Scientists take interest in asteroids for many reasons other than the potential hazards they pose. For one thing, they were formed before the planets were, and they help answer questions about the origins of our solar system. For another, asteroid impacts may have accelerated the development of life on Earth billions of years ago, bringing the "stardust" of which we and all living creatures past and present are made.

The University of Arizona–led OSIRIS-REx (Origins, Spectral Interpretation, Resource Identification, Security, Regolith Explorer) spacecraft was designed precisely to help us better understand these matters and arrive at answers to the scientific questions they raise.

OSIRIS-REx launched on September 8, 2016, from a pad at the Kennedy Space Center in Cape Canaveral, Florida. Developed by the University of Arizona Lunar and Planetary Laboratory, NASA, and Lockheed Martin—with LPL's Dante Lauretta, Regents Professor of Planetary Sciences and Cosmochemistry, serving as the principal investigator—it traveled to an asteroid formally called (101955) 1999 RQ36, arriving on December 3, 2018, after having traversed 318,431,064 miles of space. The asteroid is a C-type, meaning that it is believed to be composed primarily of carbonaceous material.

(That formal name, by the way, indicates that the asteroid was the 101,955th asteroid confirmed to exist, while 1999 indicates the year of discovery, and R, the eighteenth letter of the alphabet, indicates discovery in the first half of September; the remaining numbers indicate its sequence among the asteroids discovered in the same period. The informal name, determined in a contest won by a North Carolina third grader, is Bennu, honoring a mythological ancient Egyptian bird-god, which neatly lines up with the Osiris element of the spacecraft's name.)

After rendezvousing with Bennu, which is a mere third of a mile across, and adapting to its velocity, OSIRIS-REx photographed and assessed its carbon-rich surface and subsurface composition, using a complex battery of instruments to measure its shape, rotation rate, surface texture, chemical composition, and other features. The University of Arizona developed three cameras for the project: MapCam, which mapped the surface of the asteroid in four colors; PolyCam, an 8-inch telescope that both imaged the asteroid from 1.24 million miles away and took high-resolution, microscopic images of the surface; and SamCam, which imaged the sampling process at speeds as fast

OSIRIS-REx being prepared for launch. Photograph courtesy of NASA.

as 1.6 seconds and verified that the sampler had successfully acquired these specimens. All these data yielded both a portrait of the geology and history of the asteroid, which has been called a "time capsule" documenting the makeup of the early universe, and helped in the selection of the best site for sampling.

OSIRIS-REx touched down on Bennu on October 20, 2020, firing a burst of nitrogen to stir up the surface and loosen rocks and other materials, which were then gathered in that sampling device and brought into the spacecraft. OSIRIS-REx left Bennu on May 10, 2021, and began its two-year return to Earth. It entered Earth's atmosphere in September 2023, arriving at a speed of 27,962 miles per hour and streaking like a meteor across the western United States. After it landed, engineers retrieved the sample capsule and took it to NASA's Johnson Space Center, where scientists opened it under clean-room conditions. There the samples were analyzed to determine what minerals are in it, what the overall chemical composition is, and what quantities of water and carbon—the elements necessary for life—are present.

NASA also distributed samples to scientists for further study, while scientists at the Johnson Space Center, including researchers from the University of Arizona, began to prepare a catalog of materials gathered by OSIRIS-REx. This initial process was expected to last just a few months, but studying those materials will occupy decades to come, addressing important questions: How did the solar system form? What kinds of materials exist in the solar system? How did life evolve in the solar system? Are asteroids bringers of life or death—or both? The answers will add greatly to our understanding of how the solar system formed and how life on Earth—and perhaps other planets—began.

TO THE RED PLANET AND BEYOND

The University and the Solar System

THE TALLEST volcano in the solar system is on Mars. Called Olympus Mons, it covers an area the size of Arizona and is nearly fourteen miles high, about two and a half times taller than Earth's tallest mountain, Mount Everest. Nine of our Grand Canyons could fit inside the vast, 2,500-mile-long rift called the Valles Marineris. It has ice caps, and there is evidence that water once lay on the surface of the Red Planet.

We first learned some of these things when, in November 1971, *Mariner 9*, the first spacecraft ever to orbit another planet, arrived at Mars. *Mariner 9*, its mission aided by University of Arizona scientists, circled Mars for nearly a year, gathering data and photographing the surface of the planet. But we've learned more in much greater detail thanks to technology developed here on our campus, such as the rover cameras designed by teams led by research scientist Peter Smith, who comments, "Our rovers are designed like bloodhounds, with boundless curiosity and powerful eyes and noses. We learn from them how Mars is constructed."

One exploratory tool was the *Phoenix* Mars lander, a mission headed by Smith. Launched on August 4, 2007, it arrived near the northern pole of Mars on May 25, 2008. Developed at and led by the University of Arizona—the first NASA mission led by any university—and the first craft in NASA's new Scout class of spacecraft, its mission was to gather data that allows scientists to address three large questions, concerning the history of water on Mars, the possibility that Mars can support life, and the role of the poles in the Martian climate.

Aboard the *Phoenix* spacecraft were some of the most sophisticated scientific instruments ever built. Among them were the "eyes" of the lander, the Surface Stereo Imager (SSI), which delivered high-resolution panoramic images of the landing site. Data from the SSI helped guide the Robotic Arm, built by the University of Arizona, used to dig trenches and take soil and ice samples. The TEGA (Thermal and Evolved Gas Analyzer), also a University-built instrument, allowed scientists to conduct tests of the soil and ice and sample them for any organic matter they might contain. These and other tools made *Phoenix* the most advanced remote science laboratory that has yet visited space—and the entire mission was operated from a headquarters on campus.

Launched on August 12, 2005, the Mars Reconnaissance Orbiter carries aboard a huge camera unlike any other. Called HiRISE (High Resolution Imaging Science Experiment), the camera is not made of lenses, as an ordinary camera would be, but instead an array of three curved mirrors to focus the light from Mars onto fourteen CCDs (charge-couple devices) that capture huge amounts of visual information. So detailed are the images that HiRISE takes, in fact, that it is possible to pick out individual boulders in a scattered field— all the more impressive, given that HiRISE is flying some two hundred miles above the planet at a speed of about two miles a second, orbiting Mars once every two hours.

The individual photographs give comprehensive views of gigantic sand dunes, the depths of Mars's vast canyon complexes, the channels formed by ancient water flows, and more. In time, these images will constitute a vast library of visual data more complete than that available for any other planet in the solar system. Moreover, the stereo-paired images that HiRISE is gathering are being used to make digital elevation models precise to less than a foot, which in turn will help scientists determine the safest landing sites for spacecraft sent to Mars in the coming years. Designed by scientists at the University of Arizona's Lunar and Planetary Laboratory under the leadership of Alfred McEwen, Regents Professor of Planetary Science, HiRISE was nicknamed "the people's camera" because of the participatory science it encouraged, not just within the scientific community but also in the larger world beyond it.

Speaking of imaging, Regents Professor of Astronomy Marcia Rieke is the principal investigator for the near-infrared camera aboard the James Webb Space Telescope. The largest optical telescope in space, the Webb Telescope significantly improves on the imagery captured by the Hubble Space Telescope, launched in 1990. George Rieke, another Arizona astronomer, led the team that build the Mid-Infrared Instrument (MIRI), which, as its name suggests, measures the middle wavelengths of the infrared spectrum. The images that the Webb Telescope is sending back, courtesy of the twenty-one University scientists who worked on it, are astonishing in their detail and the phenomena they depict, serving as recruiting posters for generations of future astronomers.

Back here on Earth, a telescope array called the Event Horizon Telescope has been capturing data-based images of distant celestial objects. One, twenty-seven thousand light-years from Earth, is a black hole, the first black hole ever to be photographed. That fortunate capture is the product of a team led by astrophysicist Feryal Özel, a professor in the University's Department of Astronomy. She is now deepening her research on the origins of black holes through the Lynx X-Ray Observatory, where she cochairs the team that defines the scientific parameters of the survey of the heavens far beyond Mars.

ANOTHER WORLD

Biosphere 2

EARTH, OUR home, is Biosphere 1. How we might someday extend our home to embrace other planets lies at the heart of the work of Biosphere 2, a University of Arizona research facility located at the foot of the Santa Catalina Mountains on an old cattle ranch north of Tucson, outside the small town of Oracle. The mission of Biosphere 2 is to serve as a center for research, outreach, teaching, and lifelong learning about Earth, its living systems, and its place in the universe. Because of its unique place as a living laboratory, Biosphere 2 can make unique contributions to our understanding of questions such as the response of earth systems to environmental change. Research at Biosphere 2, for instance, has made significant scientific contributions in areas such as how ecosystems respond to elevated carbon dioxide concentrations—a pressing matter in a time of global climate change.

Biosphere 2 began with what might be called, without being in the least bit dismissive, a scenario then out of science fiction, designed as a kind of terrestrial spaceship in which eight astronauts would live and work for two years in a controlled environment like that of a spacecraft. Were it a spacecraft, granted, it would be huge. Built between 1987 and 1991, Biosphere 2 occupies an area of a little more than five and a half acres, its main area about the size of three football fields, made of 77,000 steel struts and 6,500 panes of half-inch glass. If you step inside this T-shaped building, you are in another world—or, better, other worlds. And, of course, you *can* step inside, courtesy of the fascinating tours of the facility that draw visitors from around the world.

Biosphere 2, located near Oracle. Photograph by Gregory McNamee.

A biosphere, in the scientific sense, is a complex web of life that recycles everything within it, with nothing added and nothing destroyed. In Biosphere 1, the amount of water and oxygen is constant, for example. In Biosphere 2, the eight "terranauts" who entered the closed system in 1991 and left in 1993 drank water that was recycled through waste treatment and was used to irrigate plants. The plants filtered the water, which entered the atmosphere as condensate and was harvested as rainwater, then used to drink again in a continual cycle.

The primary goal of the terranaut project was to test rigorously the hypothesis that a small artificial biosphere can replicate the principal ecosystems of Earth. Of perhaps greater interest to the public was the human dimension of the project, for with eight people living in a closed space with no option to wander out to stretch their legs and grab a cup of coffee down the road, it developed that the psychology of interaction was going to be far more difficult to predict than the behavior of machines in the day-to-day work of exploring and settling deep space.

Beyond Biosphere 2's original mission, the complex is a highly effective tool for studying how ecosystems work. The ocean biome embraces a shallow lagoon and sea depths separated by a living coral reef. The ocean is only 115 feet long and 63 feet wide, covering an area of about 7,200 square feet and containing about 750,000 gallons of water. Yet it is a very real ocean, and a self-sustaining one at that—which means that the inhabitants, numbering about thirty species of fish and many more kinds of invertebrates, feed themselves.

Nearby are mangrove wetlands, a fertile zone characteristic of tropical regions from Florida to western Africa and northern Australia. This marsh biome is a four-thousand-square-foot swamp in miniature, with both salt water and fresh water moving through it. These wetlands act, in a way, as the world's kidneys, cleaning the water as it moves along.

The world's tropical rain forests make up only some 6 percent of our planet's surface—about the same area as the United States—but they are a treasure house of diversity in terms of the world's plant and animal species. Moreover, like the ocean, these rain forests produce huge amounts of oxygen while stowing away substantial carbon dioxide. The largest of the biome's trees and plants, most of which come from the Amazon Basin and the Caribbean, can grow to 110 feet tall, while a second canopy is about half as tall and other canopies are closer to the ground.

A savannah grassland reminds us of the place where humankind emerged, while a desert biome measures the alchemy that happens when arid land meets ocean. The desert biome in Biosphere 2 looks very much like the Sonoran Desert outside. One difference, though, is that it receives its moisture from condensation rather than precipitation, as well as from irrigation.

The controlled nature of these fives biomes affords Biosphere 2 researchers the ability to study how environmental changes and stresses affect entire ecosystems, not just parts of them. More than three decades after the original terranaut experiment, drawing on the strengths of the University of Arizona in the sciences, Biosphere 2 researchers are now focusing closely on two large areas of study that are very much in the spirit of those original subjects: water and climate, and energy and sustainability. Both areas are important to us Earthlings today: we need to learn as much as we can about water and climate in a time of global change, and finding renewable, sustainable forms of energy is a pressing concern. Water, climate, energy, and sustainability will be of critical importance to the space colonizers of tomorrow as well.

PINK FLOYD AND THE PLANETS

The Flandrau Science Center & Planetarium

IF YOU were on the University of Arizona campus in the 1970s, you could, if you so chose, be among the first to savor two brand-new creations. The first was the progressive/psychedelic rock group Pink Floyd's album *Dark Side of the Moon*, released in 1973, which went on to become the best-selling album of the 1970s and is, at the moment, the fourth-best-selling album of all time. The second was a planetarium, much discussed since the 1950s, that did not materialize until the very early 1970s. It did so thanks to a bequest from a novelist and travel writer named Grace Flandrau (1886–1971). A Minnesotan, Flandrau spent her winters in Tucson, where she became a devotee of skywatching and often attended astronomy lectures. When she died, leaving an estate of $10 million (about $76 million today), Flandrau's estate made a significant gift to the University with the provision that it be used in some connection with astronomy, in her honor.

John Schaefer, then president of the University, put his head together with the head of the astronomy department, Ray Weymann, and other interested parties on campus, and they revived a dream floated by early astronomers such as Bart Bok and Gerard Kuiper—namely to construct a planetarium, open to the public, right in the heart of the astronomy complex on campus. And not just a planetarium but a museum devoted to astronomy and space sciences, geology, earth sciences, and other disciplines. And not just a planetarium and museum but a place that would serve as an educational destination for students from everywhere in Tucson, from elementary school kids to graduate students.

In 1974, ground was thus broken for the Grace H. Flandrau Planetarium, now known as the Flandrau Science Center & Planetarium. Opened in 1975, it was ideally sited: across the Mall were the Library and the Optical Sciences Building, across the street the Steward Observatory, and right next door the Astronomy Building and Lunar and Planetary Laboratory. The planetarium contained what was at the time a state-of-the-art telescope, and—here's where Pink Floyd comes in—in no time it was hosting late-night laser-light shows and astronomical viewings to the tune of *Dark Side* and other sci-fi-tinged music of the day. Throughout the years, Flandrau has hosted exhibits on nearly aspect of the sciences, from mathematics to the biology of sharks and the workings of the insect mind, delighting busloads of young students brought on field trips. A 16-inch telescope gives nighttime visitors views of distant galaxies and nearby planets alike, from the gas cloud belts of Jupiter to the far reaches of Andromeda. And in 2016, the planetarium itself was wholly remade, with a full-dome projection system, three-dimensional software that can make viewers feel they're on Mars, and an 18,000-watt sound system that can practically be heard from the Red Planet as well. It made for a fine prelude to the celebration of Flandrau's second half century—with, of course, more rock-and-light shows to come.

THE PROPER STUDY OF HUMANKIND

The School of Anthropology

"**H**OMO SUM: humani nil a me alienum puto," said the Roman playwright Terence: "I am a human: nothing human is foreign to me." That's the spirit of anthropology, which concerns living and past cultures and what are called lifeways: the foods that we humans eat, the deities we worship, the things we trade, the homes we build, the names we call our relatives and the people in the next village. It is about human bodies over the hundreds of thousands, even millions of years, far back into the protohuman past. It embraces art, history, warfare, medicine, birth, architecture, transportation, communication—all the skills and technologies we have developed over the course of millennia. And it is about the dead, for the dead join the living in telling the human story.

The University's leading place in the discipline stretches back to 1893, when the state legislature funded the creation of a museum on campus that would be devoted to "the collection and preservation of the archaeological resources" of the territory and the region. The first directors were natural historians, and it was not until 1915 that a full-time archaeologist was hired for the job in the person of Byron Cummings. On his arrival, he proposed a series of anthropology courses, of which President Rufus von KleinSmid approved a couple while ordering Cummings to concentrate on his museum duties, which, as of the year of his arrival, took place in what is now the Douglass Building after having moved from a few quiet corners of Old Main.

Emil Haury with a group of archaeology students at Snaketown, an important Hohokam site along the Gila River.

Cummings did tend to the museum, diligently—but on the side he taught, attracting young scholars who would go on to remake the field. One was Clara Lee Fraps (1905–97), who earned her master's degree in 1928. As Clara Lee Tanner, she would become one of the world's best-known students of southwestern Native American arts. Another was Emil W. Haury (1904–92), who earned his master's the same year. He and Tanner became the first faculty members in the recently formed Department of Archaeology. Haury later went to Harvard to earn his doctorate and returned in 1937 to take over from Cummings, who retired the following year. Over the years Haury would hire a succession of brilliant archaeologists whose work under his guidance established a chronology and cultural history for the Hohokam, a people whose modern descendants include the Tohono O'odham and Akimel O'odham of the Sonoran Desert. As museum director and department head, one of his first acts was to bestow on the unit the new name Department of Anthropology, better reflecting the breadth of study that he hoped to inaugurate.

That came to pass, and quickly. Scholars such as Norman Gabel, a biological anthropologist, and Edward Spicer, one of the pioneers of ethnohistory, joined the department, which, with the recruitment of other scholars, became a leader in the "four-field approach": archaeology, cultural anthropology, linguistics, and physical anthropology. That effort was significantly enhanced when, as former department head and Arizona State Museum director Raymond H. Thompson has chronicled, President Richard Harvill decided to place Arizona's Departments of Astronomy and Anthropology in the vanguard of the University's transformation to an internationally important research institution. Along the way, Haury, joined by Thompson and Spicer, helped establish the University of Arizona Press in 1959—then, as now, a leading publisher in anthropology.

When I came along in the mid-1970s, the Department—now the School—of Anthropology was a freewheeling, exciting, and very well-funded place to be, with dozens of faculty members whose research blanketed the world. Some of the best-known scholars, to name just a few, were Keith Basso, an authority on the Western Apache languages and ways of thought; Stanley Olsen, a zooarchaeologist who, among other things, established the first scientific chronology for the domestication of the dog; Susan Phillips, a linguist with a special interest in the words used in courtroom proceedings; Mary Ellen Morbeck, an outstanding student of primate evolution; Ellen Basso, a cultural anthropologist who combined a European-inclined, intellectually demanding blend of anthropology and philosophy with a fearless willingness to plunge into the South American rain forest; and Helga Teiwes, who united anthropology and photography to create a new subdiscipline—and even art form. (Teiwes's archive, comprising more than seven thousand images, is now housed at the National Museum of the American Indian in Washington, D.C.)

Headed since 2013 by Diane E. Austin, the School of Anthropology retains the four-field approach, but it has broadened in scope still further to concentrate on several strengths, including the cultural study of gender and sexuality, migration studies, medical anthropology, and, of course, the anthropology of the Southwest in all its aspects. Across the way from the school, the Arizona State Museum flourishes still, with archives and artifacts representing all the interesting ways there are, and have been, of being human.

WASTE NOT, WANT NOT

The Garbage Project

O NE OF the great contributions of contemporary southwestern archaeology began to take shape when I was an undergraduate here in the 1970s: the University of Arizona's Garbage Project—or Le Projet du Garbage, as we affectionately called it. As an anthropology student, I worked on the Garbage Project for two odoriferous years, sorting my way through plastic garbage bags full of things like rotted hamburger, slimy lettuce, overstuffed diapers, and other such unpleasantries, sifting that was necessary to fulfill the research design that underlay this definitively dirty work.

The brainchild of the brilliant Mesoamerican archaeologist William Rathje (1945–2012), the Garbage Project was an innovative application of archaeology to contemporary society, the very essence of ethnographic analogy brought to life. While studying garbage middens in Lowland Maya settlements, Rathje reflected on the many assumptions archaeologists make about ancient economies and societies based on the things people left behind in the form of discarded goods, whether a broken pot or a pile of corncobs. If modern household waste could be examined, what might it tell us about the nutritional habits, social organization, wealth, political standing, and even religious beliefs of those who threw it away?

So it was that for day after fetid day, made especially grueling in the hot months, a team of us undergraduate anthropology students stood in Tucson's main garbage dump and counted cheese wrappers, animal bones, rotting cucumbers, and beer cans, practicing what Rathje called "garbology" by comparing this hard data to what the people who discarded it said about their lives in surveys that Rathje and other researchers conducted while gaining permission to dig into those folks' trash. The stories that the surveys told had the participants eating more healthfully and certainly drinking less than their artifacts revealed, but we tried to be diplomatic when talking of such things.

Rathje's research took a turn at that point, since there was no way to survey a thousand-year-old Maya household to ask what its inhabitants consumed or whether they fibbed about it. Instead, he turned to the study of food waste, among other questions. From the data gathered, Rathje determined that Tucsonans, in the 1970s, threw away about 10 percent of their total food purchases and that the middle class tended to be more wasteful than either the wealthy or the poor. There are reasonable explanations for this: even in those days, arriving in the middle class typically required two incomes, which for busy people might mean a single trip to the grocery store each week—a schedule guaranteed to see some food wastage. Matters have gotten worse in the half century since, even in times of economic turmoil and pandemic, and follow-on studies of the Garbage Project indicate that the average American family of four now discards somewhere between one-fourth and one-half of the food it purchases. That amounts to a lot of money—and mountains of uneaten food in a time of growing hunger.

A CASE OF OVERKILL

Paul S. Martin and Tumamoc Hill

N **1966,** two University of Arizona archaeologists, C. Vance Haynes and Peter Mehringer, were surveying the San Pedro River near the city of Sierra Vista when they discovered an ancient kill site with two scatterings of mammoth bones. People of the so-called Clovis Culture had done the killing about thirteen thousand years ago, staying at the site long enough to leave behind a spearhead, butchering tools, and a bone scraper used to straighten arrow and spear shafts. The remains of an ancient bison species and other extinct animals were found there as well.

Outside of zoos and animal sanctuaries, elephants do not live North America today, certainly not in the wild. Neither are there dire wolves, camels, short-faced bears, giant ground sloths, or saber-toothed cats. Paul Schultz Martin (1928–2010), a professor of geosciences at the University, had an idea why that should have been the case, and in that same year of 1966 he published a short paper in the journal *Nature* that advanced what he called the "overkill hypothesis"—that is, the idea that the hunters who streamed into what is now the Southwest at the end of the last major ice age killed the abundant game they encountered until the megafauna, the largest prey species, were gone.

Martin painted on a wide palette. Trained as a zoologist, he made major contributions to the disciplines of ornithology and herpetology, making a still-consulted survey of the birds and reptiles of the highlands of the Mexican state of Tamaulipas. It was there, while still a student, that he contracted the polio virus, the effects of which required him to use a cane for the rest of his life. That did not keep Martin from climbing every mountain in sight and scrambling up the walls of the Grand Canyon to explore remote caves for the remains of prehistoric creatures, nor from bouncing around in his battered old pickup truck across the roughest patches of desert he could find.

Martin's overkill hypothesis had its critics, but he defended it with vast troves of data derived from fieldwork and combing the archives. Headquartered at Tumamoc Hill, several miles off campus, he gathered a groups of like-minded researchers who explored the pros and cons of his theory, which supplanted an earlier explanation—natural climate change—with human agency. As his friend Vance Haynes, who didn't always agree with him, once remarked, Martin was unusual among scholars in being willing to accept the possibility that he was wrong, and he hosted a pair of conferences, resulting in the UA Press volume *Quaternary Extinctions* (1989), that included viewpoints from several camps, including arguments that strongly challenged his own.

For a sometimes controversial scholar, Paul Martin was a relaxed sort of fellow who liked nothing better than to banter and exchange ideas with friends and colleagues over regular brown bag lunches at his hilltop office. I was privileged to be present at many of them, informal seminars that involved a mix of funny stories, groan-worthy puns, academic gossip, and sharp scientific insights. The collegial, noncompetitive scholarship that echoed off the volcanic rock walls of the old building begat dozens of articles and many books, which was entirely in keeping with the spirit and purpose of the place itself. It also helped give birth to a later insight that Martin advanced toward the end of his life: If the Pleistocene saw the extinction of many species at human hands, he reasoned, could the world not be "rewilded" with modern species that filled the same ecological niches as their forerunners or even, with advances in DNA, be repopulated by lost species themselves?

Tumamoc Hill, the site of these musings, takes its name from the Tohono O'odham phrase meaning "horned lizard." It stands next to "A" Mountain in the Tucson Mountains to the west of the city. On a shelf about a third of the way up the 3,108-foot-tall peak is a cluster of stone buildings that were built over the years beginning in 1903, when the Carnegie Institution, which later helped fund A. E. Douglass's Laboratory for Tree-Ring Research, established the Desert Laboratory on a site of just over 860 acres of rough terrain. It's a remarkable place inasmuch as, for the last 120 years, the desert there has not been significantly changed at human hands; instead, it has been altered by patterns of growth and demise that provide a biological record of climate change, plant biogeography, and other matters.

The University of Arizona took over ownership and management of this biological preserve in 1960, though most scientists, apart from Paul Martin and his desert-rat crew, kept their offices on campus. Effectively abandoned for many years, the Desert Laboratory buildings have slowly been coming back to life with structural repairs and ethnobotanical gardens and other exhibits put in place. And Tumamoc Hill itself has become one of the most popular venues in the city for a good leg-stretching, heart-pounding workout to take in views of the Old Pueblo, the laboratory, and the Sonoran Desert's striking sunrises and sunsets.

LEADERS, RELUCTANT AND OTHERWISE

Byron Cummings and the University's Presidents

BYRON CUMMINGS (1860–1954) was a reluctant president. Appointed by the Board of Regents to head the University of Arizona in 1927, he protested that he didn't really want the job and asked that his administrative duties be shared out with the deans of the College of Agriculture and the College of Mines while the search for a permanent replacement continued.

It took the Board of Regents a year to find that replacement, and meanwhile, Cummings itched for the job he had held since 1915, directing the Arizona State Museum and heading the Department of Archaeology. He also served as the dean of the College of Letters, Arts and Sciences while adding a law degree to his quiver.

On returning to the museum, Cummings undertook extensive field research, unearthing the first evidence of human inhabitants in the Sonoran Desert at the end of the last ice age, a date then established at about eight millennia before the present. (That date has since been pushed far into the past.) Energetic and restless, Cummings also campaigned for new quarters for the museum, which opened under his direction in 1936.

Cummings may have served reluctantly, but he was said to have been a solid leader who brought calm to the campus after the presidency of the mercurial Cloyd H. Marvin. A lover of culture, Cummings also inaugurated an artist and concert series that opened on November 14, 1927, with famed pianist Alexander Brailowsky, followed by performances by the London String Quartet and numerous singers, dancers, and musicians. The artist and concert series continues today.

Byron Cummings, UA archaeologist, museologist, and president, at what is now Rainbow Bridge National Monument in northeastern Arizona in 1909.

Cummings retired from the university in 1938 and lived in Tucson until his death. Of him, the anthropologist Clara Lee Tanner wrote, "Dean Cummings rests deep in the hearts of the men and women with whom he came in contact. He gave freely of inspiration, of knowledge, he gave willingly and without reservation."

Presidents of the University of Arizona

Robert C. Robbins (2017–)

Ann Weaver Hart (2012–17)

Eugene G. Sander (2011–12)

Robert Neal Shelton (2006–11)

Peter W. Likins (1997–2006)

Paul S. Sypherd (1996)

Manuel Trinidad Pacheco (1991–97)

Henry Koffler (1982–91)

John Paul Schaefer (1971–82)

Richard Anderson Harvill (1951–71)

James Byron McCormick (1947–51)

Alfred Atkinson (1937–47)

Paul Steere Burgess (1936–37)

Homer LeRoy Shantz (1928–36)

Byron Cummings (1927–28)

Cloyd Heck Marvin (1922–27)

Francis Cummins Lockwood (1922)

Rufus Bernard von KleinSmid (1914–21)

Arthur Herbert Wilde (1911–14)

Andrew Ellicott Douglass (1910–11)

Kendric Charles Babcock (1903–10)

Frank Yale Adams (1901–3)

Millard Mayhew Parker (1897–1901)

Howard Billman (1895–97)

Theodore B. Comstock (1894–95)

Frank Arthur Gulley (1890–94)

A sculpture of a wildcat, the University's mascot and symbol, graces the Mall near the Administration Building. Photograph by David Olsen.

PLACES AND SPACES

The University of Arizona began with a single building around which other structures soon rose. Central to the mission of the growing school was a library. The University's collection has grown from a few technical manuals and textbooks at its founding to millions of items and a broad range of cutting-edge services today, making the University Libraries ever more central—and essential—to learning and research. Other buildings have come to play important roles in the lives and memories of Wildcats past and present, including the Student Union and Centennial Hall. Those places are full of school spirit—and, some say, of spirits of a different kind. All of the buildings that we will meet here (and, let's not forget, the hidden tunnels beneath our feet) continue to serve important purposes on campus.

BOOKS, CONVERSATIONS, AND 3-D PRINTERS

The University Libraries

"NO UNIVERSITY in the world has ever risen to greatness without a correspondingly great library." So said Lawrence Clark Powell (1906–2001), who, after having led the University of California, Los Angeles, library system for decades, moved to Tucson in 1970 and helped found the University's Library School, now part of the School of Information. Even after retiring in 1990, Powell spent his days in the stacks and conference rooms of the Main Library, enthusiastically reading and writing about the literature of the Southwest, librarianship, and other subjects of longtime interest.

The University of Arizona boasts a vast collection that, while the numbers refuse to stand still, now comprises about 8,645,000 electronic and print books and journals, along with hundreds of thousands of maps, photographs, manuscripts, sheets of music, and other materials. These are distributed among the Main Library, the Albert B. Weaver Science-Engineering Library, and the Health Sciences Library in Tucson. Apart from these locations, other entities at the University maintain independent libraries, among them the College of Medicine–Phoenix, the Poetry Center, the Center for Creative Photography, the James E. Rogers College of Law, the College of Education, and the Arizona State Museum.

When the University opened, its library was a bookcase in the Old Main office of a volunteer curator, Frank Gulley, the dean of agriculture. Most of the books in the collection were technical manuals and treatises on agriculture, mining, and other practical sciences, in keeping with the school's early mandate. By 1893, the library had grown to about 700 volumes that, in time, threatened to overwhelm Gulley's office; in 1896, the noncirculating collection was given its own room, open to faculty and students six hours a day.

By 1900, the collection had grown to 10,000 volumes and was dangerously overcrowded, especially in a building heated by kerosene stoves, laced with questionable electrical wiring, and full of potentially volatile chemicals in the labs below. Howard Hall, an English instructor, succeeded in securing larger quarters, and in 1905, the collection, now directed by formally trained librarian Estelle Lutrell, moved to the newly constructed Douglass Building, sharing a space with the beginnings of the Arizona State Museum in what would later house the College of Law.

The state legislature approved a new library building in 1922, and ground was broken on January 17, 1924, at an assembly involving the entire student body and a large number of townspeople. Located just inside the main gate, this new library opened late in 1926, though it was not completely furnished until May 1927. The legislature's original budget of $80,000 had swelled first to $190,000 and then just shy of $475,000 (about $8 million today) thanks to some nimble negotiating on the part of President Cloyd Marvin. (Though the faculty thought him dictatorial and he didn't last long on the job, Marvin succeeded in securing funding for paved campus streets and other buildings as well, including Bear Down Gym.) The collection had by then grown to 56,000 books, housed in what is now the Arizona State Museum, one of the most handsome structures in the state.

As the collection grew, the library was twice renovated and expanded, once in 1951 and again in 1962, doubtless disturbing some of the ghosts who were said to inhabit the steel-scaffolded, penumbral stacks in the windowless new additions. But, as any bibliophile knows, books always accumulate faster than the room to contain them does. So it was that on July 27, 1973, President John Schaefer broke ground for a new library on the southwest corner of Cherry Avenue and the Mall, where the Wildcats baseball practice field had once stood. In a fine nod to the continuum of history, the shovel used in the 1924 groundbreaking ceremony was the one used half a century later.

The new Main Library was completed in November 1975 at a cost of $12.1 million (about $69 million today). In one of the periodic dollar-hostage-taking skirmishes that takes place in the state capitol, however, the legislature failed to fund the shelving and furniture, an extra $2 million then. The library, accordingly, did not open until January 1977. During the intervening year, though, the main collection was moved from the old library through a combined army of professional movers and student helpers, the latter of whom transported some books in wheelbarrows. The new library, under the direction of W. David Laird, provided a vivid, constantly evolving illustration of Lawrence Clark Powell's dictum and of the University's long pattern of growth to a world-class research institution.

The Main Library expanded again in 2002. By 2017, the University had articulated an ambitious, unique plan to enfold the old Bear Down Gym and a newer, adjacent building into

The old University Library, now the Arizona State Museum, in the 1920s.

a "Student Success District" that would join the Main Library and the Science-Engineering Library by means of sky bridges and outdoor plazas, as well as new entrances that connect each building. The achievement is more than simply architectural, forward looking though it is. As Shan C. Sutton, the eleventh dean of libraries, points out, in recent years, librarians have been rethinking what libraries can be and do. He notes an evolution from "book storage and quiet spaces"—which still exist throughout the library complex—to places where technology and collaborative learning combine to provide hands-on experiences that take place in venues such as makerspaces, offering tools and mentors that can teach students everything from sewing to assembling a circuit board. In the Main Library's Catalyst Studios, virtual reality programs and films are crafted, podcasts recorded, storyboards drawn—a hub of activity that is open to each and every student. Throughout the complex, tutoring and advising spaces also offer academic aid and guidance.

The University of Arizona Libraries and its satellites continue to contribute to our school's excellence while leading the way into the future.

BURGERS, POOL, AND HANGING OUT

The Student Union Memorial Center

CLASSROOMS, LABORATORIES, fieldwork, practicums: all are essential to education. But so, too, is hanging out with friends and classmates, discussing the issues of the day, ideas of no small import, the nature of life. The Student Union Memorial Center has long provided just the venue to do so.

On March 21, 1923, a story in the *Arizona Daily Wildcat* promised, with evident excitement, that a new building for students was going to rise that fall on campus, with an auditorium seating 2,400 and a maple-floored ballroom that could accommodate 1,200 dancers. A follow-up report in February 1924 expressed hope that the unrealized building was merely delayed, but it soon became clear, after it was dropped from the agenda of a Board of Regents meeting, that the building wasn't going to materialize anytime soon. Indeed, President Cloyd Marvin put a halt to discussions around the planned Student Union and worked on landing the new library.

The University's present-day Student Union was instead born in 1938. Sort of, anyway. That year, President Alfred Atkinson, who had just arrived on campus, appointed a faculty committee to study the school's physical-plant requirements while making provisions for a home for the union. The state legislature passed a bill combining a loan from the federal government with state funding in the amount of a little less than $1,168,000 (about $24.5 million today), with some of the funds earmarked for that home. About that time, however, inspectors discovered that Old Main was in disrepair, and the money for the Student Union was put to work renovating the structure.

That was a fortuitous move, for in the summer of 1945, Old Main itself was made into a temporary student center, with a lunch counter, soda fountain, and other amenities installed. With the influx of military personnel returning from wartime service, it soon became apparent that Old Main was too small for the job, but not until 1947 did yet another president, J. Byron McCormick, take on the task of securing funds for a new building. An architect suggested razing Old Main and putting the Student Union atop the ashes, but enough alumni objected to the proposal that the site was moved catercorner to it.

Putting a new building up was another matter, though, and faculty, students, townspeople, alumni, and legislators banded together to secure the necessary funding, which amounted to just short of $900,000 in 1949 (about $11,116,000 today). The building opened in 1951, with the costs for what was now called the Student Union Memorial Center, honoring the dead of two world wars, having swelled to $1,158,000 (about $13,500,000 today).

The new three-story building was a marvel for its day, with a sprawling cafeteria, several kitchens, lounges, offices for student government and organizations, two ballrooms, game rooms, and a post office. Giving a bit of a lie to the building's name, the Student Union also contained a faculty dining room, though students didn't seem to mind. Over time, the Union came to host a bookstore, several dining areas, and outdoor patios, and at any given time it was the busiest building on campus.

The 1951 Student Union, refurbished over the years, served the community well until 2000. It was then that builders razed the old structure and began to build a new one in its place. Completed in 2003 at a cost of $59 million (about $97 million today), the present Student Union Memorial Center enclosed nearly 400,000 square feet of lounges, meeting rooms, the Associated Students bookstore, and restaurants. Modern touches such as a computer lab and a rooftop organic garden came along later, evidence of the constant evolution of the center of student life.

FOR THEM THE BELL TOLLS

The USS Arizona *Memorial*

COMMISSIONED IN 1916, just four years after Arizona attained statehood, the battleship named in its honor sailed out of the Brooklyn Navy Yard and plied the waters off the East Coast. USS *Arizona* took President Woodrow Wilson to the Paris Peace Conference after World War I ended, then joined the U.S. Pacific Fleet. The ship fell victim to Japanese dive-bombers at Pearl Harbor, sinking to the seafloor, its crew having lost 1,177 sailors and officers.

In 1943, naval engineers salvaged the ship's two original bells, both made of silver and copper mined in Arizona. One was kept for the memorial over the *Arizona*'s resting place that was already being planned but that was not completed until 1962. The other went into storage in a naval yard on Puget Sound in the Pacific Northwest, with plans to melt it down. In 1944, however, a University alumnus and naval captain named Wilber L. Bowers learned of its whereabouts and lobbied for it to go to his alma mater. He succeeded, and the bell was sent, as a long-term loan on the part of the U.S. Navy, to the University in October 1946. After being paraded through the streets of downtown Tucson, dedicated at a ceremony presided over by University president Alfred Atkinson and navy admiral Milton E. Mills, and brought to campus, it was again stored until the Student Union was completed in 1951, when it was hung in the building's bell tower and rung on ceremonial occasions such as commemorations of December 7, as well as after Wildcat athletic victories.

In 2000, when the old Student Union was razed, the bell was again put into storage. Plans had been made to install it in Old Main, but at 1,820 pounds, it proved too heavy to mount. So, two years later, when the new Student Union was completed, the *Arizona* bell was hung in a specially built belfry. The bell is visible on the east and west exposures of the belfry, and a plaque nearby reads, "The preservation of the U.S.S. Arizona bell is dedicated to the men who lost their lives on the battleship Arizona in the attack on Pearl Harbor on December 7, 1941."

The bell is in good condition overall, though its inscription is fading and the exterior is weathered. By a happy coincidence, Bowers, then ninety-nine years old, rang it on September 11, 2002, the first anniversary of another history-changing surprise attack. It was a working bell until December 2020, but in order to preserve it for time to come, the bell of the USS *Arizona* is no longer rung.

Another memorial to the crew of the *Arizona* stands on the Mall, and a lounge room on the ground floor of the Student Union contains memorabilia and photographs of the *Arizona* and its crew. Every December 7, the University's Navy ROTC holds a commemorative ceremony at the Mall memorial, with a reading of the names of the eight Arizonans aboard the USS *Arizona* on that fateful day.

SEALS OF (U)APPROVAL

Branding the University

I N 1914, University of Arizona president Rufus von KleinSmid stopped in at a monastery in southern Indiana where a well-known religious artist, Father Albertus Kleber, was in residence. President von KleinSmid asked Kleber to design a seal for the school, one that reflected the strengths and interests of the institution while honoring the virtues of humane education generally. Sometime later, Kleber's drawings arrived, and the one von KleinSmid chose was a bold black-and-white emblem that would in time bear the University's approved blue and red colors. Von KleinSmid took the seal to the Board of Regents for approval, and it was formally adopted in 1915.

A careful look shows that Father Kleber scaled the wall between church and state by inserting a small cross into the design, annotated by the Latin word *sursum* (upward). Other elements of the seal are more workaday, including a pick and plow to indicate the importance of mining and agriculture to Arizona's economy, each flanking a key that represents knowledge. Below this stands an Aladdin-worthy lamp atop a pair of books, and around the whole is emblazoned the curiously meta motto *Sigillum Universitatis Arizonensis*—"the seal of the University of Arizona."

The seal is still in use on products like key rings, sweatshirts, and stationery, though the school's boldly branded blue-and-red "A" has taken its place in most official contexts.

The seal of the University of Arizona, in use since 1915.

GOING UNDERGROUND

The University's Tunnels

W HEN I worked on a University of Arizona archaeological project in a small town in southeastern Italy in 1977 and 1978, several local people confided to me that the catacombs that ran beneath the town's Norman cathedral extended all the way to Rome, a distance of about 210 miles. In truth, the catacombs stretched for just a couple of hundred feet, but they were spooky enough that few of the townspeople had ever checked the true distance or confirmed what turned out to be folklore.

Tales of the tunnels that run beneath the University of Arizona have a similar folkloric dimension to them. They've been said to harbor secret rooms, vast underground chambers, ritual altars, and all manner of dark secrets—the stuff of the under-the-dorm tunnels depicted in the 1985 Val Kilmer vehicle *Real Genius*. Now, it is true that these tunnels exist, dug through the hard caliche soil of the Sonoran Desert. But most of them are narrow enough to cause discomfort, crammed full of water pipes, telephone and electricity lines, heating conduits, and other utilities. I'm sorry to disappoint, but there are no subterranean palaces along their circuit—that I know of, anyway.

The first of the University tunnels was built in 1931. More tunnels, some designed by architect Roy Place to accompany the new buildings he drafted, were laid in during the rest of the decade. During World War II, some of the larger tunnels were designated as bomb shelters in the unlikely event of an enemy attack, and it was common knowledge where the entrances could be found.

In later years, though, the tunnels were mostly a challenge for adventurous students who made a kind of game of exploring them, sometimes emerging in dorms where, technically, they were not supposed to be, sometimes popping up in locked classroom and administrative buildings where, yes, they were not supposed to be. In the 1980s, when the game Dungeons & Dragons became a fad, the tunnels served as a ready-made setting for obsessive players. The University of Arizona Police Department and the Superintendent of Grounds (later Facilities Management) naturally frowned on the pastime of tunnel roaming, which was generally harmless if illegal, to say nothing of an insurance nightmare, given that the tunnels offered the possibility of being scalded by a hot water pipe or bitten by a sheltering rat or snake.

That didn't keep students from poking around in the tunnels. One explorer was Tucson native Randy Tufts, president of the student body, who was an inveterate fan of the underground, having built a bomb shelter in his family's backyard in the scariest years of the Cold War. On graduating with a bachelor's degree in geology, Randy scouted out caves around the Southwest. In 1974, following up on a tip from a miner, he and fellow alumnus Gary Tenen discovered a cave in the Whetstone Mountains southeast of Tucson and, on wriggling down into it, found two huge chambers full of hidden water—and plenty of bats. They kept their discovery secret until they were able to secure a promise for protection from the state government, and so it was that Kartchner Caverns State Park came into being. Randy Tufts later turned his attention skyward, going back to school at the age of fifty and obtaining a PhD from the University for mapping the geology of Europa, a moon of Jupiter.

A University tunnel is coated with a carbon fiber compound developed by Mo Ehsani of the College of Engineering. Photograph by Carina Johnson, courtesy of the University of Arizona.

Back to the tunnels. In 2014, the University acted on a discovery by College of Engineering professor Mo Ehsani, who developed a carbon fiber compound that could be used to reinforce existing buildings susceptible to earthquake damage. One tunnel, running between the Student Union and the Chemical Sciences Building, a distance of 850 feet, had begun to show its age. Facilities Management workers coated the tunnel with Ehsani's carbon fiber concoction, which saved all concerned the trouble of digging up the earth, pouring new concrete, and filling in the excavation. Given that the oldest tunnel is nearly a century old and that the tunnel network extends for fifteen miles, there's plenty of work left to do.

Speaking of the University's physical plant, a visitor to campus might notice a progression of building forms and styles that commemorates the school's history over nearly a century and a half. The oldest remaining buildings and other structures, such as the gabbro wall that lines Park Avenue on the west side of campus, are made of wood and stone. At the heart of the University, built over decades and stretching across much of the area between Speedway Boulevard and Sixth Street, is what's called the Red Campus, commemorating the red brick from which those buildings were made. The newer buildings that dot the campus are creations of steel and glass. The result, Tucson architect James Gresham (1928–2014) wrote, is "the unforeseen result of the very happy marriage of tradition with pragmatism," and one of the most physically attractive campuses anywhere in the nation. A former professor of architecture, Gresham was the designer of one of the University's most innovative structures, the Integrated Learning Center—which, happily enough, was built underground.

FAMILY MATTERS

Polo Village and Christopher City

I**N 1950,** the median age at which a man married was 22.8, a woman 20.3, just a touch lower than the ages for those married from 1946 through 1949. Contrast that with the ages in 2022: 30.1 for men and 28.2 for women. Contrast that further with the median age in 1940, 24.3 and 21.5, and a historical fact begins to suggest itself: after World War II, perhaps spurred by the desire of military veterans to get back to normal life, young marriage became a cultural norm. That norm persisted through the mid-1960s, when so many young men went to fight another war, after which the median age for marriage began its climb.

The number of young newlyweds did not go unnoticed in the administrative offices of the University of Arizona in the months following the surrender of the Axis powers. When the veterans began to stream back to Tucson, the site of numerous military training installations, many of them brought new spouses, some even young children. The University responded by taking an on-campus military field, a polo ground where cavalry troops and ROTC students had trained, and surrounding its central stable with 114 surplus metal Quonset huts, each partitioned to house two families.

Within a few years, with the take-charge attitude of GIs who were older than their civilian student counterparts, the eight hundred residents of Polo Village, as it was called, had organized themselves into a miniature town complete with a governing council, nursery school, laundromat, and small grocery store. Thanks to generous federal funding, the rents were low, and the veterans were able to use their GI Bill benefits year-round, which, in time, meant that the Quonset huts were equipped with newfangled "swamp coolers" to make them

Residents of Polo Village, the UA's first married-student housing complex, in the early 1950s. Photograph courtesy University of Arizona.

bearable in summer. The veterans planted trees and gardens, erected fences, and made the best of quarters that were meant to stand only temporarily, until new dormitories could be built that did not remind them so much of military barracks.

Temporary stretched out for years. Portions of Polo Village stood until 1984, and the University rented out Quonset hut apartments until 1979 at the bargain rate of $52 a month (about $225 today). Polo Village stood square in the path of the steadily expanding University Medical Center complex, however, and block by block its metal buildings, which were in sad disrepair in all events, were periodically removed throughout the mid- to late 1960s, with the College of Medicine even appropriating a few huts to house the medical library until its new building could be erected.

Meanwhile, during the presidency of Richard Harvill, the University acquired a property then, at six miles away, thought to be far distant from campus. Called Christopher City and located on the northwest corner of Fort Lowell Road and Columbus Boulevard, that property, an apartment complex occupying seventy acres, had originally been intended for Catholic families. A year after opening in 1963, though, only a small number of units had been rented out, and in 1966 the Federal Housing Administration foreclosed. The Tucson City Council contemplated using it for public housing but then offered it to the University, which acquired the property in 1967 for $2.45 million (about $22 million today). Christopher City—it retained its old name—opened for rental in 1968, and the University refurbished its 420 apartments one by one from 1969 to 1971, the last year of Harvill's presidency.

Designated as married student housing, Christopher City was upscale compared to the Quonset huts of old. It had a swimming pool and recreational facilities, and the rents were reasonable enough, but the complex wasn't particularly well built to begin with. In 2000, the University condemned Christopher City as uninhabitable and, after selling it to private developers, got out of the—by then anachronistic—business of married student housing. A sprawling residential complex now occupies the site, while Polo Village is but a memory buried underneath the University Medical Center.

AN AUDITORIUM FOR THE AGES

Centennial Hall

A GREAT UNIVERSITY needs many things: a great library, great professors, great students. It also demands a great auditorium, one of those community-building spaces that can do many things, from staging student recitals and professional performances to serving as a lecture hall and site for commemorations, graduations, and inaugurations.

It wasn't until 1909, though, toward the end of his term, that President Kendric C. Babcock put an auditorium on the to-do list of buildings to be erected on campus when anyone could get around to it. First had to come classrooms, laboratories, a library, and other obligations. Arthur H. Wilde was more insistent: when he became president in 1911, he demanded that an auditorium be built within four years. Alas, Wilde did not last out those four years as president, and his successor, Rufus von KleinSmid, found other priorities. Cloyd Marvin reinstated the demand, but he didn't last long either.

Finally, President Homer L. Shantz found both the funding and the necessary approval for an auditorium. So grand was it in design that a member of the Board of Regents objected that it could never be filled. He called the auditorium "Shantz's folly," but it was built all the same. When it was dedicated on April 22, 1937, Shantz was gone too, replaced the preceding year by not one but two presidents.

Why did it take nearly thirty years to put up that auditorium? Well, there were other priorities, as noted. Funding was always an issue. Then there was the all-too-human dimension of pride of place: some property and business owners near the western gate wanted the auditorium there, while their counterparts to the east of campus wanted it on the east side. (Of course, there were also the contrarians, the west-siders and east-siders who didn't want the thing in their backyards.) In the end, the west side won out, only because with the clearing of ground and the removal of athletic fields, greenhouses, an aviary, and assorted other structures over the years, there was room for a new building across the way from the library.

The auditorium filled to capacity immediately after World War II, when returning GIs swelled student enrollment. The first classes to be held in the auditorium were the vastly popular, standing-room-only first-year Psychology 1a and 1b courses. (Thirty years later, as a first-year student, I had Psych 1a there.) Other large introductory lecture courses in economics, chemistry, humanities, and other disciplines met in the auditorium until the 1980s, while at night the building offered public lectures, dance performances, and a few near brawls when contending political factions debated on- and offstage. It saw countless luminaries of all political stripes, including President John F. Kennedy, Joseph Campbell, Dr. Martin Luther King Jr., Eleanor Roosevelt, Jackie Robinson, William Kunstler, Gloria Steinem, and Hunter S. Thompson, and almost every night for years on end, it seemed, the hall was packed to the rafters.

The auditorium offered musical performances as well, with its superb acoustics and ability to seat nearly three thousand audience members at a time. When the building began to show its age in the early 1980s, President Henry Koffler found the funding for a complete overhaul that honored the work of the initial architect, Tucsonan Roy Place, while thoroughly modernizing the auditorium as a performance space. Completed at a cost of $4 million in 1985 (about $11.25 million today) and named Centennial Hall to honor the University's hundredth year, the auditorium has seen an extraordinary range of performances ever since, from the rock band Wilco to the musical *Hamilton* to plays, ballets, symphonies, stand-up comic acts, and even the occasional lecture. With its 2,400 seats, it is the largest performance venue in Tucson. And contrary to that regent of old, UA Presents, the arts organization in charge of booking performances, seems to have no trouble whatever in filling Centennial Hall every time.

GHOST STORIES

The University's Haunted Places

T**HE YEAR** was 1914, and the University of Arizona, entering its fourth decade, was brimming with incoming students who needed somewhere to live. President Arthur Wilde fast-tracked a request to the Board of Regents for funds to build a new dormitory. The board approved it, but it wasn't until 1920 that Maricopa Hall, the oldest residence on campus still used for that purpose, was completed. By then, Wilde had moved on, and it was the pleasure of his successor, Rufus von KleinSmid, to declare the building open to women students.

One of the intended residents was a young woman, her name lost to history, who, it's said, discovered that her fiancé was seeing another woman behind her back. Distraught, the student went into Maricopa Hall, still under construction, and hanged herself from a plumbing pipe. It's further said that von KleinSmid stopped in to check on the progress of the building and discovered the body—and never visited Maricopa Hall again. He did arrange for the funding to add a third floor to the dorm in 1921, but by that time von KleinSmid, perhaps as a result of his ghastly encounter, was also gone, having accepted the presidency of the University of Southern California. The young woman's ghost stayed, though, and walks the halls to this very day. Said one resident to a *Wildcat* reporter in 2003, "I've never seen the ghost. My friend Danielle said she saw her, but I think she was drunk."

The young woman's ghost isn't the only specter to haunt University residence halls. Room 480 of the old stadium dorm was said to be the favorite hangout of a ghost called Harry. A custodian who worked in several buildings reported that he'd seen clocks fall off the walls

To the President of our Student Body, John (Button) Salmon, deceased, who gave the last and best years of his life to Arizona, and left bequeathing to us for all time his own slogan, BEAR DOWN.

John Byrd "Button" Salmon in the 1926 yearbook, commemorated for coining the University slogan "Bear Down."

for no apparent reason and on a couple of occasions had heard knocks coming from inside locked storage rooms.

Ghosts are said to tread the boards of two performance spaces. Opened in 1956, the University's Marroney Theatre is believed to be haunted by a former director who, it seems, couldn't get enough of the place after shuffling off his mortal coil. After it opened in 1937, the ghosts of a man and a woman occupied what is now Centennial Hall. Apparently known to each other in life and not particularly friendly to each other in death, the pair agreed only that it's fun to frighten technicians, performers, and audience members alike. Both ghosts are said to have died in the Spanish colonial period, and why they should be on a campus that was open desert in their day is a mystery.

More fitting to the campus, undoubtedly, is the spirit of John Byrd Salmon, the University football team's quarterback and baseball team's catcher. In 1926, Salmon, nicknamed Button, was driving home from Phoenix when he overturned his car on the winding highway. He ruptured his spinal cord, an injury from which there was no recovery. Salmon died on October 8 of that year, but before he did, athletic director James Fred "Pop" McKale visited him in the hospital and asked whether he had anything he wanted to say to his teammates. Button replied, "Tell the team to bear down!" That phrase has become immortal. The same is true, it seems, of Button Salmon, whose jersey-clad ghost has often been seen outside Bear Down Gym, which opened the year he died. So has the ghost of the original Wilbur Wildcat.

It makes sense that the oldest building on campus, Old Main, should have a ghost to call its own. In this instance, the ghost is said to be that of Carlos Maldonado, a construction foreman who angered a worker while Old Main was going up and was murdered for his troubles. Carlos took up residence where he fell, choosing the building's attic as his domain

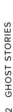

but occasionally wandering down to the lower floors and frightening more than one living soul. Carlos hasn't been seen since the building was renovated in 2014, but it could be that he's just taking a break.

Whether you believe such tales or not, these ghost stories are a longtime part of campus culture. Perhaps it's because we love to be frightened just a little, which, explains ghost story collector Jerry Hogle, University Distinguished Professor Emeritus of English, has a physiological function: "When we are in a situation of being terrified but also safe, our endorphins are aroused, and there is pleasure in that." Just take someone with you if you go into Centennial Hall in the middle of the night or climb into the Old Main attic.

James S. "Big Jim" Griffith plays his beloved banjo with a group of norteño musicians at a memorial service for Bernard L. "Bunny" Fontana at Mission San Xavier del Bac. Photograph by Gregory McNamee.

BEING HUMAN

A university is very much more than a collection of buildings, however beloved, historical, or beautiful they might be. More than a physical plant, a university is a place where people gather to teach and to learn, to grow and to explore. Some of that learning concerns the lives of people who have come before us and the beliefs they have held about their times and conditions. Some of that learning concerns how we might improve our own understanding in order to live better, more fulfilling lives, asking questions of both personal and universal application, such as what it means to be human. And some of that learning concerns how we might best express our stories. In all of these pursuits, the University of Arizona excels.

LEGENDS, MYTHS, AND LEGENDARY FIGURES

Frances Gillmor and Southwestern Folklore

L IKE MANY a southwesterner, Frances Gillmor arrived in Tucson as a result of illness—in this case, that of her mother, who, as was the custom of the day, was advised
to partake of the sunshine and fresh air of the Sonoran Desert to improve her delicate
health. Born in Buffalo, New York, in 1903, Gillmor had gone to the University of Chicago
on scholarship, but she left after two years to work as a reporter for a series of Florida newspapers. Arriving in Tucson, she enrolled at the University of Arizona, completing a BA and
MA in English while living with her mother in a bungalow owned by Louise Foucar Marshall
(1864–1956), the university's first woman professor and namesake of the still-active Marshall
Foundation. Gillmor's master's thesis was on John and Louisa Wetherill, famous traders who
had establish a trading post on the Navajo Nation at Kayenta. She expanded that thesis into
the 1934 book *Traders to the Navajos* and recorded her experiences among the Navajo people
in her 1930 novel *Windsinger*.

Gillmor moved to Albuquerque for a couple of years after completing her MA, teaching
at the University of New Mexico, but returned to Tucson to take a position in the Department of English at the University of Arizona. She alternated between writing novels and literary studies, branching out into anthropology and history. She even returned to journalism
when, in 1937, she traveled to Mexico City to study Nahuatl (Aztec) language and culture;
while there, she covered the Russian revolutionary Leon Trotsky's long-distance defense
in a show trial mounted against him by Josef Stalin's regime in Moscow. Gillmor traveled
between Tucson and Mexico frequently over the following two decades, and although she

had already earned tenure for her inexhaustible work and didn't need the degree, strictly speaking, she earned a doctorate from the Universidad Nacional Autónoma de México in 1957. As with her MA thesis, she expanded her doctoral dissertation, on the life of the emperor Montezuma I, into the well-regarded historical study *The King Danced in the Marketplace* (1964).

All the while, Frances Gillmor was teaching undergraduate and graduate courses in English, suspending her research during the regular school year to concentrate on her students and then, over the winter and summer breaks, plunging into her scholarly work. She took time over the summer of 1946 to travel to Indiana University to study folklore with the eminent folklorist Stith Thompson. She then formed an interdisciplinary committee on the folklore of the Southwest and established the University of Arizona Folklore Archive, the forerunner of the Southwest Folklore Center. Gillmor and her fellow researchers, including the famed anthropologist Edward Spicer, traveled widely throughout the region to gather folktales, songs, oral histories, art, and other materials in Spanish and English, with Native American materials placed under the care of the Department of Anthropology.

She continued to work on the folkloric archive long after her retirement in 1973, and students and colleagues continued to seek her out for her breadth and depth of knowledge of all things southwestern. Confident and thoroughly independent, Frances Gillmor was beloved as a teacher and highly regarded as a scholar. She died in 1993 at the age of ninety.

It's a matter of coincidence that an important modern mythologist was once a presence on the University campus at about the same time. Born in 1907, Evangeline Wilna Ensley suffered from respiratory ailments all her life, but it was not until 1940 that she moved to Tucson from Indiana. Availing herself of the University Library, she continued to work on a series of novels, published under the nom de plume Evangeline Walton, that were based on the medieval Welsh cycle of myths and legends called the *Mabinogion*. The first book, called *The Virgin and the Swine*, did not sell well when it appeared in 1936, but Walton was undeterred, going on to work on a trilogy of novels based on the legendary Greek hero Theseus. She also wrote a well-liked horror novel called *Witch House* and several other books and stories, finally attaining fame in the early 1970s when the *Mabinogion* series appeared in mass-market paperback editions as *The Island of the Mighty*, *The Children of Llyr*, *The Song of Rhiannon*, and *The Prince of Annwn* and became favorites of fantasy-fiction buffs. It was after reading these books and visiting Walton at her home near campus, by the way, that Stevie Nicks wrote her hit song "Rhiannon," which Fleetwood Mac performed at their storied concert in the University football stadium soon afterward.

Evangeline Walton could often be seen working in a corner of the Student Union cafeteria when I was an undergraduate in the 1970s. She couldn't be missed, for the silver nitrate with which her bronchial infections had been treated in childhood caused her skin to turn a bluish gray late in life, lending her an ethereal and even mythological look all her own. She was lovely and friendly. She died in 1996. Like Frances Gillmor's, her papers are housed in the University Libraries' Special Collections.

A SCHOLAR OF THE PEOPLE

Big Jim Griffith

D R. JAMES S. Griffith was seldom addressed by that name or title. Instead, he was universally known as Big Jim, a moniker he came by honestly: he stood, after all, six foot seven, and he had an outsize personality to match—courtly, genial, and constantly curious, among other personal qualities that made him one of the best ambassadors that the University and southern Arizona ever boasted.

Big Jim came to Tucson in 1955 from his hometown of Santa Barbara, California, and immediately fell in love with the Sonoran Desert. He earned degrees in art history and anthropology, participating in the ferment of the antiwar and countercultural movements by helping found a satirical newspaper called the *Frumious Bandersnatch*. After finishing his doctorate in 1973, he faced the terrible prospect of moving elsewhere to find a job in academia, but instead he scraped together a living until Lawrence J. (Larry) Evers, a professor of English and head of the University of Arizona Folklore Committee, recruited him to run the University's Southwest Folklore Center. Housed in a little pink bungalow across from the football stadium, the Folklore Center soon became a hive of activity, scholarly and popular, and a place that like-minded researchers could call home. Big Jim headed the Southwest Folklore Center from 1979 to 1998, during which time it moved from the aegis of the English Department to the University Library under then librarian W. David Laird.

Along the long way, in 1974, Big Jim founded one of our city's best-loved annual events, Tucson Meet Yourself, which, though nicknamed "Tucson Eat Yourself" because of all the different foods on sale, highlighted the many different cultures that make up our region, cultures from all over the world. The community showed its thanks in many ways, turning up in the tens and even hundreds of thousands to enjoy his efforts. Said Peter Yucupicio, chairman of the Pascua Yaqui Tribe, appreciatively, "There's only one Big Jim. And the thing he did was to bring awareness of all the different types of ethnicities and races living here, and the beauty of bringing us all together."

Big Jim, as the saying goes, never met a stranger. Gregarious, with an irreverent streak (as he put it, he liked to "cock a snook" at authority), and with an unfortunate love of groaningly bad jokes and even worse puns, he was a natural magnet for artists, musicians, and creators of all kinds. He put them to work, recruiting a small army of bluegrass players to support him as he played his ever-present banjo, championing forgotten heroes such as the Chicano musical legend Lalo Guerrero, organizing dances and celebrations around the year, working side by side with his equally energetic wife, Loma, and often paying for the costs of his community-oriented, community-building projects out of his own pocket.

I first met Big Jim the same year he founded Tucson Meet Yourself. Growing up in Northern Virginia and with a love of music, I often rode my bicycle into Washington for various cultural events, but that year one of them, the American Folklife Festival, was relocated to Wolf Trap Farm Park a few miles from my home. I rounded a bend and saw a group of Native American dancers. Watching them was a towering, bearded fellow whom I approached to ask what we were seeing. "These are Papago dancers," he answered, using the then-current name for the Tohono O'odham, "from outside Tucson, Arizona." I said that I was planning to apply to the University, he gave me his card and said to look him up, I did when I arrived in Tucson in the summer of 1975, and we were friends ever since.

(Those Tohono O'odham dancers, by the way, returned to their nation west of Tucson, and with Big Jim's help soon thereafter created the Tucson Waila Festival, one of the most popular Native American dance events in the country.)

Big Jim was a popular television and radio presenter and a vigorous popular writer. He was also a respected, serious scholar. Big Jim loved just about everything about our place, from candle wax–scented altars to lowriders, from norteño ballads to bluegrass flailing to Native American etiological myths and cowboy poetry, to say nothing of our region's spectacular food and drink. His home with Loma near the San Xavier Mission southwest of town was a veritable museum of regional folk art and Native American carvings, stuffed with books, scratchy records, and musical instruments of all kinds. More than anything else, he loved hearing and telling a good yarn, saying, "Neither of my parents was particularly terrified of the sound of their own voices and neither of them was terribly interested in letting stark truth get in the way of a good story, and so I've grown up in a world where stories were told."

Though he retired from the University in 1998, Big Jim remained active on campus in many ways. Calling himself "an academic butterfly flitting from blossom to blossom," he passed away in 2021 at the age of eighty-six. It seems safe to say, however, that his spirit will be with us for time to come, continuing to teach us all how to be better citizens of the Sonoran Desert.

PLACES AND PEOPLES

Bunny Fontana and the History of the Sonoran Desert

BERNARD L. FONTANA (1931–2016), known to one and all as Bunny, was a living encyclopedia of the peoples and past of the Southwest, and he was no stranger to any place or thing in the region, whether leafing through the pages of a Spanish colonial inventory or visiting a Tohono O'odham village far from the nearest road. Like Big Jim Griffith, Bunny was originally a Californian, born in Oakland in 1931, but he made saguaro country his *querencia*—the place, in the Spanish term, where he felt he truly belonged, his heartland.

Bunny came to the University of Arizona in 1955 to study anthropology, having been encouraged to do so by a faculty member doing fieldwork whom Bunny met while he was serving in the U.S. Army in Alaska. He earned his PhD in 1960, but there were no jobs to be had. Fortunately, the perceptive librarian of the University, Fleming Bennett, invented a position as "field historian" for him in the Special Collections division before Bunny could be lured away to some other school.

Two years later, Department of Anthropology head Emil Haury hired Bunny as the Arizona State Museum's first ethnologist. The museum's director, Raymond H. Thompson, wasn't quite sure of what to do with a cultural anthropologist in the midst of a community of archaeologists. Still, Bunny told an interviewer from the Tohono O'odham Nation, Jacelle Erin Ramon-Sauberan, who wrote her University master's thesis in American Indian studies on him, "Well, you know if you have jobs with no job description what do you do? You do whatever you want to do as long as you can get away with it." Bunny was thus not often to be found in his office, given freedom to roam, and he collected oral histories, folktales, and autobiographies from Indigenous peoples across the region while researching the history of Spanish colonial settlements and missions on both sides of the border.

In 1978, President John Schaefer returned Bunny to the library as field historian for the entire university. Bunny lived in a paradise of books, maps, and historical documents even as he got plenty of dust on his boots, getting away with it for another two decades, his office door always open when he was in residence.

Along the way, writing a dozen books and hundreds of articles and constantly traveling, Bunny was instrumental in founding many important groups and institutions in both the university and the community. He served on the committee that established the Southwest Center, got the Southwest Mission Research Center on its feet, and worked around the clock for the Patronato San Xavier as the organization's secretary. For the latter, Bunny helped raise millions of dollars over the years to preserve Mission San Xavier del Bac south of Tucson, bringing in art restorers from Italy who trained numerous Tohono O'odham artists—and who then returned the favor by traveling from the Tohono O'odham Nation to Rome to help restore works of art in the Vatican. Bunny attended Mass at San Xavier nearly every Sunday, and he made his home on the edge of the Tohono O'odham enclave that encompassed the mission, the core of that *querencia* for the next half century. His magnum opus was *A Gift of Angels: The Art of Mission San Xavier del Bac* (UA Press, 2010), a book that weighed more than nine pounds and contained more than 375 brilliant color photographs by Edward McCain.

Bunny retired from the University in 1992, but it was only to become busier than ever. He wrote, traveled, researched. Ever generous with his time, he plunged himself into raising still more funds for the mission while entertaining visits from dozens of scholars and students who learned, as his colleagues had known for years, that if you had a question about nearly anything having to do with the Sonoran Desert, Bunny was the man to see: if he didn't know the answer, he knew who would. Yet Bunny was self-effacing always—or, as Ramon-Sauberan told Tucson journalist Ernesto Portillo, "He was like the O'odham. He was humble."

"Nothing human is foreign to me." Bunny Fontana approached his life and work in the Sonoran Desert in that anthropological spirit, knowing that it's not enough to have the right zip code or to pay state income tax to be an Arizonan—not a true citizen of Arizona, anyway. That comes with a recognition of and willingness to drink copiously from the three great rivers that flow into this place: the Indigenous, the Hispanic, and the Anglo. The University of Arizona has long led the way in fostering this awareness, and Bunny Fontana was at the very vanguard of this effort over a long career.

DEFINING OUR REGION

The Southwest Center

IN 1964, Supreme Court Justice Potter Stewart issued a famous threshold test for the definition of obscenity. He said, "I shall not today attempt further to define the kinds of material
I understand to be embraced within that shorthand description; and perhaps I could never
succeed in intelligibly doing so. But I know it when I see it."

That's pretty much the way it is with the Southwest. We don't exactly know where it is, but
we know it when we see it—dust, mountains, cacti, enchiladas, all the things that define our
region. Indeed, the noted librarian and collector of southwestern literature Lawrence Clark
Powell echoes Justice Stewart on that note: "The Southwest," he wrote, "has many hearts,
synchronized by configuration and color. Even though we cannot define and delimit the
Southwest to the satisfaction of all its lovers, we all know when we have reached it."

We know, but questions remain. Do we include Oklahoma? How much of Colorado?
Where in Texas does the South end and the Southwest begin? Does Los Angeles count?

These are all questions that concern the scholars from many disciplines and institutions
who gather at the Southwest Center, a kind of intellectual clearinghouse for every sort of
exploration of our region—and fittingly, for the Southwest has for millennia been a cross-
roads of cultures, languages, crops, trade, customs, and ideas. Its diverse ethnic and social
makeup lends the Southwest a distinct identity, different from every other place in the
United States and the world.

It was in recognition of its unique nature that the Southwest Center was first conceived at
a *convenio* held, again fittingly, at Mission San Xavier del Bac in 1978. President John Schaefer

The heart of the Sonoran Desert along the U.S.-Mexico border near Tule Well.
Photograph by Gregory McNamee.

and field historian Bunny Fontana planned an institution that would be on the freewheeling side of things, not tightly tied to any one academic home at the University but instead welcoming to scholars and students in every discipline, from anthropology to zoology.

It took eight years to pull together the funding for the Southwest Center, but finally, in 1986, it was inaugurated. It soon came under the direction of Joseph C. Wilder, a philosopher by both training and disposition. Joe built a powerful network of advisors, contributors, and researchers that looked far beyond the borders of wherever the Southwest lies, with representatives from universities all over Mexico and Latin America as well as Europe, to say nothing of dozens of institutions within this country and Native nations of the greater Southwest, which includes northwestern Mexico. Soon the Southwest Center was abuzz with conferences on politics, literature, photography, plant geography, linguistics, ecology, folklore, intellectual history, architecture . . . well, the list goes on, and it's a long one.

No single academic discipline or approach can encompass all that there is to know about this place, and so practitioners of these diverse disciplines appreciate the many realms of knowledge and many approaches that are needed in order to comprehend it. The Southwest Center has thus become both a leader of regional research and a hub for multidisciplinary, collaborative projects. Among these have been studies of Yaqui Indian ethnopoetics, a large-scale ecological survey of the forbidding Camino del Diablo region of southwestern Arizona, histories of the cultures of northern Mexico, and ethnobotanical studies among Native cultures throughout the Southwest. The Southwest Center has sponsored the creation and development of photographic, manuscript, and oral history archives, and its efforts have been central in numerous historic preservation projects involving the architecture of the region.

One arm of the Southwest Center's mission is to publish exemplary work of scholarship that also, along with those conferences, reaches out to the broader public. To this end, the Southwest Center publishes the influential quarterly *Journal of the Southwest*, as well as award-winning books such as Eileen Oktavec's *Answered Prayers: Miracles and Milagros Along the Border*, Charles Bowden and Jack W. Dykinga's *The Sonoran Desert*, Cathy Moser

Marlett's *Shells on a Desert Shore: Mollusks in the Seri World*, and Bill Broyles and Michael P. Berman's *Sunshot: Peril and Wonder in the Gran Desierto*, among several dozen other titles.

Five decades on, now under the direction of Jeffrey Banister, the Southwest Center stands at the heart of studies about our region, hard to define though it might be. It also coordinates an undergraduate minor program in Southwestern studies, training new generations of scholars to take the multifaceted knowledge of our home far into the future.

HONORING ANCESTORS

Abe Chanin and the Bloom Southwest Jewish Archives

THE GENERAL course of Arizona history, in the years of Spanish and Anglo-American settlement, goes something like this. First came the conquistadores, looking at the lay of the land and the best way to get around on it. Then came clerics, who scouted out locations for missions that would serve as combination church, farm, trading post, and fort. Then came miners, followed shortly by soldiers, followed shortly by freighters and teamsters who hauled in supplies. Then came merchants, who settled in places that easily served all these constituents, including a little border town called Isaacson after a Jewish immigrant who arrived from Russia in 1880 and established a general store there, in what is now called Nogales. Other Jewish families arrived, bearing names such as Emanuel, Levy, and Bracker, and made their homes in the region.

Ten years before Jacob Isaacson's arrival in Arizona Territory, a German Jewish immigrant named Jacob Mansfeld (1832–94) established Tucson's first bookstore and newsstand. Other Jewish arrivals in Tucson included Samuel Drachman (1833–1911), Selim Franklin (1859–1927), and Charles Moses Strauss (1840–92). In 1883, the same year Isaacson was renamed Nogales, Strauss became Tucson's first Jewish mayor, while Franklin, a legislator, helped negotiate the founding of the University of Arizona in Tucson. It was Mansfeld who sought out the location for the University of Arizona and convinced the owners of various parcels to part with forty acres to accommodate it. Fittingly, one descendant of an early Jewish immigrant family, Esther Capin (1934–2013), served twice as president of the Board of Regents during her sixteen-year term there.

It's entirely fitting, too, that the University of Arizona should house a significant archive of materials related to the Jewish history of the Southwest. Funded by local haberdasher David A. Bloom and his wife, Leona G. Bloom, the archive was the brainchild of Abraham S. Chanin. A graduate of Tucson High School, Abe Chanin had been a student at the University of Arizona and edited the *Arizona Daily Wildcat* from 1941 to 1943. On graduation, he enlisted in the U.S. Army and served as an infantryman in World War II, fighting in Italy, France, and Austria. He returned to Tucson after the war and resumed his work as a journalist, becoming a sports reporter for the *Arizona Daily Star*. After a thirty-six-year career there that included stints as sports editor and editorial page editor, as well as separately publishing the *Arizona Jewish Post* and the *Collegiate Baseball Newsletter*, he retired to teach journalism at the University until 1988, the year the Bloom Southwest Jewish Archives opened. All the while, Chanin nurtured his love of both sports and Jewish history with several books, including a history of University athletics, *They Fought Like Wildcats*, and *Cholent and Chorizo*, which describes the interactions and, often, intermarriage between Jewish and Hispanic families in southern Arizona.

To the end of his life in 2014 at the age of ninety-two, Abe Chanin continued to gather oral histories, books, recipes, photographs, diaries, and other materials to add to the archive, which is now housed in Special Collections at the University Libraries. "Whether Jewish or not," he observed, "everyone should know about Southwest Jewish history. Jewish pioneers are forerunners to the building of the Southwest."

KEEPING THE BOOKS

Documentary Relations of the Southwest

T HE SPANISH, who colonized what is now southern Arizona from the 1600s until Mexico won independence in 1821, were punctilious record keepers. Every now and again, a colonial military officer would be dispatched to New Spain's northern frontier to report on defenses, commerce, and the relative state of war and peace with the Indigenous peoples, returning with reams of notes. Missionaries—literally, those who established and served missions such as San Xavier del Bac south of Tucson—filled page after ledger page with notes on languages, agricultural production, irrigation, and many other topics, sometimes complaining of the fieriness of the local cuisine or the obstinance of Native people who refused to accept Spanish customs and religious norms.

Wrestling this wealth of information, which amounted to more than a million pages of manuscripts retrieved from the Vatican Library and other sources, into usable form was the work of the scholars of the Documentary Relations of the Southwest (DRSW) project, now called the Office of Ethnohistorical Research at the Arizona State Museum. Its driving spirit was Charles W. Polzer (1930–2003), a Jesuit priest and historian who set out to gather Spanish-era records from his religious order in 1974. He soon realized that, rivalries aside, the Franciscans who succeeded the Jesuits in the 1700s left an equally rich trove of records behind, and then there were masses of government reports made by functionaries and soldiers on top of all that. With support from the National Historical Publications and Records Commission and the National Endowment for the Humanities, Polzer and a small group of researchers and students developed guides and indexes to the documents, as well as biographical files for some nineteen thousand people whose names appeared in them.

As well as conducting this exhaustive—and exhausting—archival work, which made innovative use of (at the time) new personal computers, Polzer and his associates prepared editions of key texts published by UA Press. One, for instance, gathers an inspection report by an official named Pedro de Rivera Villalón ordered by Spanish king Philip V, which resulted in a new set of military and civil regulations for the frontier promulgated in 1729. With Thomas C. Barnes and Thomas H. Naylor, Polzer also wrote *Northern New Spain: A Research Guide*, which historians of the colonial era have long considered an essential resource.

When not working on the collections, Polzer pressed for the nomination of Eusebio Francisco Kino, the Jesuit missionary who founded San Xavier, to sainthood in the Roman Catholic Church. Those wheels turn slowly: only in 2020 did Pope Francis elevate Padre Kino to "venerable" status, a step away from joining the calendar of saints.

Says Michael M. Brescia, an ethnohistorian and curator at the Arizona State Museum, "It was Father Polzer's dream to establish a New World archive here. Those documents let us know about the civil, political, military, religious, and ecological contexts to the Spanish Empire in our own backyard." With that treasure house of documents, microfilms, books, and other historical records made usable and useful for scholars working to this day, Charles Polzer clearly achieved that goal.

An exemplary work in the field of ethnohistory is the product of Thomas E. Sheridan, a former DRSW researcher and noted anthropologist with the Southwest Center. Sheridan's *Arizona: A History* has been lauded for its blend of historical narrative and anthropological analysis, introducing its readers to Arizona's wealth of cultures and their interactions over centuries. Published by UA Press in 1995, and again in a second edition in 2012, *Arizona* doesn't shy away from controversies such as land fraud, the disenfranchisement of ethnic minorities and historical mistreatment of Indigenous populations, and inequitable resource distribution. The eminent Yale historian David J. Weber hailed the book as one that "reveals processes—pacification, exploitation, and transformation—rather than relating one damn thing after another." Bunny Fontana, himself a pioneer of ethnohistory, remarked in an appreciative review of Sheridan's book, "My greatest disappointment concerning *Arizona: A History* is that I didn't write it."

WOMEN'S WORK

Myra Dinnerstein and Women's Studies

MYRA DINNERSTEIN arrived in Tucson in 1970, accompanying her husband, Leonard Dinnerstein, a noted scholar of anti-Semitism in America who served as a professor in the Department of History from 1970 to 2004. Armed with a doctorate in history from Columbia University, and a specialist in colonial southern Africa, she taught a continuing education course here and there until finally being invited to teach a course in women's history in 1974, a time when the field was new and neither well supported nor well understood.

All that changed when she planned out a curriculum that brought scholarly rigor to the study of women's roles in every aspect of society, leading, in 1975, to the establishment of a committee on women's studies. Despite the grumbling of a few legislators, some offended by its inclusion of lesbians in that curriculum, the program proved a popular minor until a major was approved in 1983. Even so, the Department of Women's Studies—now the Department of Gender & Women's Studies—was not formally created until 1997. Two years later, some of the aforementioned legislators tried to defund the department, but to no avail, with Dinnerstein commenting simply that their efforts amounted to "trying to keep women quiet." To add insult to injury, the department was first housed in the Mathematics Building, which in those benighted times had no women's bathrooms.

All the same, the indefatigable Dinnerstein had long before established alliances all over campus, drawing in scholars in literature, the social sciences, the arts, and other fields to build an interdisciplinary curriculum. In 1976, she worked with Laurel Wilkening, a professor of chemistry and planetary science, and later dean of sciences and vice president for research, not just to create the department but also to add to it a strong science and engineering component, encouraging women to enter fields that had effectively been closed to them for generations.

The Women's Plaza of Honor, near Centennial Hall. Photograph by David Olsen.

Indeed, Dinnerstein, Wilkening, Barbara Babcock, Susan Hardy Aiken, Patricia MacCorquodale, Judy Nolte Lensink, Billy Jo Inman, and other scholars at the University of Arizona ensured not just that women would be heard but that it would be unthinkable to exclude them from any part of academic life and beyond. One vehicle for this was the field of women's studies itself. Another, which Dinnerstein helped found in 1979, was a center of both research and activism, the Southwest Institute for Research on Women. Thriving today, SIROW engages scholars from all over campus—and all over the world—to improve the lives of marginalized communities in areas extending from education and employment to health care, the law, the arts, history, and many other realms. The program in science and engineering has meanwhile grown to include medicine, supporting women's involvement in every branch of STEM (science, technology, engineering, and mathematics) education and research and creating outreach and interdisciplinary pathways to do just that.

Myra Dinnerstein retired from teaching in 2003. Appropriately, she was one of the first members of the university community to be given a place in the Women's Plaza of Honor.

THE RICHNESS OF OTHER CIVILIZATIONS

Gail Lee Bernstein and the History of Japanese Women

I**F YOU** were a student of Japanese history in the 1960s, you might be forgiven for thinking that Japanese women, where they were mentioned at all, were either members of the nobility or geishas. Some were, of course, but very few as compared to farmers, shopkeepers, tailors, cooks, nuns, poets, artists, and all the other sorts of workers whom Gail Lee Bernstein uncovered in her historical research on Japanese women from the 1600s to the present.

Bernstein, a native of New York, came to Japanese studies somewhat accidentally. As an undergraduate student at Barnard College, she became friends with the daughter of Japan's ambassador to the United Nations. She recalled, "The study of Asia was still considered an exotic occupation in the late 1950s," one that she jumped at, enrolling in a doctoral program with the noted historian Edwin O. Reischauer at Harvard University and completing her dissertation in 1968.

Bernstein arrived in the History Department as an assistant professor in 1967. She was named an associate professor in 1972, about the time she began the research project that would result in the book *Changing Roles of Women in Rural Japan* (1976). The same year, she also published her study *Japanese Marxist: A Portrait of Kawakami Hajime, 1879–1946*, for which she won the prestigious John K. Fairbank Prize of the American Historical Association. Promoted to a full professorship in 1984, she followed those books with numerous contributions to edited volumes on Japanese women, and then, in 1983, with the prizewinning book *Haruko's World: A Japanese Farm Woman and Her Community*. Over the next three decades, she continued to expand on a field of study that she essentially invented here at the University of Arizona, all the while teaching generations of undergraduate and graduate students through courses across the breadth of Asian history generally.

Before her time, as Bernstein wrote, "It is as though the female factory workers, office workers, artists, teachers, preachers, entrepreneurs, volunteers, and political activists . . . never really existed." In the years since she became a professor emerita, Japan, Korea, and especially China have become ever more prominent players on the world stage, and Gail Lee Bernstein's work has been critically important in helping us understand the lives of women in that context. That understanding, she adds, fulfills what she long regarded as her scholarly duty—namely "to disseminate knowledge of Asia that will make the richness of non-Western civilizations available to more persons and that will equip them to work and live in the twenty-first century."

WHAT IT MEANS TO BE HUMAN

Donna Swaim and the Power of the Humanities

PROFESSORS WHO bring skill and dedication to their teaching command respect from all but the most grudging students. Some professors are well liked. But few are beloved, a rare category of which Donna Swaim was an outstanding representative.

Donna was born a full generation ahead of her classmates at the University of Arizona, of whom I was one. In partnership with one of Tucson's most successful architects, Bob Swaim, she had raised a family, and then decided to return to school to pursue her love of literature and the classics. Though she technically was an undergraduate in her late thirties, having grounded herself in courses in a dozen disciplines before settling into her chosen academic home, Donna was well beyond the rest of us not just in experience but also in a lifetime of constant reading and thinking, a fact her professors instantly recognized and surely appreciated.

Donna became a passionate advocate of the humanities, a large field that embraces disciplines such as folklore, history, religious studies, classical studies, and literature, so called because these areas of study ask, in various ways, what it means to be human and how to do so better. Such matters were her great preoccupation, generating questions that we classics undergrads would bat around over coffee late into the evening at the Student Union: What can literature teach us in a time of impending nuclear annihilation? (The Cold War was still going strong.) Can one be both virtuous and wealthy? What constitutes the good life?

While she was studying, earning both a master's degree and doctorate, Donna was also teaching, and eventually the University—always reluctant to hire its own—awarded her with a faculty position with a home in what evolved from the Humanities Department into the College of Humanities. In that role, Donna taught a whirlwind variety of courses in religious studies, humanities, literature, medical humanities, and English. She tutored student athletes, who became her biggest fans just as she was theirs. She worked with incarcerated people, counseled anyone who came to her for advice, and led students on two dozen humanities-oriented trips abroad, visiting countries around the world. She taught in Dr. Andrew Weil's Center for Integrative Medicine. She was everywhere at once, and the word was out for fifty

Donna Swaim, beloved professor of humanities and religious studies. Photograph courtesy of Katy Brown.

years: Whatever else you do at the University, take a class with Donna Swaim. Countless students took that advice, and it was no accident that they dubbed one of her most popular courses, on spirituality in the arts, "Friendship 101."

Donna Swaim died in 2020 at the age of eighty-six, having retired from teaching while continuing to mentor, read, and learn. It is fitting testimonial to how beloved she was that hundreds of her former students attended a memorial service for her the following spring.

Donna Swaim helped build the College of Humanities into a powerhouse, ranked tenth among public universities in the nation in 2021. That was a distinction earned by many other humanists at the University, from early department heads such as Fred Dye and Robert A. Burns to immensely popular lecturers such as Christopher Carroll. The first dean of the College of Humanities, Richard P. Kinkade, was the model of a Renaissance man, a scholar of medieval Spanish literature who was also a gifted musician and a skilled pilot who built his own airplane. His successor, Annette Kolodny, was among the best-known feminist scholars of her generation, a pioneer in the now well-established field of ecoliterary studies.

The work of all of them continued through a robust humanities faculty, exemplified by Karen Seat, who is head of the Department of Religious Studies and Classics, Donna Swaim's precinct. Beginning in 2012, Seat rebuilt the department brick by metaphorical brick, adding lines of study in New Testament language and literature, religious studies for health professionals, and online classics and religious studies minors. The current College of Humanities dean, Alain-Philippe Durand, has helped launch ventures in digital and applied humanities, fields such as Africana studies, and institutes such as the Center for Buddhist Studies to complement and enrich more traditional disciplines.

What does it mean to be human? There are many answers to be found in that flourishing intellectual community.

GOING MEDIEVAL

Scholars of the Middle Ages

THEY'RE LIKELIER to gather in city parks these days, but back in the 1970s and 1980s, devotees of the medieval/Renaissance cosplay Society for Creative Anachronism gathered on the Mall, jerkins taut and bells all a-jingling. They may have been in on a well-kept secret: namely, in buildings all across campus, University scholars were working on questions concerning medieval and Renaissance history, art, music, literature, science, and society.

Foremost among them, I'm sure those scholars would agree, was the historian and theologian Heiko A. Oberman (1930–2001). A native of the Netherlands, Oberman taught at Harvard Divinity School and the University of Tübingen. It was in the damp climate of southern Germany that Oberman arrived at the thought that a warm, dry climate might be just the thing for his wife's arthritis, and, after he made his interest known, he was invited to join the history faculty here in 1984. Soon thereafter, he founded the Division for Late Medieval and Reformation Studies, teaching courses that were popular among students of every and no religious denomination—for, although he was considered to be among the most important historians of early Protestantism, he was delighted to share his mission of turning his students into "world citizens" with broad horizons, telling them of his Dutch homeland, "One cannot be parochial in a country so small that speeding sends you into another country." Named a Regents Professor in the inaugural class of 1988, he wrote or shepherded into being more than thirty books and hundreds of articles, perhaps the best known of them a somewhat controversial biography, *Luther: Man Between God and the Devil*. His vast research library is now housed within the University Libraries.

In the English Department, no teacher was more enthusiastic about his subjects, which included *Sir Gawain and the Green Knight* and other medieval texts, than Christopher Franklin Carroll (1937–2013). His middle name is an embodiment of the history of Tucson and the University, for Chris—always Chris, never "Professor"—was a direct descendant of founding father Selim Franklin, living in Franklin's downtown home after he and his wife, fellow English professor Susan Hardy Aiken, thoroughly renovated the 1898 structure. Sitting cross-legged on a desk, Chris was a born storyteller, acting out scenes from Chaucer, Dante, and other medieval writers. He held the rank of lecturer for decades because he was more interested in teaching than research, but all the same, the University very rightly saw fit to name him a distinguished professor in 1995. Chris passed away in 2013 at the age of seventy-six, a teacher to the last.

Sigmund Eisner (1920–2012) was more reserved than Chris Carroll, but he had a droll sense of humor that he accentuated, back in the days when people smoked in class, by puffing on a pipe. A devotee of medieval ballads, he was also among the world's leading Chaucer scholars, writing a critically lauded study of Chaucer's use of the astronomical device called the astrolabe—which, along with his studies of other medieval astronomers, made him well known to his colleagues down the Mall in space sciences. Just down the hall from him, Frederick Rebsamen (1926–2009) was, among other things, a translator of *Beowulf* and a scholar of Old English, while downstairs in the Modern Languages Building, classicist Richard Jensen (1936–2010), a popular teacher of ancient Greek and Latin, translated the difficult medieval Latin of Italian poets Domenico Silvestri and Coluccio Salutati. Meanwhile, back in the English Department, there were enough Shakespeare scholars at work to inspire the joke that Tucson should be renamed "Stratford on the Santa Cruz."

If you wanted to know about a word in Latin, Greek, Old English, or any of several dozen languages, then Richard Diebold (1934–2014) was the person to see. A professor of anthropology but at home in many disciplines, Richard was a linguist of extraordinary breadth, working in such modern fields as sociolinguistics (the study of how people actually *use* language) while at his happiest puzzling out such things as the words for salmon and wheel in the conjectured ancestor of the Indo-European languages. A medievalist as well, Richard would have told you that the name Beowulf is a kenning, a kind of linguistic riddle, deriving from the Old English names for bee and wolf—a creature, that is to say, that raids beehives, namely a bear.

Historian Donald Weinstein (1926–2015), a specialist in the history of Renaissance Italy, liked to ask big questions. "How," he wrote, "did the Middle Ages, with its religious, world-denying culture, give way to the world-embracing, life-affirming culture known as the Renaissance?" He answered such questions by digging deep into the archives—eight hundred biographies of Catholic saints, for example—in order to look at the social and political issues that underlay why one person might have been chosen over another for honors bestowed upon the worthy dead. It was Don Weinstein, incidentally, who hired Heiko Oberman, an event he considered to be one of the greatest things ever to happen at the University.

Oberman's Division for Late Medieval and Reformation Studies flourishes to this day. Across campus, the medieval cosplayers long gone, fewer scholars and students than in the days of yore are working away on the likes of Shakespeare and Eleanor of Aquitaine. Still, those who do—historians, art historians, linguists, literary scholars, librarians—find that the people of that not-so-distant medieval past are alive and have much to say.

THE WANDERING PROFESSOR

Francis C. Lockwood

B ORN IN Illinois as the Civil War was coming to a close, Francis C. Lockwood (1864–1948) was a man of parts. He tried his hand at farming, briefly, then decided to become a teacher. After a time living in Kansas, he moved east to earn a doctorate in literature. He became a Methodist minister, taught and preached in Utah and, again, Kansas, became active in local politics, moved to Pennsylvania to head the English department of a small religious college, went to England to study at Oxford University—and then, in 1916, having lived the life of an itinerant scholar for two decades, was lured to the University of Arizona as a full professor of English.

Tucson was a small town of twenty-two thousand then, and the University had a student body of just over a thousand. Arizonans paid no tuition, while out-of-state students paid $15 a semester (just shy of $430 today). As it has continued to do, the English Department taught grammar and composition as well as literature, and Lockwood fielded all manner of courses. He took a leave of absence when the United States entered World War I, lecturing on literature and other topics on troop ships crossing the Atlantic, then, on returning to Arizona, became a roving professor who traveled back and forth to towns such as Douglas, Yuma, and Winslow to bring higher education to places then without schools of their own. His travels inspired an interest in cowboy life, folklore, Native American cultures, and Arizona history, to all of which he would soon return.

But first a task awaited him for which he professed a touch of reluctance. In 1922, President Rufus von KleinSmid abruptly resigned, having been offered the same job for much more money at the University of Southern California. With three deans and ninety professors and instructors of various ranks to choose from, the Board of Regents immediately appointed Lockwood. He accepted the presidency only on the condition that the board find a permanent candidate forthwith, and for the next six months, until September 1922, he headed the University with vigor and diligence. When his successor, Cloyd Marvin, proved to harbor rather tyrannical leanings, Lockwood headed the loyal opposition—which earned him expulsion from the faculty offices in Old Main and banishment to a distant building.

For all that, Lockwood was named dean of the College of Liberal Arts. At the same time, having written books on such topics as the philosopher Ralph Waldo Emerson, study techniques for college students, and the fundamentals of public speaking, he began to work on a succession of studies on Arizona and the West. "When I came to Arizona, at once I found myself wanting to know all about it, but the facts were as elusive as the desert mirages I saw about me, as whirling and tricky as the dancing dust devils that disported themselves everywhere on the broad mesas," he wrote in his 1928 book *Arizona Characters*. He read everything, and more important, he talked to everyone he could, befriending pioneers such as Will Croft Barnes, the author of *Arizona Place Names*, as well as White Mountain Apache elders whom Barnes had fought against four decades before. He spent time with fellow professor A. E. Douglass, the doyen of dendrochronology and observational astronomy, and with priests in small villages across the Sonoran Desert. He took his questions to diners, retirement homes, remote ranches. He wrote prodigiously, mastering both history and anthropology, with his books *The Apache Indians* and *Pioneer Portraits* remaining standard texts for decades. In his spare time, he researched the history of the Spanish missions founded by the missionary Eusebio Francisco Kino, successfully lobbying for a memorial to the Jesuit explorer next to Tucson's City Hall. Naturally, he wrote a book about those missions too.

Frank Lockwood retired in 1941 but remained active on campus, living a couple of blocks away in a tidy bungalow that still stands on First Street. He died in 1948. His papers—several carloads of them, a colleague recalls—are housed in what is now the Arizona Historical Society just to the west of campus.

LIVING IN WORDS

The Creative Writing Program

IN **1936**, the University of Iowa established the first master of fine arts (MFA) degree in creative writing. It was alone for many years, but then a few other schools developed programs of their own, and by 1975 about 50 offered MFAs. (About 250 offer them today.) The University of Arizona was one of the pioneers, establishing a track in creative writing in 1972 and, for the purpose, funding appointments for one professor, two assistant professors, an instructor, and a lecturer for the following year. One of those new assistant professors was the novelist Robert Houston, who remained on the faculty for nearly forty years, teaching generations of students. (The other was Richard Shelton, about whom more in a moment.) "It was a three-year program when we started," Houston recalls, "but then, when tuition started going up, we switched to a two-year program in order to spread financial aid more widely." Now headed by novelist and editor Kate Bernheimer, the three-year program has since been restored as an option, and the University of Arizona MFA is one of the few that fully funds its students so that they can concentrate on their work. Bernheimer was preceded by Manuel Muñoz, a short-story writer and novelist who was awarded a MacArthur Fellowship for his work in 2023.

The faculty grew in the boom years of the late 1970s and 1980s, with both full-time and visiting professors, many of them well known in the world of literature: novelists Vance Bourjaily, Elizabeth Evans, and Joy Williams; poets Joy Harjo, Carolyn Kizer, and Tess Gallagher; memoirist and novelist N. Scott Momaday—the list goes on. One memorable part-time faculty member was the novelist and environmental firebrand Edward Abbey, whom

Houston was able to hire as a full-time professor. Abbey was renowned for being gruff, irreverent, and contrarian, especially when it came to any kind of authority figure (think a department head), but he took his teaching duties with utmost seriousness. One of the students he mentored, perhaps improbably given his leanings, was the feminist and religiously inclined essayist Nancy Mairs, who extolled Abbey as "a sure-handed editor, thorough, tough, and good-humored." Mairs went on to publish a number of award-winning books, including *Plaintext* and *Waist-High in the World: A Life Among the Nondisabled*. Other notable graduates of the program include the novelist Richard Russo, famed for books such as *Nobody's Fool* and the Pulitzer Prize–winning *Empire Falls*; novelist and essayist David Foster Wallace, who, also in contrarian mode, rejected the Raymond Carver–influenced minimalism of the time for overstuffed narratives that brimmed with footnotes, such as *The Broom of the System*; poet David Wojahn, whose first book of poems, born as an MFA thesis, won the Yale Series of Younger Poets award in 1981; and poet, essayist, and short-story writer Alberto Ríos, who went on to become Arizona's poet laureate.

Those three are among the thousands of students who have passed through the MFA and undergraduate creative writing programs over the last half century. And if the best-selling writers to come out of the University were outside the English Department—novelist Barbara Kingsolver was a biology student, though she did join the English faculty after becoming established as a writer, while the sociologist and Catholic priest Andrew Greeley wrote a series of steamy potboilers—those writing students and their faculty have been prodigiously productive. Indeed, it's estimated that collectively they've written and published more than a thousand books, a number that grows with each year.

A POET TURNS TO PROSE

Richard Shelton and *Going Back to Bisbee*

T BEGAN with an idle suggestion in the course of an unhurried lunchtime conversation on a hot summer day: "Dick, with all these great stories you tell, you really should get to work writing a memoir." Richard Shelton (1933–2022), renowned as a poet, seemed to wave off the thought of turning to prose—but a year later, he was back with the manuscript he called *Going Back to Bisbee*, a manuscript that was in every way splendid, without a wasted word, full of good and sometimes rueful humor. Here, for instance, is a passage celebrating a beloved van in which he traveled the country, with a ding provided by his wife, Lois Shelton, onetime director of the University of Arizona Poetry Center:

> Blue Boy is badly faded now, like my eyes, from years of Arizona sun, and he has a gash near the rear where my wife backed him into a paloverde outside our garage. (When asked how it happened, she said, "God moved a tree," and she sticks to that story.) He is a little loose in the joints and has many rattles as the result of some of the worst roads on the North American Continent, but he continues to purr along like the perfect traveling machine he is.

Shelton first came to Arizona from his native Idaho courtesy of the U.S. Army, which drafted him and sent him to Fort Huachuca for training. When his time in the service was over, he took a job teaching school in nearby Bisbee, an old mining town within eyesight of Mexico, and began to work on a graduate degree at the University of Arizona. With a

Richard Shelton, poet and author of the UA Press best seller *Going Back to Bisbee*. Photograph by LaVerne Harrell Clark, courtesy of the University of Arizona Poetry Center.

doctorate in hand some years later, he joined the faculty of the English Department and fast became the ideal academic entrepreneur, helping launch the creative writing program and its associated MFA degree, bringing in poets from all over the world to read from their work, chasing down grants, teaching literature and writing to incarcerated men, and racking up awards, all the while publishing a couple of dozen books of poetry. "Thousands of students—both at the university and in the prison system—count him as a mentor and guiding influence," says Tyler Meier, executive director of the Poetry Center, and that's exactly so.

And then there was that book of prose, *Going Back to Bisbee*. Published in 1992, it won the prestigious Western States Book Award and was named a "notable book" by the *New York Times*. It remains one of UA Press's best-selling titles—and thirty years on and more, it continues to take readers down winding desert roads into the shimmering past.

LIFE IN VERSE

The Poetry Center

EDWARD ALBEE. Sandra Cisneros. Lucille Clifton. Carolyn Forché. Allan Ginsberg. Joy Harjo. Jane Hirshfeld. W. S. Merwin. N. Scott Momaday. Kenneth Rexroth. Adrienne Rich. Luci Tapahonso. If a distinguished poet has drawn breath at any time after 1960, the chances are very good that poet has given a reading at the University of Arizona Poetry Center.

The origins of the center lie in the generosity of Ruth Walgreen Stephan, in whose name lies the source of her great fortune. A scholar of Indigenous South American folklore, Stephan had been wintering in Tucson throughout the 1950s, writing well-regarded historical novels and amassing a collection of hundreds of books of poems in a cottage just north of the old campus on Highland Avenue. She bought the house next door as well. In 1960, Stephan donated both houses to the University with the stipulation that they be used as a poetry library and a sort of hostel for visiting poets, together intended, as Stephan said, "to maintain and cherish the spirit of poetry."

On November 17, 1960, Robert Frost, the most popular American poet of his time, came to Tucson and, with Stephan and U.S. representative Stewart Udall, inaugurated the Poetry Center. (Over a drink after the event, Udall and Frost hit on the idea that a poet should be on the podium at the next presidential inauguration, a tradition that has endured ever since.) Shortly afterward, LaVerne Harrell Clark became the Poetry Center's first director, and with the help of a generous endowment provided by Stephan, she began to build out the poetry collection and to establish a reading series by which leading poets from around the world would be invited to showcase their work.

Lois Shelton, director of the Poetry Center, in 1979. Photograph courtesy of the University of Arizona Poetry Center.

The first poet to participate in the series was Stanley Kunitz, who read in February 1962. The following month, the highly regarded poet and translator Kenneth Rexroth arrived from San Francisco to read from his work and conduct a workshop with students in the English Department. Robert Creeley came to read more than once over the years, as did Gary Snyder, Robert Bly, Denise Levertov, Galway Kinnell, and, later, Jane Miller, Diane Wakoski, Joy Harjo, Jorie Graham, Seamus Heaney, and Luis Alberto Urrea.

The poets who have participated in this reading series—the earliest of them gathered in a two-disc recording edited by Stephan—have grown used to reading before standing-room-only crowds, but perhaps the best attended reading of the 1960s was that by librarian of Congress Archibald MacLeish, who drew a crowd of 2,600 on November 2, 1965. Later readings have been consistently well attended, indicating the great interest poetry and its writers hold for both the University community and the larger community of Tucson, with audiences so numerous, indeed, that former director Alison Hawthorne Deming once joked that readings might better be held in the McKale Center.

In 1979, when the Poetry Center was directed by Lois Shelton, the Russian poet Yevgeny Yevtushenko began a long-standing tradition of writing on the wall of the poets' house, with mostly humorous messages. Those inscriptions—Yevtushenko's read "I bless everybody unblessed by God / Those in shoes and those unshod"—are now part of history, for, once it became clear that the original cottages were falling into disrepair, the Poetry Center moved to three other small houses on the periphery of campus. The original cottages disappeared, victims of a street widening project, and the new quarters—again, old buildings that had originally been homes—were later paved over for a parking lot for the expanding University Medical Center.

In 1990, the Board of Regents approved the building of a new home for the Poetry Center. It took more than a dozen years of fundraising to secure the nearly $7 million in construction costs for this new home, which is located not far from Stephan's original cottages. As Alison Deming observes, the architects and builders faced several design challenges, including creating a space that could house a huge collection of poetry and host several hundred audience members while also providing private, quiet space for study. Tucson architect Les Wallach met the challenge admirably, working under the slogan "contradiction = inspiration."

Its new home inaugurated in 2007 thanks to an endowment campaign headed by Helen S. Schaefer, for whom the building is named, the Poetry Center has grown to house a library containing thousands of books, manuscripts, recordings, and other materials. It is the site of workshops, classes, seminars, school field trips, and, of course, readings—and, best of all, the creation of new poems by rising generations of poets.

A READER'S PARADISE

The Tucson Festival of Books

A UNIVERSITY, AS we've noted, is a living confluence of books, ideas, and people. (Handsome buildings and grounds are a lagniappe.) This confluence is visible everywhere in the everyday interactions of students and teachers, scholars and peers, researchers and staff members, all the people who make up the University of Arizona. But it is also wonderfully evident when, each year, the university as both place and intellectual construct embraces the larger community of Tucson and, indeed, readers and writers from all over the world in the event known as the Tucson Festival of Books.

The festival has its origins in a happy idea that came to Tucson home builder and bibliophile Bill Viner: namely to gather booksellers, readers, and writers to celebrate the community of books. But where to do so? Nowhere was so conducive as the University to hosting a large and varied crowd and the hundreds of booths and lecture halls that would be needed, but landing such a thing on top of a working campus would disrupt schedules right and left. Summer was too hot, the end-of-year holidays too deserted—but then someone hit on the happy idea of staging the festival on the opening weekend of the University's annual spring break, allowing a full week to disassemble, pack, clean up, and close down.

The University, in partnership with the Tucson Pima Public Library and other institutions, was instantly on board, and the Tucson Festival of Books launched—had its first edition, as Viner and his founding committee dubbed it—March 14–15, 2009. About fifty thousand visitors were expected, but the crowd was larger than that, drawn to campus by dozens of authors and vendors. The numbers grew steadily larger year by year, as best-selling and emerging authors alike led workshops, gave readings and talks, and appeared on panels. Two years on, one of those best-selling writers, the great mystery doyen Elmore Leonard, was honored with the inaugural Festival Founders Award. Other winners since have included the Western novelist (and bookseller) Larry McMurtry, of *Lonesome Dove* fame, along with his screenwriting partner, Diana Ossana; children's author R. L. Stine, who blends juvenile horror with a terrific sense of humor; Richard Russo, the writer and University alumnus perhaps best known for the picaresque novels *Empire Falls* and *Nobody's Fool*; and Luis Alberto Urrea, a festival favorite and a triple threat as essayist, poet, and novelist.

From its comparatively humble origins, the Tucson Festival of Books has grown to embrace more than three hundred exhibitors and more than five hundred participating authors each year. Meanwhile, attendance has long exceeded the one hundred thousand mark, making the festival the third largest in the United States and one of the largest in the world.

The University of Arizona Hospital, now known as the Banner–University Medical Center Tucson. Photograph by David Olsen.

HEALING ARIZONA

The University of Arizona was entering its ninth decade when its enterprising president surveyed the scholarly landscape around him and detected a missing piece, a large gap in the curriculum that urgently needed to be closed: namely, the University lacked a medical school. Political rivalries underlay that absence, but once it was addressed, they were set aside, and the College of Medicine and numerous allied institutions were soon on a fast track to the future. They remain resolutely forward looking, and today the University of Arizona is a font of innovation in every imaginable aspect of medicine and health care, with pioneering multidisciplinary programs in medical robotics, cardiac surgery, oncology, nursing, public health, drug discovery, and many other avenues of research and treatment that benefit a vast community of humans—and, with a new school of veterinary science, animals too.

HEALING ARIZONA

The College of Medicine

THE RIVALRY between the University of Arizona and what is now Arizona State University (ASU), two hours up the interstate, dates back nearly ninety years—if, that is, a certain story about football recruiting violations is to be trusted, about which more later. That rivalry has been fought out not just on the athletic field, though. For many years, for instance, the two schools played an elaborate game of cat and mouse with the Arizona State Legislature to be named the host of Arizona's first medical school, with the University of Arizona winning by just a single vote in both chambers—and then, it's said, only because President Richard Harvill had quietly gotten a jump start on funding, with a shovel-ready site selected on the distant northeastern side of campus.

The legislature approved the College of Medicine in 1963. Four years later, the Health Sciences Building was completed and the first class of future doctors, numbering thirty-two students, was enrolled. Four years later, twenty-nine of them graduated, a solid showing for a staggeringly challenging program. By that time, other buildings were rising in what would become the medical complex, including the first iteration of the University Medical Center and a building devoted to clinical and laboratory studies, all requiring the demolition of dozens of homes dating back to the early years of the twentieth century.

From the very beginning, the College of Medicine concentrated on medical problems that were specific to the desert, such as respiratory medicine, the outcome of an elderly population afflicted by tuberculosis and endemic diseases such as valley fever. Tuberculosis is now uncommon, but the University is a leading center of research on asthma and valley fever, an illness caused by a bacterium that lives in desert soil, two-thirds of all cases of which occur in Arizona.

In service to the community, as well as to dogs and other animals that are susceptible to the illness, the College of Medicine operates the Valley Fever Center for Excellence, whose researchers, in 2023, developed a vaccine for what is technically called coccidioidomycosis, a vaccine that may be available to both pets and humans before the target year of 2030. Significant drug discovery and development also takes place at the R. Ken Coit College of Pharmacy, one a medication that prevents Alzheimer's disease by impeding the formation of plaque and "tangles" in the brain. Named for an alumnus who has donated more than $50 million to it, the College of Pharmacy also operates the Arizona Poison and Drug Information Center, a source of vital information for anyone who may have ingested a harmful substance or, as all too commonly happens, is bitten by a venomous insect or reptile.

One need not be advanced in years to benefit from College of Medicine research. One of the most important pediatric treatment centers in the nation is the Diamond Children's Medical Center. Allied with it is the new University of Arizona Health Sciences Center for Advanced Molecular and Immunological Therapies (CAMI),

Richard Harvill, president of the University from 1951 to 1971, a period of dramatic growth. During his tenure, President Harvill founded both the College of Medicine and the College of Nursing. Courtesy Special Collections, The University of Arizona Libraries.

another locus for advanced drug discovery, which, in November 2022, received a $10 million gift from the Steele Foundation to develop treatment modalities for autoimmune diseases that affect children, such as type 1 diabetes, juvenile arthritis, and lupus.

Cancer and heart research were also emphases from the outset, with the freestanding University of Arizona Cancer Center established in 1986. The Cancer Center offers a strong example of the College of Medicine's dual focus on research and practice. Founding director Sydney E. Salmon (1936–99), who studied philosophy at the University as an undergraduate before turning to medicine and rising to the rank of Regents Professor, was a pioneer in treating breast cancer, saving many lives. Dr. Salmon held eight patents, wrote more than four hundred scholarly papers, and edited twelve books on cancer research and treatment, all

good reason for one of the Cancer Center's buildings to be named in his honor. One of his successors as director, Dr. David S. Alberts (1939–2023), continued Salmon's strong research program by developing molecular-level chemotherapeutic agents used in the detection and treatment of bladder, colon, prostate, skin, and many other kinds of cancer.

Regents Professor of Medicine and cardiologist Dr. Marvin Slepian has been working on bioengineering technologies developed through his laboratory at the Sarver Heart Center. One is a ventricular assist device that replaces the imperfect blood-circulating abilities of a diseased heart, affording a kind of intermediary until a human heart is available for transplantation. Biomedical engineers have also been working on a battery-free pacemaker that doesn't require the extensive invasive procedures involved in installing other such devices—and, as a bonus, bypasses the heart's pain receptors, reducing the discomfort many pacemaker wearers feel.

The story of medicine at the University of Arizona reiterates that of departments, centers, institutions, and laboratories across the campus: research and scholarship thrive at the margins, drawing on the talents of thinkers from many disciplines. It is not surprising to note that medical faculty members hold positions elsewhere on campus, from entomology to computer science to mechanical engineering and beyond. The future of our health will lie in many hands across the campus, all working to improve lives everywhere.

On that note, the work of Dr. Mohab M. Ibrahim stands out for bringing relief to those who suffer from chronic pain owing to conditions such as fibromyalgia and migraine. The anesthesiologist has been working with what is called green light therapy to reduce levels of pain, and those patients whom he has treated report a substantial decline in the burden of misery they carry. Watching a woman die of cancer in agony because pain-relief medications were unavailable after Iraq invaded his native Kuwait sent Dr. Ibrahim on his path: "That experience really shaped me," he says, "and made me want to understand pain better and find ways to manage it."

Dr. Allan J. Hamilton, a longtime professor of surgery, has been leading the way for technology-assisted operations that leverage artificial intelligence to help decide the safest and most efficient procedures to produce the best possible outcomes. An award-winning popular author, Dr. Hamilton notes that these projects are extensions of a human and humane medicine, and that his training for his students emphasizes both compassion and care. That training will carry far into the world and the future, for the College of Medicine and, through Health Sciences, its many allied colleges and centers host a student body numbering more than four thousand. Said President Robert C. Robbins, "The presence of those assets is truly unique and is a model for delivering an innovative care system throughout the state of Arizona."

CAMI, incidentally, the recipient of $150 million in funding from the State of Arizona, is located in Phoenix. A Wildcats fan might take pleasure in thinking how it must have rankled ASU veterans of the first fight to see the founding of a Phoenix-based medical residency program in 1992. Fifteen years later, that was followed by the four-year University of Arizona College of Medicine–Phoenix, a toehold in ASU's backyard and a key step in revitalizing the capital city's downtown as part of the Phoenix Bioscience Core.

INTEGRATIVE MEDICINE

Andrew Weil and the Future of Healthcare

T BEGAN as a grand experiment. In 1994, James E. Dalen (1932–2024), the dean of the College of Medicine, approved of a suggested curriculum for a new course of study in "integrative medicine," to be led by a Harvard-educated physician and ethnobotanist named Andrew Weil. The bearded, jeans-clad Weil didn't cut the usual medical figure; he was friends with hippies, beatniks, poets, and scholarly outliers, had studied the medical applications of marijuana while working toward his medical degree, and was deeply interested in such matters as medicinal plants and Asian healing traditions—not the usual stuff that figures on the MCAT, that is to say.

Weil had been lecturing since the 1970s on alternative approaches to treatment and healing, and while some of his colleagues were skeptical, his talks were well attended and proved popular among students. So it was that Dean Dalen approved a two-year residential fellowship in integrative medicine, which embodied such studies as the mind-body relationship, spirituality and health, homeopathic and naturopathic remedies, holistic treatment, meditation, and Ayurvedic and Chinese traditional medicine. Perhaps the most important component was Weil's insistence that physicians communicate openly with their patients both as a matter of common courtesy and as a means of investigating the causes and consequences of illness.

Those skeptics aside, Weil's program in integrative medicine has trained several thousand physicians over the years. At the same time, more than seventy-five medical schools in the United States now incorporate at least some of the elements of the integrative-medicine

Andrew Weil, a pioneer of integrative, holistic medicine. Photograph courtesy of the Andrew Weil Center for Integrative Medicine.

curriculum. In 2007, Weil took an endowed chair in integrative rheumatology, the first of its kind in the country, and the following year took the leadership of the newly established University of Arizona Center for Integrative Medicine. In 2019, honoring its founder, the institute was renamed the Andrew Weil Center for Integrative Medicine. In 2022, ground was broken for a new building for it that will include classroom and laboratory spaces and serve as a model for a healthy workplace.

The center's curriculum, meanwhile, has expanded to interact with nearly every field of medicine, from family practice and pediatrics to oncology and environmental medicine. At the same time, Andrew Weil has proved to be a nimble intellectual entrepreneur, writing best-selling books such as *The Natural Mind*, *Eating Well for Optimum Health*, and *Spontaneous Happiness* and founding a line of natural-food restaurants. His 2017 book, *Mind Over Meds*, is a timely examination of the problem of overmedication and offers suggestions for natural remedies in the place of pharmaceutical interventions. His website, www.drweil.com, is a popular source of medical information that illustrates the eclectic nature of integrative medicine.

TRADITIONS OF CARE

Jennie R. Joe and Native American Medicine

DELIVERING HEALTH-CARE services is difficult under any circumstances. It is all the more difficult when serving remote communities and, sometimes, people for whom speaking of illness and death is circumscribed.

Enter Jennie R. Joe. Born into the Diné people, she grew up on the Navajo Nation, attending school in New Mexico and later Oklahoma. In 1964, she earned a degree as a public health nurse, served as a medical officer in the U.S. Navy, and worked with the Indian Health Service. She also served as a clinician during the Native American activist occupation of Alcatraz Island in 1969 before completing a doctorate in medical anthropology.

Joe came to the University in 1986 to work with medical researchers and clinicians on developing rehabilitation services and assistance programs for disabled people in Indigenous communities. The following year, Joe became a professor in Native American studies and, in 1990, director of the Native American Research and Training Center, working with Indigenous students to teach constituents about such health problems as diabetes and substance abuse. She was appointed a full professor in the Department of Family and Community Medicine and taught courses in the Graduate Interdisciplinary Program in American Indian Studies, and in her research and outreach work she developed training curricula that helped coordinate the work of physicians and traditional healers working on the Navajo Nation, a collaboration that, long thought impractical if not impossible, is now flourishing there and in other Indigenous communities. Her later work has also centered on pediatric care, developing culturally appropriate ways of addressing health concerns. Altogether, thousands of students passed through the doorways of her classrooms over the thirty-five years she taught full time, and by far the greater proportion of them went on to work in medicine and health care.

Born in Arizona in 1866, a boy named Wassaja was removed from his Kwevkepaya (Yavapai) family and sold to a photographer named Carlos Gentile. The Gentile family moved to Chicago, where Wassaja, renamed Carlos Montezuma, excelled in his studies and enrolled in medical school, becoming the first Native American to earn a doctorate in medicine.

Returning to Arizona, Montezuma served his people not only as a doctor but also as an activist whose labors assured that the Yavapai would retain their reservation lands along the Verde River northeast of present-day Phoenix rather than be removed to serve the interests of developers. He died in 1923, an exemplar of a doctor who cared for his patients not just as individuals but also as members of a community grounded in a particular place and time.

Given that example, it is entirely fitting that in 2021 Jennie Joe, now a professor emerita, should have led the ceremonies honoring the renaming of her Native American Research and Training Center for him. It is now called the Wassaja Carlos Montezuma Center for Native American Health, continuing its original missions of sponsoring health-related research and training Native American students to pursue health-care careers.

One important entrée to furthering this work has been the University of Arizona's Pre-Medical Admissions Pathway (P-MAP), which offers Indigenous and other minority students a yearlong preparatory program before they enter medical school, many of them not having had the advantages of students who did not grow up in rural communities under socioeconomically disadvantaged conditions. Of P-MAP's inaugural cohort in 2015, five of the ten students were of Native American descent. One of them, a San Carlos Apache scholar named Sylvestor Moses, already held a doctorate from the University in biochemistry and molecular and cellular biology but wanted to become a medical doctor. "I believe that in becoming a physician," he remarked, "I not only can provide health care to my San Carlos Apache community, but I can serve as a role model for our Apache youth."

Moses, who as of this writing is completing a residency in internal medicine, is not alone. Of the 2019 medical school class of 102 graduates, eight were Native American—the largest cohort of Native students in any class to date. Their numbers have grown in the years since, and the University of Arizona ranks at the top of institutions training Indigenous students to bring health and healing to their communities and beyond.

SPIDERS AND SNAKES

Leslie Boyer and the Mysteries of Venom

S OME KINDS of plants and animals are poisonous. Some kinds of animals are venomous. The distinction between these two terms is more than fine, though both are matters of life and death.

A venomous animal has to deliver its poison directly to some other organism, often by injecting it through a fang or stinger to which a venom-producing organ is attached. The ability to produce and deploy this venom is an evolutionary adaptation that serves both defensive and offensive ends: the venom can be used in protecting an organism against a predator, or it can be used in preying on other organisms.

By contrast, a poisonous organism does not deliver its toxins directly. A poisonous frog, for instance, needs only to be handled or licked in order to transmit its poison to some other organism; it doesn't need to bite or sting in order to do so, and instead of the poison being produced by a single organ, its entirely body can carry the toxin. This is the case with many kinds of butterflies, moths, and beetles—and, of course, many kinds of plants as well.

Animals that produce venom have been doing so for eons. Humans have only recently learned how to make antivenin to counteract the effects of, say, a rattlesnake bite. The University of Arizona is a world-renowned center for the research and development of such lifesaving substances.

Leading this charge for many years was Dr. Leslie V. Boyer, the founding director of the Venom Immunochemistry, Pharmacology and Emergency Response (VIPER) Institute in the College of Medicine. When she was a young girl, she recalls, she was fascinated by funnel spiders, a venomous family whose bite can be fatal to humans. "I spent many hours feeding

Leslie Boyer, renowned physician and developer of antivenins. Photograph courtesy of VIPER/Leslie Boyer.

moths to funnel spiders," Dr. Boyer says with a smile. After medical school, she was confronted with what she calls "a baffling scorpion sting case," which put her on the path to a career in medical toxicology, about which she's formulated some interesting statistics—for instance, the fact that most male snakebite victims are young men who mess with a rattler on a dare, while most female victims are in their later years and simply didn't see the critter that bit them. Either way, Dr. Boyer observes, a Sonoran Desert dweller would do better to be bitten by a venomous creature in Mexico, where rattlesnake antivenin sells for a hundred dollars a dose, than in the United States, where the cost multiplies to a bill many dozens of times higher.

Developing effective and, it's hoped, cost-effective antivenins is one of the jobs of VIPER. One of Dr. Boyer's projects included the development, through cross-border cooperation, of an antivenin for scorpion stings called Anascorp, which has been proven highly effective through clinical trials, and which has been attributed with saving both lives and medical costs, replacing intensive care treatment with, in most cases, outpatient care. Since three hundred thousand North Americans are stung by scorpions every year, this adds up: in 1994, in Mexico alone, three hundred people died of scorpion envenomation, but by 2010, when Anascorp was in wide use, the figure had fallen to just fifteen.

Antivenin is produced by injecting an animal—a horse, a goat, even a cat—with small amounts of venom. The animal will produce antibodies, components in the blood that fight against the toxin, neutralize it, and protect the host organism from ill effects. Blood serum containing these antibodies is drawn from the animal and processed to remove unwanted proteins while isolating the active ingredient in the antivenin. Antivenins are in great demand, and it takes effort and time to produce them, for which reason Dr. Boyer once told an interviewer that the greatest challenge in producing them is simply mustering up the necessary perseverance to see the job through.

Leslie Boyer retired in 2020, but she continues to research and write. And, she says, "I still feed moths to spiders when nobody is looking."

SAVING LIVES IN VIOLENT TIMES

Peter Rhee and Gabby Giffords

IT **WAS** one of the most horrific moments in Tucson's history. On January 8, 2011, a young mentally ill man burst into a meet-and-greet event that U.S. representative Gabrielle "Gabby" Giffords was holding inside a northwest-side grocery store and began shooting. He aimed carefully, shooting Giffords in the head, and then fired wildly, killing a federal judge, a nine-year-old girl, a congressional aide, and three other Tucsonans.

Giffords's intern, a twenty-year-old University of Arizona student named Daniel Hernández Jr., and Tucson paramedic Aaron Rogers applied first aid, preventing Giffords from drowning in her own blood. Within minutes, she was rushed to the University of Arizona Medical Center, where chief trauma surgeon Peter Rhee set to work. Born in Seoul, South Korea, in 1961, Rhee had proved a brilliant student on immigrating to the United States as a ten-year-old, then enlisted in the U.S. Navy on completing medical school. As a combat surgeon, he was one of the first medical personnel to arrive in Afghanistan with allied forces in 2001. He served in combat there and in Iraq, returning to the United States to treat wounded evacuees. In 2007, he joined the faculty of the University of Arizona as a professor of surgery and chief of the critical care and trauma units, and it was there that he encountered the unfortunate victim. When she squeezed his hand, Rhee later recalled, he was sure of her survival, saying, "She will not die."

She did not die. Instead, Rhee, working with neurosurgeon Michael Lemole Jr. and ophthalmologist Lynn Polonski, saved Giffords's life, plain and simple. He removed part of her skull to relieve swelling and bleeding, then placed her in a medically induced coma to allow her to begin recovery. On January 12, she opened her eyes for the first time.

A sea of well-wishing cards, balloons, stuffed animals, and other objects laid before the University of Arizona Hospital honored U.S. Rep. Gabrielle "Gabby" Giffords after she was severely wounded by a would-be assassin in 2011. Photograph by Gregory McNamee.

That fact was reported to a standing-room-only audience in McKale Memorial Center by President Barack Obama, who was doubtless thinking of Giffords's medical team and those first responders when he remarked, "These men and women remind us that heroism is found not only on the fields of battle. They remind us that heroism does not require special training or physical strength. Heroism is here, all around us, in the hearts of so many of our fellow citizens, just waiting to be summoned."

By January 21, under Rhee's constant care, Giffords was stable enough that she could be moved to an advanced treatment center in Houston. After months of additional care and therapy, she appeared on the floor of the U.S. House of Representatives on August 1, 2011. She left office the following year and began to campaign for gun control, joined by her husband, retired astronaut Mark Kelly, who was elected to the U.S. Senate from Arizona in 2020. Years later, she continues both her recovery and her activism.

Peter Rhee continued to serve at the University of Arizona until 2016, two years after publishing a memoir, *Trauma Red: The Making of a Surgeon in War and in America's Cities*, that focused closely on the Giffords shooting in order to describe the work of a trauma surgeon. He went on to take a chair at the Uniformed Services University, teaching future combat surgeons.

The gun control debate continues. One of its foremost students is University of Arizona sociologist Jennifer Carlson. In her 2020 book, *Policing the Second Amendment: Guns, Law Enforcement, and the Politics of Race*, Carlson observes that the Second Amendment right to carry firearms does not apply equally to members of all communities, and that easy access to an inventory of firearms that far outnumbers people disproportionately affects members of ethnic minorities. As Carlson writes, "structural racism intersects with gun policy to aggravate, rather than ameliorate, vulnerabilities facing communities of color." So significant is her work that in 2022 Carlson was named a MacArthur Foundation fellow and recipient of what is popularly called a "genius grant," perhaps the most prestigious intellectual award in the country. Her current work examines the rapid proliferation of firearms in recent years, driven by political unrest, ethnic tensions, and personal and financial insecurities wrought by the COVID-19 pandemic.

CURING WHAT AILS US

The College of Nursing

I F YOU follow the news or, heaven forfend, have had to pay a visit to the hospital recently, you know that the health-care industry suffers from a shortage of nurses. So it has always been—and especially in Arizona, where, until World War II made the need for nurses especially urgent, there was no instrument for learning the profession short of going to a neighboring state for training. That began to change in 1942, when St. Joseph's Hospital in Phoenix established a quick-turnaround, three-year diploma program. Four other hospitals had followed suit by 1944, but then the war ended, and so did the urgency.

By 1955, Arizona was the only state in the country that had no formal baccalaureate program in nursing, and the few hospitals that maintained a nurse-training program had to bring in faculty from out of state. One was an accomplished University of Colorado professor of nursing named Pearl Parvin Coulter (1902–2002), whom President Richard Harvill hired away in 1957 to head the new School of Nursing. She must have wondered what she was getting into when she was taken to the new school's headquarters and sole classroom, a disused conference room in the Liberal Arts Building. The first class of forty-two students were crammed together in ways only a pandemic could love, but Coulter, a skilled administrator, soon negotiated more space, eventually moving into the basement of the Home Economics Building and, later, the football stadium.

All along, Coulter had been planning to expand the baccalaureate program to master's and doctoral degree tracks, with the former approved the same year she retired, 1967. The School of Nursing became the College of Nursing in 1964, but it still seemed something of an afterthought, even with its scores and then hundreds of students, until finally, in 1968, it was moved, now under the direction of Gladys Sorenson, to its own building alongside the site of the planned College of Medicine.

Coulter's hoped-for doctoral program was also approved in 1975, and in its first decade, seventeen doctorates were awarded. At the same time, the College of Nursing initiated a program of cross-cultural study, learning traditions and developing networks in Native American and Hispanic communities throughout the Southwest. Half a century later, those links still endure. So, too, do electronic ones, for the College of Nursing has been a pioneer in education in cyberspace, offering an online doctoral program and teleconferencing to serve students in rural areas and internationally.

There's still a shortage of nurses everywhere, but with schools in both Tucson and Gilbert, Arizona, and with ample scholarship opportunities, the University of Arizona is doing its part to meet it, graduating 143 nurses with undergraduate and graduate degrees in 2023.

One of the scholars who lent strength to the cross-cultural aspect of nursing education was trained both as a nurse and as a medical anthropologist. Holding a doctorate from the University of Arizona, Margarita "Rita" Artschwager Kay brought scholarly rigor to the field and was at home in the remotest of reservation communities and farming hamlets everywhere in the state, bringing both health-care practice and research questions with her as she traveled.

Among the most noteworthy nursing educators of her time, and retiring as a full professor in 1992, Rita Kay had many crowning achievements. Perhaps the most important of them, apart from all the nurses she taught over the decades, is her book *Southwestern Medical Dictionary*, first published in 1977, which enabled speakers of Spanish and English to work their way toward describing a medical condition and remedying it, looking up words and pointing to anatomical pictures. Science, folk culture, and language all meet in its pages, where you'll find "triglycerides/*triglicéridos*" right next to "tripe soup/*menudo*," the latter, of course, a proven cure for much of what might ail you.

CHASING DOWN THE PANDEMIC

COVID-19 Research at the University

I**T WAS** 1918, and even as World War I was winding down, a virus was sweeping across the world. When the so-called Spanish flu—Spain being the first place it arrived in Europe, though it was born in China—finally ebbed, two years later, it left somewhere around one hundred million people dead worldwide.

A variant of the SARS (severe acute respiratory syndrome) family of viruses, the Spanish flu was the deadliest epidemic in human history to date, overshadowing the death toll of more famous epidemics such as the Black Death. No place was safe, and certainly not the United States, where some seven hundred thousand people died. The University of Arizona was not exempt, and in October 1918, the campus was closed as student after student retreated to homes and dorm rooms, deathly ill.

A hero emerged in the person of Byron Cummings, known as "the Dean," who was then the director of the Arizona State Museum and head of the Department of Archaeology. Dean Cummings and his wife, Isabelle, donned masks and went from dorm to dorm, nursing and feeding the ill. They turned Herring Hall, then the University's gym, into a hospital, while the campus was kept under quarantine well into 1919. Said A. E. Douglass, the famed scientist, of the Dean, "I have always felt that his help day and night in the campus hospital at that time when nurses were scarce and students were dying, saved the lives of many students." Of Isabelle, the faculty senate declared on her death in 1929, "Particularly do we recall the service she rendered night and day to the students and in the homes of faculty during the influenza epidemic of 1919."

For all the Cummings's efforts, some three hundred Tucsonans, mostly young adults, some of them students, died of the flu.

Fast-forward to 2014, when Michael Worobey, a professor in the Department of Ecology and Evolutionary Biology, determined that the Spanish flu indeed began in China and was born when an avian flu jumped over to human hosts. Working with colleague Guan-Zhu Han, Worobey was able to link the virus to a horse flu that had broken out in the United States in 1870, crippling the economy even as it was recovering from the ruinous financial effects of the Civil War. Worobey's paper, published in the influential journal *Nature*, recommended a vigorous program of vaccinations for people of all ages in the event of a similar pandemic, which limited the spread of the disease in the American cities that implemented it between 1918 and 1920.

Now fast-forward to January 2020, when reports began to circulate in the United States of a "novel"—meaning hitherto unknown—form of coronavirus, the same family of bugs that yielded the Spanish flu. Under the leadership of President Robert Robbins, an experienced physician, the University was placed under quarantine in March, with all in-person classes suspended and converted to online instruction. That pivot was disruptive, a cost of lost time and effort borne by thousands of students and faculty, but it turned on a proverbial dime, and for the rest of the year the campus was a virtual construct.

University scientists, though, donned masks and went to work to help monitor and predict the path of illness. One project, and certainly not a pleasant one, led by microbiologist Ian Pepper, tracked pathogens in sewage, a process known more politely as wastewater-based epidemiology. In a program that would come to be employed widely around the world, those scientists studied where concentrations of the virus occurred, enabling them to then study the conditions of affected communities and concentrate treatment and containment efforts. This tracking was subsequently put into play three years later to follow the path of a drug-resistant fungus called *Candida auris* that threatened to spread, via reclaimed wastewater, throughout the agricultural fields outside Yuma, Arizona, which produces 90 percent of the U.S. winter vegetable crop. A collaboration of University microbiologists and the College of Agriculture's Yuma Center of Excellence for Desert Agriculture kept the fungus from spreading—and certainly saved countless lives.

University microbiologist Floyd "Ski" Chilton made another important discovery during the COVID-19 outbreak—which, as of January 1, 2024, had killed more than seven million people worldwide. His work, drawing on the talents of a team of scientists and students, concerned the physical conditions that led to fatality, and it concluded that an enzyme very similar to rattlesnake venom caused severe inflammation in some COVID patients, which in turn allowed the virus to destroy vital organs. Controlling the secreted phospholipase A2 group IIA (sPLA2-IIA) enzyme may well prove to be the difference between life and death for those now suffering from what has been called "long" COVID.

More than four years after it landed on these shores, as I write, COVID is still with us, a pandemic representing "a protracted battle between a generation-defining virus and scientists working at a breakneck pace to fight it," as University surgery and immunobiology professor Deepta Bhattacharya puts it. Bhattacharya has been studying how immune systems respond to the virus and, more important, how immunity is maintained by quickening the response of immune cells and boosting antibodies to keep people from becoming sick as the virus evolves into new variations. The science is complicated, but the message we take from it is clear: get vaccinated, get boosted, and stay safe. Or, as Bhattacharya counsels, "There's been a sort of emerging narrative saying that we're all going to get it. And you know, over the course of our lifetimes, I think that's probably true. But it doesn't mean that you have to get it right now."

AN OUNCE OF PREVENTION

The Mel and Enid Zuckerman College of Public Health

S MOKING. BINGE drinking. Overeating. Not exercising. We humans do all sorts of things that are deleterious to our health, knowingly and unknowingly, racking up enormous medical and societal costs even as we cut our lives short.

It's against that uncheerful background that the scholars, researchers, technicians, and students of the Mel and Enid Zuckerman College of Public Health do their work. It's a vast canvas. Some researchers look at the health effects of aging, others at addiction, still others at the role of genetics in health and illness. Some examine environmentally conditioned illnesses, others pandemics, others how the intersection of poverty and social isolation impact the incidence of illness. These researchers take an interdisciplinary approach, working with scholars and practitioners in other departments and schools, as well as with community-based organizations and government agencies, blending research and service to improve the health of us all by battling, for example, diabetes, youth violence and self-harm, and industrial pollution.

One easy way to make oneself unwell in the Sonoran Desert is to spend too much time outdoors in hot weather, willingly or not, or to live in circumstances where cooling is unavailable. Thanks to the efforts of researchers at the Zuckerman College led by epidemiologist Heidi Brown, all of whom worked closely with other epidemiologists, health-care providers, and architects, health-related risks have been lessened with the establishment of "cooling centers" where people lacking shelter or air conditioning can spend time in a climate-controlled environment and be provided with drinking water and other hydrating beverages. The team also created an online map that allows agencies to direct clients to the nearest centers in Arizona's urban areas, potentially saving many lives each torrid summer.

Another Zuckerman College initiative recognizes that working as a firefighter carries the risk of developing cancer as a result of exposure to chemicals in fire-suppressive materials. The job also carries a heightened risk of cardiovascular disease. Researchers are now working to determine if plasma or blood transfusions can help reduce the levels of harmful chemicals in the bloodstreams of these first responders, doing service to those who themselves do essential service on behalf of the community. While Zuckerman College scientists are studying these matters, others are looking at stress, post-traumatic disorder, and other issues that can affect the mental and physical health of first responders.

Still another Zuckerman College program is called One Health, which works from the thesis that human health is inseparable from environmental health and animal health. Addressing economic inequality, climate change, zoonotic disease transmission, and other broad-scale problems, researchers seek to build community-based approaches to complex public health problems.

Zuckerman College offers master's and doctoral degrees in public health, as well as numerous dual master's degrees that match public health studies with law, medicine, pharmacology, and other fields. It also offers graduate degrees in biostatistics, environmental health sciences, epidemiology, and health promotion. The Mel and Enid Zuckerman College of Public Health is relatively new, established only in 2000. Yet its work has already taken on international significance, and a growing student body, graduate and undergraduate, is vigorously addressing diverse matters of health and wellness.

The north face of the Eller College of Management. Photograph by David Olsen.

OF COMMERCE, JUSTICE, AND GOVERNMENT

The demand curve. The writ of habeas corpus. The bicameral legislature. The blockchain. All are terms of art in disciplines in which the University of Arizona has emerged as a leader of increasing distinction. The Eller College of Management, whose name honors a homegrown entrepreneur, is a world leader in business and economic education, and within it the Department of Management Information Systems has been ranked the country's best. University researchers there have done critically important work in cybersecurity, a pressing need in our time. The James E. Rogers College of Law, endowed with a $115 million gift from the attorney and business leader whose name it bears, has been an important innovator in the administration of justice, with particular concern to the needs and rights of Indigenous people and members of minority communities. And political leaders have cropped up on every corner of campus, from the model courts in that law school to—not at all least—the basketball court.

TAKING CARE OF BUSINESS

The Eller College of Management

I**T SPEAKS** volumes about the economic history of Arizona that, as we've seen, the first schools founded at the University were devoted to mining and agriculture, extractive enterprises that relied on distant markets and saw profits shipped far from home. It wouldn't be until a quarter century later that the school turned its attention to developing a homegrown economy in the form of business education, establishing a bachelor of science degree in what was called commerce in 1913 and then, at the dawn of the roaring twenties, a master of arts degree in economics.

The requirements for entering business school were fairly stringent at the time, including a prerequisite of two years of passing grades in English and competence in penmanship, an art long since lost. Still, both programs proved immediately popular, so much so that enrollment swelled to more than 550 students by 1927—more than 1 in every 4 of the 2,033 students enrolled at the University that year. That growth fueled the creation, that year, of the School of Business and Public Administration (BPA), which took over much of the real estate in Old Main and held on to it for the next decade.

In 1938, BPA found a new home in an old dormitory building called North Hall. The move was meant to be temporary, and the administration barred BPA from making any changes to a structure that it intended to revert to a dormitory one day. A dozen years later, BPA was still there, and it wasn't until 1952 that the College of Business and Public Administration, so designated in 1948, found a home of its own, a newly constructed building catercorner to Old Main and across the street from the College of Engineering. The new

A bungalow, photographed around 1900, once owned by groundwater specialist and University agriculture professor G. E. P. Smith. Most of the extensive neighborhood north of campus is now the site of the hospital, the James E. Rogers College of Law, and other units.

building was the first on campus to be fully air-conditioned—and the first to offer access to students who used wheelchairs.

The college was well served by the four-story building and its two dozen classrooms and three dozen offices for the next few decades, but then the second wave of baby boomers hit campus and swelled the enrollments in business, economics, public information, and, in 1985, the newly minted discipline of management information systems, its faculty initially endowed by a grant from IBM. Two essential gifts made the next evolution possible in the form of large donations from alumni Karl Eller (1928–2019) and Norm McClelland (1927–2017). Both had made sizable fortunes, Eller as the chief executive of the Circle K Corporation and, later, Columbia Pictures Communications, and McClelland as the owner-operator of Shamrock Dairy, Arizona's largest dairy. In 1982, McClelland Hall rose as one of the new complex of buildings north of Speedway. Built at a cost of $20 million (about $65 million today), it is a four-story structure with a roomy 180,000 square feet of office, classroom, and laboratory space to accommodate thousands of students and hundreds of faculty and staff members. The structure is one of the most visually striking late modernist buildings on campus.

Karl Eller's contribution came in the form of millions of dollars in donations over four decades, beginning in 1984 and continuing until his passing. More than that, Karl Eller was constantly on hand, encouraging students as a mentor and critic of their entrepreneurial projects—one reason why the Eller College of Management, as it was renamed in 1998, has long proved a hive of innovation and hustle.

Today the Eller College offers graduate and undergraduate programs in economics, finance, marketing, entrepreneurship, accounting, business management, and operations management, with the college ranked overall in the top two dozen business schools in the United States. The Department of Management Information Systems is rated the best in the country, the MBA program consistently in the top five. Eller has also developed interdisciplinary degree programs with the College of Law and the College of Medicine.

THE DISMAL SCIENCE AS ENTERTAINMENT

Gerald J. Swanson

T**HOMAS CARLYLE,** the Scottish historian and curmudgeon who called economics the "dismal science," might well have changed his mind if Gerald J. Swanson (1940–2020) had been his contemporary. Gerry (he was a first-name sort of fellow) had a profound mastery of both the qualitative and quantitative aspects of the discipline, which is both art and science, and he enjoyed it all, thinking of numbers as an intellectual game and social observations as a blend of intuition and sentiment—very much in the old school of Adam Smith, while also absolutely up to the minute.

Unusually for academic economists, Gerry came into the discipline from industry. A capable mathematician with a keenly logical mind, he had been steered into engineering by a high school counselor, then took his degree at the University of Illinois and went to work for General Motors. He didn't much like it, he admitted, but he learned the workings of real-world business. He decided he wanted to teach instead, aiming only for a master's degree and a high school teaching certificate until discovering that he could push forward to a doctorate in economics with the investment of just a little more time. He finished that degree in 1971, having honed another talent along the way: he was a natural at the lectern, with a great sense of humor and a gift for patient, clear explication of some very complex topics.

That led him to the University of Arizona, where he was hired to teach baby-boomer-swelled introductory economics classes before as many as a thousand students at a time. His lectures were so popular that his colleagues in what became the Eller College of Management noted a phenomenon they called the "Swanson effect": whenever Gerry was on leave or sabbatical, the number of enrollees in introductory courses as well as declared majors and minors dropped markedly.

Gerry was often on leave, because apart from teaching and research, he was also a prolific writer and public speaker. Having written his dissertation on tax policy, he was a frequent advisor to governments, including the Arizona State Legislature. His co-authored book *Bankruptcy 1995* warned that policies that putatively lowered taxes while not reining in costs was a recipe for financial ruin, and while he pointed that book particularly at the policies of the George H. W. Bush administration, he would later note that no one since then was doing much to wrestle with a deficit that was growing into the trillions of dollars. Vice President Dick Cheney may have muttered, "Deficits don't matter," but Gerry's follow-up book *America the Broke* argued precisely otherwise. Both books were best sellers, and both contained messages that Gerry pressed for years to come.

Although Gerry doubted that politicians would ever do anything meaningful to curb deficit spending, he made it a cornerstone of his economic thinking, and though his projections could be, well, dismal, he presented them with a smile. It was a contagious smile at that, for, as a natural proselytizer for the discipline, one of his great accomplishments was to establish, with his business leader friend Thomas Brown, a program to teach economics to high school and intermediate school teachers so that they in turn could teach economics to their students. A highlight of the year for all those teachers was a breakfast at which Gerry delivered a genial lecture that concluded with a quiz with questions such as "What percentage of the federal budget is mandatory spending?" and "How long has it been since the 'great recession' officially ended?"

The answers were all over the board, which proved a useful illustration of a grand principle: economics, he noted, is as much a matter of perception and feeling as much as it is of hard numbers. He concluded his final Brown lecture, from 2019, with encouraging words: "Good news—our economy is growing. We are not in a recession." With a nod to that dismal bit, though, he added that the recovery from the Great Recession was still ongoing, the slowest recovery since the Great Depression. And that was before coronavirus hit, an event that Gerry did not live to witness.

Hopeful, engaged, and constantly cheerful, Gerry spent nearly half a century in the classroom, introducing thousands on thousands of students to economics. It is a fitting honor that the University should have named its undergraduate teaching award, given annually to five teachers from full professors to graduate teaching assistants, the Gerald J. Swanson Prize for Teaching Excellence.

AI AND CYBERSECURITY

Hsinchun Chen and Management Information Systems

T**HE INTERNET** is an essential utility, as necessary to every household as running water and air conditioning. It is also an invisible, globe-spanning realm where very bad people are constantly on the prowl, looking to steal state secrets from governments, intellectual property from companies, passwords to bank accounts from individuals, and so forth. Cybercrime is rampant, organized by hostile governments, denizens of the dark web, and ordinary hackers, and while there are things we can do to keep ourselves safe from them, the black hats always seem to be one step ahead of the good guys.

Enter Hsinchun Chen. A Regents Professor of Management Information systems in the Eller College of Management, Chen is a world-renowned expert in what is called "data mining," or extracting information from the petabytes of ones and zeroes that float about in the cybersphere. Some of the applications of data mining are the daily bread of researchers and students, for without it there would be no search engines, no usable digital libraries, no informatics. Among the most prolific of scholars in the field, Chen, a native of Taiwan, has published scores of books and book chapters and hundreds of articles that have influenced the growth and direction of the field.

Chen, who began teaching at the University in 1989, founded the Artificial Intelligence Laboratory and is its director. Through the lab, he has coordinated numerous cybersecurity research projects. One is the Dark Web project, which breaks through the firewalls and other bulwarks that criminals and terrorists use to disguise their activity, tracking, for instance, supposedly anonymous messages to their true authors. His Hacker Web project similarly developed algorithms and software to help understand and interdict hacker activities. The NSF awarded Chen a $4.2 million grant to development a cybersecurity curriculum, with special emphasis on minority recruitment and retention, bringing in students from under-served communities as well as military units and Native American tribal colleges.

On the less nefarious side of informatics, Chen is developing medical intelligence systems that are of use in home health care, especially for older people living alone, as well as remotely tracking health conditions among diabetic patients. As active an entrepreneur as he is a scholar and researcher, Chen had founded numerous spin-off companies that use data mining in such fields as fraud detection, defense intelligence, and medicine.

LAYING DOWN THE LAW

The James E. Rogers College of Law

U**NTIL THE** late 1970s, the area along the north side of Speedway bordering the University campus was a congeries of hundreds of small brick and adobe bungalows, rambling apartment buildings, two-story garages, and fence-lined alleys. Many of these buildings housed the faculty and students from the earliest days of the University, and most, nearly a century on, were a little worse for the wear—all good reason for the University to buy them up and replace them with new structures on a rapidly expanding campus.

Apart from the Medical Center, the first new building to go up north of Speedway was the College of Law. Founded in 1915, the law school had by this time graduated thousands of attorneys over the years, and, with a burgeoning enrollment in the baby boom era, it had long since outgrown its quarters in first the old Douglass Building, where the Arizona State Museum had originally been housed, and then, after 1955, in what is now the Franklin Building, so renamed in 1980 to honor the attorney and legislator Selim Franklin, one of the founding fathers of the University of Arizona.

There had been some discussion before the new building went up of moving the college to offices downtown, near the city and federal courts, but in those days downtown was in disrepair, public transportation was iffy, and not many suitable places were available to solve the college's problem of space. The new building solved all that problem, allowing for a large library, seminar and classrooms, and mock courtrooms, a spacious place to house a program that would soon grow from the standard doctor of jurisprudence to include, today, a master's degree in legal studies, a preparatory bachelor's degree in law, an advanced doctorate in juridical science, a master's degree in Indigenous governance, and graduate certificates in Mexican law and health law. With some five hundred students enrolled at any given time and with a body of alumni numbering more than seven thousand, the James E. Rogers College of Law is a thriving, always busy intellectual center with a diverse student body and faculty from three dozen countries—and one that is highly ranked nationally.

It was not always so diverse. Breaking down barriers came about at the hands of progressive faculty and administrators, but not without some institutional resistance. An early exemplar is Lorna Lockwood (1903–77), born in the mining town of Douglas when Arizona was still a territory. Lockwood earned a bachelor's degree in Spanish at the University in 1923, then went on to receive her JD in 1925. She passed the bar exam on her first try. Even so, in a time when only men, it was thought, had a lawyerly mind-set, she was limited to working as a legal stenographer until 1939. Then, with fellow attorney Loretta Whitney, she founded her own law firm. In the meantime, she had run for and won a seat in the Arizona House of Representatives, a post she held intermittently until becoming a judge—and then, in 1961, she became the first woman to serve as chief justice of the Arizona Supreme Court. She was a strong candidate for a seat on the U.S. Supreme Court, but it would not be until 1981 that another Arizona woman, Sandra Day O'Connor, won appointment to the bench.

Joyce Edline Holsey, the first Black woman to graduate from what is now the James E. Rogers College of Law. Photograph courtesy of the University of Arizona.

Joyce Edline Holsey (1927–2006) earned a degree in chemistry from Hunter College in New York City when she was only nineteen, then took a master's degree in education for the visually impaired. With her husband, a physician, she moved to Tucson in 1958 and, a decade later, enrolled in the College of Law, excelling in coursework and argumentation even as she experienced a growing loss of eyesight that would become nearly total. In 1971, she became the first Black woman to graduate from the school, passing the bar exam that year and becoming a renowned attorney working for Southern Arizona Legal Aid on behalf of abused women and children.

Two decades earlier, Carrasco Lawrence Huerta, a member of the Pascua Yaqui Tribe of Tucson, became the first Native American to graduate from the College of Law. A brilliant student and able administrator, he went to work on issues of Indigenous sovereignty and devoted himself to expanding educational opportunities in Native communities, becoming chancellor of Navajo Community College before returning to Tucson to draft the Pascua Yaqui constitution. A scholarship in his name, administered by Regents Professor of Law Robert A. Williams, has supported more than three dozen Native students, part of a cohort of more than two hundred who have earned law degrees from the University of Arizona.

Students at the College of Law in the years from 1991 to 2004, incidentally, had a front-row view of some of the most momentous years in the history of the U.S. Supreme Court thanks to retired chief justice William Rehnquist, who began his legal career as an attorney in Phoenix before he entered government and, in 1971, became an associate justice. Serving on the highest bench for four decades, he wrote more than a thousand legal opinions that were known for their scholarly depth, which served Rehnquist well in the courses he taught on the Supreme Court and its not always transparent ways.

It's been said that the United States graduates far too many lawyers. That may or may not be so, but in recent years, nine out of ten James E. Rogers College of Law students were employed in their chosen field within a year of graduating—an admirable record in nearly any discipline.

JUST WORDS

The National Center for Interpretation

EVERYONE IS entitled to a fair trial. This is a central guarantee of the U.S. Constitution, a fundamental right of anyone charged with a crime. So, too, everyone is entitled to a trial by a jury of one's peers. But what defines a peer? If one is a monolingual speaker of, say, Russian or French, must the jurors all share that linguistic competence? Of course not, for otherwise the legal system would grind to a halt as abilities, qualities, and characteristics were parsed out, an obviously impossible task.

It was the insight of the eminent Spanish professor and linguist Renato Rosaldo, in the mid-1970s, that the desired fair trial could be achieved if the accused had an accurate, skilled interpreter on hand. A young colleague of his, Roseanne Dueñas González, had spent several years working in the Arizona Superior Court system for Pima County providing interpretation into and out of English for Spanish speakers, the subject of her doctoral research, and all concerned noted a marked improvement in the conduct of the bilingual proceedings.

The question was how new interpreters would be conjured into being. Rosaldo took a look around at some of his advanced undergraduate students, from an air force spouse from Spain to an aspiring lawyer from Indiana and a rancher's son from south of Yuma, Arizona, and divined an answer: he would take the most talented speakers he could find, immerse them in legal vocabulary in Spanish and its English equivalent in a semester-long intensive course, and set them to work interpreting in court cases in the city and county judicial system.

The program proved successful, and so, in 1979, was the National Center for Interpretation (NCI) born. As González, who was also affiliated with the Center for English as a Second Language, rose to lead NCI, her doctoral program became the foundation of a competence test for federal-level translators. Other languages were added, including, over time, Cantonese, Navajo, Haitian Creole, Iñupiat, and American Sign Language; in 2012, González and NCI published the definitive second edition of the 1,500-page book *Fundamentals of Court Interpretation*, the flagship publication in a growing field.

NCI continued to center on the law in its first years, but other applications were obvious, especially in medicine and health care. As the success of Margarita Kay's *Southwestern Medical Dictionary* had recently proved, there was a strong demand for interpretation between medical personnel and monolingual patients, and those two fields were drawn into the program. Business was an obvious addition as well, especially given the critically important cross-border commerce between Mexico and the United States, and the Spanish and Portuguese undergraduate program accordingly added business to its certification program. To gain credentials as a translator, students now complete three online tracks in medical, legal, and business translation. A parallel online track provides certification as an interpreter, work that centers on oral rather than written communication.

NCI remains a leader in the field. While it is one of the lesser-known success stories of the University of Arizona, practitioners of law, medicine, and international commerce know it as a go-to resource for training and standards. Its work has changed countless lives, ever helping to bridge cultures and languages with the aim of attaining equity—at least equity of words—for all.

POLITICOS PAST AND PRESENT

*Raúl Castro, Barry Goldwater, Morris and Stewart Udall,
and Other Leaders*

BORN IN 1916 in the mining town of Cananea, Sonora, Raúl H. Castro was a middling student until a teacher pulled him aside and encouraged him to read beyond the stuffy classroom primers, adding books such as *Don Quixote* and Mexican folktales to his diet. When he was ten, his family moved across the border to another nearby mining town, Douglas, Arizona, and Castro, by then an exemplary student, edited his high school newspaper, read everything he could, and won a football scholarship to Northern Arizona University.

Graduating in 1939, Castro returned to Douglas and applied for a teaching position. Told that he was disqualified because of his ethnicity, he moved south to Mexico again, finding work as a clerk for the American consulate in Hermosillo, Sonora, and taking an interest in the law. He traveled north to Tucson and, the story has it, marched into the office of the dean of students, telling him, "I can teach Spanish better than any of your instructors can. Please do me a favor: call the dean of the law school and tell him to admit me, since they don't admit Mexicans." Impressed by the young man's self-confidence, the dean did just that. Castro was admitted to law school, and he taught Spanish while studying the law, graduating with distinction in 1949.

Castro practiced law on his own until being elected Pima County's attorney in 1955. He then served as a judge in the Pima County Superior Court until 1964, when President Lyndon Johnson named him the U.S. ambassador to El Salvador and later to Bolivia. He returned to law practice in Arizona, then made history in 1974 by being the first Mexican

American elected governor of the state. He served only two years of his term before President Jimmy Carter named him the U.S. ambassador to Argentina. In 1980, he returned to Arizona, establishing a law practice in Nogales and working until 2003, when he retired. He died in 2015 at the age of ninety-eight. His papers are housed in Special Collections in the University Libraries.

On the opposite end of the political spectrum, Barry Goldwater (1909–98) arrived at the University of Arizona in 1928. He had been a poor student in his first year of high school in Phoenix, whereupon his parents packed him off to military school in Virginia. The banishment had the desired effect: Goldwater excelled in both his academic pursuits and as an athlete, lettering in football, swimming, track, and basketball. Moreover, he ran for office in student government, won, and carved out the beginnings of a path he would follow. Regrettably, Goldwater attended the University of Arizona for only a year. His father, the owner of a popular department store in Phoenix, died, and Goldwater was forced to drop out to take over management of the family business. His later career as an Arizona politician, serving five terms in the U.S. Senate, is well known. Less well known is Goldwater's superb photography, much of it documenting the Indigenous peoples and remote places of Arizona. Honoring the quality of his work, his archives are housed in the Center for Creative Photography.

Incidentally, a Republican colleague of Goldwater's in the Senate, Bob Dole (1923–2021), also attended University for a year. Badly wounded in combat in World War II, he endured a long series of operations between 1945 and 1947, then came to Tucson to continue his recuperation in the warm climate of the Sonoran Desert. He enrolled as an undergraduate in 1948 and completed the school year but then returned to his native Kansas to be closer to family. After earning a law degree, he served in the Kansas Legislature for ten years, then ran for U.S. Congress in 1960, serving in both chambers until 1996. That year, Dole left the Senate to run for president, retiring to private life after losing the election to Bill Clinton.

Born in 1922 in the Mormon farming community of St. Johns, Arizona, Morris K. "Mo" Udall had both law and politics in his blood, his father having been a judge on the Arizona Supreme Court for several terms. Following military service during World War II, Udall enrolled at the University of Arizona. Not only did he excel in classwork and serve as president of the Associated Student Government, but Udall also emerged as the leading scorer on the Wildcats basketball squad, taking the team to its first ever National Collegiate Athletic Association (NCAA) playoff and racking up 371 points in the 1947–48 school year. After

Morris K. "Mo" Udall, the future U.S. representative, as a champion Wildcat basketball player in 1948. Photograph courtesy of Special Collections, The University of Arizona Libraries.

earning his bachelor's degree, he played professional basketball in Denver, Colorado, for a year, then returned to Tucson to take a law degree, graduating in 1949. He practiced law in Tucson until 1961, then entered the U.S. Congress, where he served until retiring for reasons of health in 1991. Along the way, he ran for the U.S. presidency, wrote the best-selling book *Too Funny to Be President* after losing in the Democratic primary race, and worked with organizations advocating for civil rights and health-care reform. Mo Udall passed away in 1998. His archives are in Special Collections, as are the materials of an extensive oral history project with interviews with Udall and many of his contemporaries.

Mo's older brother, Stewart (1920–2010), played Wildcat basketball as well. He entered the University in 1938 but left to serve in World War II, earning an Air Medal and other honors. He returned to Tucson in 1946, entered law school, and was admitted to the bar in 1948. While at the University, he and Mo had helped integrate the previously segregated dining facilities in the Student Union, and as lawyers both led the way in desegregating Tucson's public schools. Elected to Congress in 1954, Stu Udall proved a strong advocate of the environment, for which reason President John F. Kennedy named him secretary of the interior—according to historian Douglas Brinkley, the best ever to have held that office—in 1961. In that role, he added numerous national parks and monuments to the nation's holdings, and he also helped establish cultural organizations such as the National Endowment for the Humanities and the Kennedy Center. His papers are also in Special Collections.

Regina Romero. Raúl Grijalva. Jon Kyl. Esther Tang. Dennis DeConcini. Paul Fannin. Ron Barber. Juan Ciscomani. Ayọ Tometi. Annie Dodge Wauneka. Jim McNulty. John Rhodes. Ann Kirkpatrick. Emory Sekaquaptewa. Name a politician, activist, or community leader in Arizona, and you're likely to land on a Wildcat. Something in the water, perhaps . . .

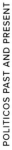

The eastern exterior wall of the University of Arizona Poetry Center. The holes in the wall are binary code spelling out a line from a poem by Richard Shelton, "you shall learn the art of silence." Photograph by Gregory McNamee.

THE
GIFT OF
TONGUES

How many languages are spoken in the world? By one conservative estimate, some five thousand, although that number has been declining as language systems, like ecosystems, fall before dominant species of speech: Mandarin, Spanish, English. And how do those languages work? The University of Arizona is home to a scholar who has been pondering that question for eight decades. He is not alone: we know much about languages living and extinct because of a long tradition of outstanding research in linguistics here. Our own Tucson home has heard hundreds of languages, from Native ones of long presence to languages spoken by recent newcomers from all over the world. In tribute to those Indigenous languages and cultures, too, the world's most important and most distinguished series of books of Native American literature is edited and published here.

BREAKING THE CODE

Noam Chomsky and the Hidden Rules of Language

THE GREEK historian Herodotus tells us that an Egyptian king named Psammetichus once ordered that two newborn boys be brought up by a voiceless shepherd, away from all people, in order to find out what their first original utterance would be. Both of the boys said the same thing, *bekos*, the Phrygian word for bread. Thus, Psammetichus concluded, the original language of humankind was Phrygian. QED.

In a roundabout sense, Noam Chomsky has devoted a lifetime of linguistic study to a similar quest, trying to identify the "deep structure" neurological rules that allow humans to generate language. Languages—five thousand or so are spoken around the world—differ, of course, but those rules, Chomsky holds, are universal and innate; hidden deep within the brain, the deep structures that produce those rules allow humans to learn their native languages correctly and, usually, to be intelligible as they speak of events past, present, and future.

Beginning in the 1950s, Chomsky's work neatly coincided with the development of computer languages, where it was highly influential in helping develop disambiguating if/then rules and the like. His "context-free grammar" is a central part of the algorithms underlying numerous computer languages and programming, including voice-command-parsing applications such as Alexa and Siri. His work has also shaped cognitive science, psychology, mathematics, education, neuroscience, philosophy, and his own home discipline of linguistics.

The author of books such as *Aspects of the Theory of Syntax* and *Language and Mind*, Chomsky taught for decades at the Massachusetts Institute of Technology (MIT). He tried retirement but, just shy of ninety years old, instead joined the faculty of the University of Arizona in 2017, saying, "We fell in love with Tucson—the mountains, the desert" and praising the university's intellectual community. He had visited the school many times, giving standing-room-only lectures in Centennial Hall, and now he both taught in the Department of Linguistics and gave public lectures on a variety of topics that broadly ranged across disciplines such as politics, history, and economics.

Apart from his work in linguistics, Chomsky is renowned as a political activist and firebrand, a stern critic of American interventions in places such as Iraq and, long ago, Vietnam. The *New York Times* has called Chomsky "the most important public intellectual" at work today, and he likes nothing better, it seems, than to hold open lectures (he calls them "office hours") when members of the always overflowing audience can ask him whatever is on their minds. To their delight, he has yet to be stumped—no surprise, for, along with his pathbreaking professional publications, he has written more than a hundred books.

As of 2024, in his ninety-sixth year, Noam Chomsky is both laureate professor of linguistics and the chair of the Agnese Nelms Haury Program in Environment and Social Justice. It's no surprise that many faculty members in linguistics trained with Chomsky at MIT and that much of the scholarship out of the department bears his stamp, addressing not just high-level questions on language acquisition, computational linguistics, semantics, and the like but also the social applications of language in addressing matters of justice, equality, and misinformation.

A MULTITUDE OF TONGUES

The Center for English as a Second Language

THE INTERNET connects distant corners of the world. So do highways, shipping lanes, airline routes. But perhaps the strongest connector, since the end of World War II, has been the English language, the lingua franca of Earth.

In large part because of its strong programs in the sciences and its first-class laboratories and research facilities, the University of Arizona has long been a lure for students from all over the world. Some come to the University with a strong command of English, but many more do not, and that's where the Center for English as a Second Language (CESL) comes in.

That story begins in 1968, when President Richard Harvill asked around to find someone who might teach speakers of other languages, through immersive techniques, how to read, write, and speak English. Harvill had been busy recruiting international students for several years, only to have faculty members tell him that many of them were at a disadvantage in the classroom, and the search was urgent. It finally led Harvill to the English Department and a young graduate student named Frank Pialorsi, who, inexperienced in administration, asked Harvill how he should proceed. Assuring him of a generous budget, Harvill replied with instructions to set his goals high and make it "the best program in the country."

Pialorsi took his charge seriously. He hired faculty members who were not only talented language instructors but also had international experience, many as Peace Corps volunteers or military veterans. Students began to arrive, their countries of origin reflecting changes in international politics and alliances. Mexico has always had a strong presence in CESL's student body, but over the years, there have been groups of students from China, Vietnam, the Soviet Union and Russia, Libya, Venezuela, Kazakhstan, Brazil, the Ivory Coast, and Saudi Arabia. All have faced the same program of instruction, which promises "superior English language instruction to native speakers of other languages through excellent teaching, an engaging curriculum, and programs which support learning, collaboration, and community-building." Through the English Department, CESL also provides a venue for teachers of English as a second/foreign language to train in pedagogical methods, and it offers specialty courses for members of the professions, focusing on the vocabulary of medicine, toxicology, agriculture, and avionics, for example.

Frank Pialorsi retired from CESL at the end of 2001. The center has faced challenges in the years since, all traceable to world events—two global financial crises, a pandemic, and the vagaries of international relations among them. Even so, CESL remains a world leader in language instructions, just as President Harvill had directed. As one gauge of its importance, CESL has taught nearly fifty thousand students from 128 nations, many of whom have returned to their native countries to continue the work of teaching English to their compatriots.

PALABRAS PROFUNDAS

Miguel Méndez and the Rise of Chicana/o Literature

S IX YEARS of elementary education, six of intermediary and secondary. Four years of undergraduate school, another two or three for a master's degree, another four or five for a doctorate. That adds up, for most aspiring academics, to a quarter century or more of education before getting to work.

Born in Bisbee, Arizona, in 1930, Miguel Méndez took a different path by necessity. Both his parents were from the neighboring Mexican state of Sonora, and when the Great Depression lingered well into the 1930s and jobs proved scarce, they returned to their homeland, settling in an agricultural hamlet. There Méndez attended elementary school through the fifth grade, when he went to work on his parents' small farm. Fortunately for him, though, his parents shared a love of reading, with a small home library of books and magazines, and they encouraged him to read widely and write stories of his own.

When he was still a young teenager, Méndez moved by himself to Tucson, where a wartime shortage of labor had led to a great demand for *albañiles*, or construction workers. He learned masonry and bricklaying on the job, becoming skilled at both, meanwhile continuing to read and write by candlelight at night and to haunt Spanish-language bookstores in Tucson and Nogales. In 1969, his first short story, "Tata Casehua," was published, and in 1970, despite his lack of formal education, Pima Community College hired Méndez to teach courses in Spanish language and literature. In 1974, he published his prizewinning, nowclassic novel *Peregrinos de Aztlán* (Pilgrims of Aztlán), and in that same year, he joined the Department of Spanish and Portuguese at the University of Arizona. Beginning as a lecturer,

The cover of Miguel Méndez's best-known novel, *Peregrinos de Aztlán* (Pilgrims of Aztlán), published in 1974.

he was promoted to full professor in 1986. He continued to teach in the department until 2000, then retired, but was active on campus and in Tucson's literary community until his death in 2013.

Over those years of teaching and service, Miguel Méndez came to be hailed as one of the most influential and gifted practitioners of Chicana/o literature. Well versed in the classics of world literature, he wove together elegantly written, linguistically rich narratives that featured all the cultures in play along the Arizona-Mexico borderlands—Hispanic, Tohono O'odham, Yaqui, Anglo—in all their complexity. To that mix he added folklore and myths, especially Arabic ones that had found their way into the medieval Spanish tradition, reinterpreting them for a modern audience. A champion of the working class and of the underdog, he wrote empathetically of ordinary struggles and the difficult history of his time, especially the Vietnam War era and the aftermath of the Mexican Revolution, enacted by desert dwellers and urbanites alike.

Miguel Méndez wrote novels, short stories, poems, and essays, some forty books, all in Spanish. And as for that lack of education? The University awarded Méndez an honorary doctorate in humane letters in 1984, about the same time he received Spain's highest award for literary merit. He was even nominated for the Nobel Prize in literature.

THREE CULTURES

Esther Don Tang and Chinese Tucson

LIFE WAS not easy for nineteenth-century Chinese immigrants to Arizona and the West. They were confined to building railroad lines, working as laborers on construction projects and in mines, spending long hours in kitchens and laundries. Forbidden to marry anyone other than other Chinese people, they lived in segregated communities, usually alongside marginalized African Americans, Mexican Americans, and Native Americans.

In Tucson, those Chinese immigrants lived south and west of the present-day city center. Prejudice and de facto apartheid governed their lives, but within their community, social and family networks grew and economic connections formed. If in the 1880s, as archaeological evidence shows, poverty reigned—putting the lie to the Chinese name for America, Gold Mountain—by the early twentieth century, a prosperous middle class of merchants and traders had begun to emerge, and most small grocery stores in the city were owned by first- and second-generation Chinese Tucsonans.

We know many details of Chinese American life in our city because of the diligent research of Esther Don Tang (1917–2015), who grew up in Tucson's Chinatown. Her father, Don Wah, was American-born, but even so, because of those racist laws, he had to travel to China in order to find a spouse. After he married, he worked as a chef on Southern Pacific trains until moving to Tucson in 1905, where he founded the small city's first commercial bakery.

Esther Tang attended Mansfeld Junior High School and Tucson High School, graduating from the latter in 1937. She then moved to San Antonio, Texas, to live with a married sister and work in a family business while attending business college. Returning to Tucson, she married David Tang (1914–2002) in 1942. David Tang became a leader in the business community, founding Tucson's first supermarket and investing in real estate while rarely failing to attend a Wildcats home game, no matter what the sport.

Meanwhile, Esther Tang attended the University of Arizona, graduating with a bachelor's degree in nutrition and sociology. While working with her husband at their stores and managing a real estate portfolio, she volunteered for such positions as a board member for the YMCA and the Community Chest, raising money to promote girls' and women's sports. In 1966, she became the executive director of the Pio Decimo Community Center, bringing health, social, and educational services to a poor neighborhood for the next twenty years. She went on to help lead a construction firm that built homes for underserved communities—and hired their members to do so—in Tucson and Phoenix. Another of her firms built retirement and assisted-living homes, and Esther Tang became an active volunteer with the Pima Council on Aging.

Esther Tang was elected to the board of Pima Community College in 1975, and she did much to build the school's east side campus. And even with all those enterprises going on at once, she remained active in fundraising and community outreach efforts at the University while collecting material related to the city's Chinese community, highlighting its importance as a component of our multicultural, multiethnic city. As she recalled late in life, "As we grew up, my eight sisters, one brother and I not only celebrated the Chinese traditions but the Mexican culture and American holidays. We learned three languages simultaneously and still enjoy and cook the ethnic foods for our families. It's really marvelous when one can select the good things in each culture."

Historian, activist, community leader, and native Tucsonan Esther Don Tang in 1955. Photograph courtesy of the Tucson Urban Renewal Project.

Trilingual in Cantonese, Spanish, and English, Esther Tang was a force for those good things at the University and in the larger community. She earned many honors in her lifetime, including Tucson Woman of the Year, Tucson's Outstanding Citizen, and the University Alumni Award. She served as a charter member of the College of Humanities Advisory Board, and in 2002 the courtyard, conference room, and two galleries in the newly built Learning Services Building were named in her honor. A plaque in the University of Arizona Women's Plaza of Honor also commemorates Esther Don Tang's life and achievements.

A HALLMARK OF NATIVE AMERICAN LITERATURE

Sun Tracks

A T THE beginning of 1971, three young Diné students at the University of Arizona decided to launch a quarterly journal of Native American literature. They found a faculty sponsor in Edward P. Dozier, a Tewa scholar who was the first Native American professor to receive tenure in any anthropology department in the United States. Ethnohistorian Bunny Fontana pulled in a small grant for the project, while Dozier—who sadly died that year at the far-too-young age of fifty-five—assembled a board of advisors that included several English Department faculty members. The journal *Sun Tracks*, the first such Indigenous literary magazine to be published in America, appeared in October 1971. Three more numbers appeared, but then the three original editors graduated, and *Sun Tracks* suspended publication.

Two years later, a young English professor named Larry Evers arrived on campus. A specialist in Native American literature, Evers brought in new grants and, working with Indigenous students across campus, renewed the journal, securing contributions by N. Scott Momaday, Gerald Vizenor, Leslie Marmon Silko, Simon J. Ortiz, Paula Gunn Allen, and many other then-rising writers.

In 1980, the sixth volume of the series focused on literary works by Hopi, Diné, Tohono O'odham, and Yaqui writers. The following year, the Sun Tracks editorial group—"both a project and a place name," as Evers writes in the anthology *Home Places: Contemporary Native American Writing from Sun Tracks*—reprinted *The South Corner of Time: Hopi, Navajo, Papago, Yaqui Tribal Literature* in book form with UA Press. Unusually for the time, the book contained bilingual texts in each of the four Native languages, a practice that a young poet named Ofelia Zepeda would follow in 1982 with her Tohono O'odham / English bilingual text *When It Rains: Papago and Pima Poetry / Mat Hekid O Ju: O'odham Na-cegitodag*. (The current English title replaces "Papago" with "Tohono O'odham.") Other UA Press books followed, including *Spirit Mountain: An Anthology of Yuman Story and Song*, representing numerous Native nations along the Colorado River; Acoma writer Simon J. Ortiz's book of poems *A Good Journey*; a collection of black-and-white images called *Hopi Photographers, Hopi Images* co-edited by the Hopi writer and filmmaker Victor Masayesva Jr.; *Secrets from the Center of the World*, a collection of poems by Joy Harjo, who would go on to become poet laureate of the United States, accompanied by photographs by astronomer Stephen E. Strom; and many other books. More than half a century on, Sun Tracks is the most distinguished Native American literary series ever published.

Every book in the series is a standout, but I confess a special fondness for Larry Evers and Felipe S. Molina's groundbreaking book *Yaqui Deer Songs/Maso Bwikam*, for which I was the in-house editor at UA Press. "The book combines extensive bilingual song texts, verbatim commentaries by knowledgeable Yaquis, sensitive accounts of ethnographic and mythological background, and detailed scholarly reference to the literature both on Yaqui culture and on American Indian oral poetry," wrote the distinguished linguist William Bright in a review of the book, adding, "one is unaccustomed to such riches." That's exactly right, and, in continuing Sun Tracks' insistence that Native American literature is truly literature, the book is exemplary.

GATHERING THE RAIN CLOUDS

Ofelia Zepeda

W HEN OFELIA Zepeda arrived in Tucson in the mid-1970s, she did not come with the sense that she would one day be a well-published poet. Neither did she have any expectation of becoming the first member of the Tohono O'odham Nation to earn a doctorate in linguistics, far less of attaining the illustrious rank of Regents Professor at the University of Arizona. That she did all those things over a long career was a matter of accident, Zepeda says, and one that began with a chance encounter with another student of languages.

That student was Kenneth Hale, a brilliant linguist from MIT who once reckoned that he could pick up the basics of a language he'd never heard before in the space of about fifteen minutes. Born in 1934, Hale grew up on an Arizona ranch, and he may have been one of the few professors at MIT ever to don cowboy boots to begin with, much less wear them in the classroom. By the time he died in 2001, he had mastered more than fifty languages, and he seemed a little surprised if you had not.

When Hale learned that a young woman who had grown up speaking O'odham at home had arrived on campus, where he was a visiting scholar, he helped steer grant money to her—with the proviso that she study linguistics.

"When I came here, I didn't know the field existed," she says. "I thought I might want to be a teacher, and I wanted to find a way to teach O'odham people how to read their language. There was a dictionary and a book of folktales, but when I bought them, I stared and stared at them—they just made no sense to me, a native speaker. I couldn't connect the orthography to the words I knew."

Zepeda addressed that problem by writing the first full grammar of the O'odham language, first published as *A Papago Grammar* by UA Press in 1983. (The Tohono O'odham were formally known as the Papago until shortly thereafter, while their cousins the Akimel O'odham, "People of the Flowing Water," were known as the Pima.) The orthography she established in that book, working with Hale and other speakers and scholars, is now the official standard for written O'odham, and the book has been used to teach thousands of students. The first sentence one learns is this: "*'I:da 'o'odham 'o ñeok*" (This person is/was speaking).

Tohono O'odham linguist and poet Ofelia Zepeda. Photograph by Cybele Knowles, © 2015 Arizona Board of Regents. Courtesy of the University of Arizona Poetry Center.

Zepeda undertook fieldwork in the Sonoran village of Quitovac, "a vibrant place with a natural water source," she says, "which is what *vac* means." There, two groups of O'odham intersect: the Tohono O'odham, whose name has been translated as "Desert People," and the Hia C-ed O'odham, whose name means "Sand People," and whose homeland is drier and more austere than the saguaro-studded lands of what the Spanish called the Papaguería.

Not much had been known about the lifeways of the Sand People until Zepeda undertook a series of oral histories, gathering stories from elders about significant places and customs, the use of food plants and knowledge of animals, the changing seasons and the work and ceremonies appropriate to each. Zepeda went on to establish the American Indian Language Development Institute (AILDI), which trains Native American teachers in methods of instruction to help transmit to new generations languages and knowledge that might otherwise have disappeared. In the years since its founding, more than two thousand students have been through the AILDI program.

It was from her study of her language, Zepeda says, that she became interested in writing poetry. "At first I used traditional songs. The writing came because of the students—I had to write in order to give them something to read, and it wasn't as though you could go to Amazon in those days and order up a Tohono O'odham novel. I asked my students to write stories that we could all share, things from their lives, and my own stories came out as poems.

Many of my students were singers, and so they often transcribed songs that they knew, and we all learned together." The materials that she gathered with her students became part of *The South Corner of Time*, the first book in the Sun Tracks series published by UA Press. In time, Zepeda would become the editor of the series herself, encouraging emerging Native writers in several genres.

Songs and poems: in Ofelia Zepeda's hands, the two are not easily distinguished, and many of her original works contain traditional formulas—repeating choruses or elements, for example. Many of her poems, in books such as *Ocean Power* (1995), are written in both English and Tohono O'odham.

Zepeda still returns to Quitovac to attend the rain ceremonies that she has commemorated in many poems, songs to help pull down the clouds and urge them to deliver their burden of water to the thirsty land below. Anyone who wishes to be a true citizen of this part of the Sonoran Desert, a land at once austere and generous, will want to have her songs in memory, close to our hearts.

AT THE PINNACLE OF LEARNING

N. Scott Momaday and the Regents Professors

H OUSE MADE *of Dawn* is a novel that, in an ordinary publishing season, might have enjoyed a quiet, short life and then disappeared, the fate of so many books. But there was something about it that caught the zeitgeist when it appeared in 1968, recounting, in a terrible time of war, a Native American veteran's difficult adjustment to life at home following military service. That debut novel earned its author, N. Scott Momaday (1933–2024), a Pulitzer Prize. It was the first of many honors for Momaday, who, in 1982, would join the faculty of the University of Arizona as a professor of English and American Indian studies and who would, in 1988, be enrolled in the first class of faculty members to be honored with the designation of Regents Professor.

That distinction is not something one applies for, but instead something one earns through teaching, research, writing, and outreach—the ordinary work of professors, that is—at the very highest level of accomplishment. The process of selection is not widely advertised, but the award is certainly broadly distributed across the faculty. With Momaday in 1988, for example, Victor R. Baker, a professor of geosciences, earned the honor as well. Baker is an extraordinarily prolific scholar in a field he practically created, namely the geological study of ancient floods. The inaugural class included another hydrologist, Shlomo P. Neuman, a visionary scholar of the movement of water in underground aquifers, as well as religious historian Heiko A. Oberman and philosopher Joel Feinberg, among others.

Every year since, a minimum of two Regents Professors have been named, although in most years the number is five or six. They come from every field of inquiry. Humanities scholars have included critical cultural theorist Barbara A. Babcock, poet and linguist Ofelia Zepeda, and historian Oscar J. Martínez. From the social sciences have come law professor and water-policy scholar Robert J. Glennon, archaeologist John W. Olsen, and geographer and resource analyst Sallie Marston. The sciences have been especially well represented, in keeping with the University's leadership in scientific research and scholarship, with honorees that include astrophysicist Renu Malhotra, hydrologist and atmospheric scientist Hoshin Vijai Gupta, oncologist Allan Hamilton, and geoscientist Jonathan Overpeck. At this writing, the most recent cohort of Regents Professors includes Sama Raena Alshaibi, a professor of photography and videography in the College of Fine Arts; Juanita L. Merchant, a professor of medicine and leading researcher in gastroenterological diseases; and Jean-Luc Brédas, a professor of chemistry who has led the way in developing new high-efficiency materials for telecommunications devices.

The visually stunning courtyard of the Environment and Natural Resources 2 Building, completed in 2015. Photograph by David Olsen.

THE WORLD AROUND US

Astronomy and geosciences have long provided the scientific intellectual underpinnings of the University. But excellence in many other branches of science is a hallmark here, too, and advances in all of them have propelled the postwar growth of the University of Arizona as a research institution of international renown. The flagship has long been atmospheric sciences, since expanded to incorporate hydrology, both areas of urgent importance in a changing climate. Optical sciences have provided the eyes, so to speak, for cameras and telescopes that are now traveling to the outer reaches of the universe, while cognitive science is probing into the innermost workings of the mind. Another strength is insect science, an interdisciplinary approach involving the study of insect minds, bodies, and behavior through many lenses. These and other sciences afford happy examples of intellectual teamwork in action.

PIECES OF Π

Mathematics and the Mathematics Building

IN MATHEMATICS, pi (represented by the Greek letter π) is the ratio of a circle's circumference to its diameter. It's a neat party trick to recite the number out to more than a few decimal places, and few people can go beyond 31 of them—that is, 3.141592653589793238 4626433832795.

Archimedes, the ancient Greek scientist, made a very accurate estimation of π, arriving at a value of 3.1418. Scientists in centuries following worked laboriously to make the calculation even more accurate, extending the number of decimal places; by the time Isaac Newton was at work, he was able to calculate π to 16 places. A bit more than a century ago, the Indian mathematician Srinivasa Ramanujan found new infinite sums that in turn could be used to find many more digits of π.

In 1997, Japanese computer scientists Yasumasa Kanada and Daisuke Takahashi used a fourth-order convergent (that is, superfast) algorithm to calculate the value of π to 51,539,600,000 decimal digits. In September 2002, Kanada used a modified algorithm to compute the value to 1,240,000,000,000 decimals, a calculation that took one of the world's most powerful supercomputers more than 400 hours to complete.

These pieces of the history of π are of a piece with the story of the University's Department of Mathematics, which took time—plenty of time—to progress from a rather dutiful, there-because-it-has-to-be portion of the curriculum to a world leader in both theory and application.

That story begins in 1892, when a few mathematics courses, "pure" and "applied," were placed under the purview of the College of Mines. Most of these courses, such as algebra and geometry, are taught in high school today, but territorial Arizona had few teachers capable of fielding them even at the college level. It took another dozen years for the University to create a mathematics major, and the first bachelor's degree was awarded to Josephine Walters in 1918. The first master's degree went to Samuel Ridgely three years later, but not until 1962 was the first doctorate awarded, this one to Marcus Bernard.

The doctoral program in mathematics was the result of a number of, beg pardon, factors, among them the elevation of a top-grade mathematician, Harvey Cohn, to department head in 1959. The United States was galloping along in the first stages of the space race, initiated with the launch of the Soviet satellite *Sputnik* in 1957, after which federal money began to flow to the sciences at unprecedented levels. At the same time, Cohn wisely used Tucson's natural beauty and agreeable climate to lure mathematicians who had retired from teaching elsewhere, enabling him to stretch out the budget and expand the department rapidly.

Today, seven decades on, the Mathematics Department is a mature program that boasts nearly a hundred faculty members, ranging from lecturers and instructors to full professors, who work in every corner of mathematics. Some specialize in geometry and algebraic topology, which is often called "rubber sheet geometry," since it deals with properties that do not change when an object is stretched but not cut. (For example, a rubber band can be formed into a square, a circle, an ellipse, and similar shapes without changing its fundamental properties, though transforming a circle into a line segment requires it to be cut, altering its essential nature.) Others specialize in the mathematical discipline of probability, which concerns itself with the chances that some event will occur—for instance, the prediction that there will be, say, a 20 percent chance of rain on a given day. Still others specialize in mathematical logic, using game theory to make optimal choices among a range of possibilities, a theory that has been widely applied in such far-ranging fields as economics and diplomacy. Differential geometry, number theory, computational analysis: as with the Mathematics Department of 1892, our modern mathematicians work in both theory and practice, but at dazzling levels of accomplishment, and often backed by supercomputers that Srinivasa Ramanujan could never have dreamed of—the kind that, even today, add digits onto π, for today we can calculate it to trillions of decimal places.

Harvey Cohn retired in 1967. Two years later, the Mathematics Department moved from the Physics Building into its own quarters. Tucked away in a quiet corner a couple of blocks south of Old Main and completed in 1968 at a cost of $800,000 (a bit less than $7,000,000 today), the Mathematics Building was built in the "brutalist" style on an X-shaped plan that suggests the multiplication sign (or perhaps the algebraic variable x). Four stories were originally built, with the cantilevered structure so sturdily constructed that more floors could be added. Two more floors were indeed added in later years. Even though the building could use some refreshing—a perennial exercise for architecture students—on a campus full of interesting buildings, the Mathematics Building is perhaps the most unusual.

SEEING INTO THE FUTURE

The Wyant College of Optical Sciences

"**D**ON'T YOU know that fields are for cattle?" So thundered Kenneth Rexroth, one of the first poets to read at the Poetry Center in 1962, urging his audience to ask questions of the world as broadly as possible without surrendering to shallowness. As we have seen throughout this book, many of the most exciting intellectual developments—cognitive science, AI, cultural studies—in recent decades have come when scholars from several disciplines converge to make something new.

Optical sciences is a case in point. Now, scientists have been studying optics since well before Isaac Newton published his *Opticks* in 1704. But it has really been only since the post–World War II era and the development of lasers and other precision devices that optical sciences—blending such fields as mathematics, physics, materials science, electrical engineering, and medicine—has come into its own. In that development, the University of Arizona has played a leading role.

The story begins with Aden Meinel (1922–2011), whom we met earlier. A Californian who began his scholarly career in aerospace and mechanical engineering, Meinel became fascinated by astronomy, volunteering at the Mount Wilson Observatory in Los Angeles and eventually becoming an apprentice optician, where he learned to make specialized plates for cameras without optical aberrations, tools essential for the study of space. He later added to the inventory with an invention of his own, a spectrograph that allowed him to study chemiluminescence.

In 1957, the NSF tasked Meinel with finding the site for a new observatory within the continental United States. After a careful search, Meinel settled on Kitt Peak, in a mountain

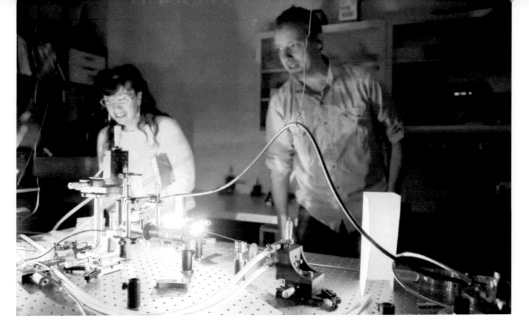

The **VECSEL**, or vertical external-cavity surface emitting laser, developed by University optical scientists. It can generate "tunable" light at all ends of the spectrum, with many practical applications. Photograph by Paul Tumarkin, courtesy of Tech Launch Arizona / University of Arizona.

range southwest of Tucson on the Tohono O'odham Nation. He negotiated with tribal leaders to lease the mountaintop, then installed the original Steward Observatory telescope and other instruments at the new facility and began observations. In 1961, the University invited Meinel to join the astronomy faculty and become director of Steward.

A month later, the Optical Society of America approached Meinel and asked him to lead a study group to build a curriculum in optical sciences. The University of Rochester, in the New York city where Eastman Kodak was located, was the nation's leader in the area, but Meinel, who was not without a competitive streak, decided he wanted to build an even better center at UA. At whirlwind speed, he made a pitch for an Optical Sciences Center (OSC), securing funding from the U.S. Air Force to the tune of $5.25 million (about $42 million today) in direct and indirect funds for a building across the Mall from the astronomy and space sciences complex of buildings. OSC opened in 1970, its entrance graced by a brilliant sculpture by Tucson artist Don Cowen that is both arresting to the eye and enigmatic, perfectly in keeping with the nature of the optical sciences enterprise.

Aden Meinel headed the new center until 1973, then settled back into the role of professor until retiring in 1985, eventually turning his scholarly attention to developing better optical receptors for collecting solar energy.

Over the years, OSC accumulated a number of world-class scientists who brought with them research laboratories and large grants from industry and government. One of them was Willis E. Lamb Jr., winner of the 1955 Nobel Prize in physics. Another was James Wyant (1943–2023), who became director in 1999. With ample experience in both academia and industry, Wyant built the center steadily, all the while quietly making plans to convert it into a college of its own. That happened in 2005, when he became the first dean of the newborn College of Optical Sciences, now called the Wyant College of Optical Sciences in his honor.

Countless innovations have come from OSC and the Wyant College since 1964. Regents Professor Harrison H. Barrett, for example, developed numerous imaging instruments that have proven of use in both astronomy and medicine—and even in wildlife management, developing radio-tracing tools for small mammals in the field. Illustrative of the cross-disciplinary nature of optical sciences, Barrett, now an emeritus professor, held appointments in mathematics, medicine, and biomedical engineering as well as in his home college. David Brady, who holds an endowed chair, heads the Camera Lab, which, in 2012, developed the first gigapixel camera, which gathers nearly a hundred million times the visual information as the camera invented by Louis Daguerre in the 1830s. Also on the camera front, Michael W. Marcellin—a Regents Professor with appointments in mathematics and electrical and computer engineering as well as in optical sciences—is one of the primary scholars behind the JPEG2000 protocol, a vastly improved standard for image compression over the familiar, ubiquitous JPEG.

Roger Angel, an astronomer and inventor, has been working for years on improving solar photovoltaic cells, a fitting field of endeavor in a sun-drenched place such as Arizona. Less obvious, perhaps, is Brian Anderson's declaration that the Wyant College "is home to the coldest spot in Arizona"—namely a lab in which laser light captures atoms and cools them to the thinnest of a hair above absolute zero, all in the interest of improved imaging techniques. As to imaging, Meredith Kupinski has earned honors for her work in using polarized light to detect cervical cancer, among other applications. Similarly, Jennifer Barton, with appointments in biomedical engineering and several other departments and who serves as director of the BIO5 Institute, a collaborative research center, has developed miniature endoscopes that use multiple optical imaging techniques, evaluating them as tools for early detection of cancers, and has contributed to an innovative technique employing lasers to treat blood-vessel disorders.

Mohammed Hassan, a physicist and optical scientist, has been working to develop a fast-switching computer with the potential to be a staggering million times faster than the computer on your desktop. Whether you need a computer so speedy isn't quite the point, though—the exciting application of his invention is the transmission of data to and from outer space. The university's mirror-building projects, so essential for the exploration of the universe, have involved optical scientists for decades, ever since the first mirror optician joined the faculty in 1964. And here on Earth, specialists in remote sensing are improving on radiometry and GPS to take the margin of error from meters to millimeters, something an astronaut landing a spacecraft on a distant planet will someday surely appreciate.

Dozens of research projects are under way at any given time at the Wyant College of Optical Sciences, where, forgive the pun, things are always looking up. A world leader in optical physics, photonics, optical engineering, and remote sensing, and with hundreds of students at every level, it's one of our crown jewels.

THUNDER AND LIGHTNING (AND DUST)

The Department of Hydrology and Atmospheric Sciences

S TUDY THE skies around Tucson in midsummer, and you're likely to see plenty of cumulonimbus clouds, whose towering anvil-head formations mark not just the arrival of life-giving water but also the possibility of life-ending danger. Those clouds can rise to thirty thousand feet and more. They're full of water but also ice, and, as a mix of both, ice crystals coated with water and hail called graupel. Water, ice, hail—all can be terribly damaging. So, too, are the explosions of lightning within the clouds, explosions that can create evanescent temperatures five times hotter than the surface of the sun.

We know all this thanks to scientists at the University of Arizona, an international leader in lightning research beginning as long ago as the early 1940s. It was here that the noted scientist Leon E. Salanave did much of the work for his 1980 book *Lightning and Its Spectrum*, still a standard reference in any meteorologist's library.

The faculty and affiliates of the Department of Hydrology and Atmospheric Sciences have much material to study, for 8.6 million times a day, somewhere on Earth, a bolt of lightning is firing. We can quantify that particular datum thanks in good part to an emeritus member of the atmospheric sciences faculty, E. Philip Krider, who has been studying methods and technologies of lightning detection for half a century. His work has been instrumental in the development of the National Lightning Detection Network, a network that feeds data on lightning strikes into a central processor, not just recording past blasts but also helping predict the path of future storms—unquestionably a lifesaving technology.

Speaking of lightning, it can strike twice in the same place. A dozen times, even. It need not even have a visible cloud to set lightning in motion. Reminds Mike Crimmins, a professor of environmental sciences, "If you can hear thunder, you can be struck by lightning," good reason to stick close to shelter when a monsoon storm is brewing.

It's not just lightning that the University's atmospheric scientists study. In 2023, Xubin Zeng of the Climate Dynamics and Hydrometeorology Collaborative used laser imaging and output from models to develop an algorithm to measure wind speed and direction by the water vapor in the air, an innovation that promises to be useful in helping predict hurricanes and their future paths. Closer to home, William A. Sprigg, a research professor emeritus in the Department of Hydrology and Atmospheric Sciences, was a longtime student of the formation of dust storms, which, in Arizona, can involve the wind's kicking up tons of dust and dirt in the air—material that contains more harmful stuff, such as the, well, dust from livestock feedlots, chemicals, fungi such as the species that causes valley fever, bacteria, and toxic chemicals. In a place such as Phoenix, where one of the world's largest dust storms—a hundred miles wide and nearly twelve miles high—was recorded in 1991, such an event can be fatal to those who suffer from pulmonary ailments. And dust storms frequently are fatal when they blow up onto Arizona's interstate highways. The work of Sprigg and his colleagues has helped meteorologists and traffic safety agencies alike predict the track of dust storms, saving lives and billions of dollars in medical expenses.

A postscript: The best local lightning story that I've heard comes, as so many of the best stories do, from the late University folklorist Big Jim Griffith, who pointed out in passing that the seventeenth-century filigree cross atop Mission San Xavier del Bac is a cleverly disguised lightning rod. It seems that the uncle of a friend of his, a cowboy in Mexico, was out riding fences one day when lightning blew a leg off his horse. The horse keeled over, of course. So the vaquero held up a slab of *queso blanco*, or Chihuahua cheese, and waited for the next stroke of lightning, which immediately followed. (As our atmospheric scientists can tell you, lightning often strikes more than once in the same place.) The lightning melted the cheese, which he applied to the horse's leg, gluing it back onto the unfortunate steed's body, and off the two rode.

"The point of the story," Big Jim told me with his Cheshire-cat grin, "is not really about lightning. It's about the meltability, elasticity, and all-around wonderfulness of Chihuahua cheese."

NOR ANY DROP TO DRINK

Helen Ingram, Hydrology, and Water Policy

T IS scarcely necessary to point out that the University of Arizona lies in a desert, and a desert by definition is a place in which water is at a premium. Yet, for somewhat less than a couple of hundred years now, Arizonans have been behaving as if water were abundant, mining deep groundwater aquifers and building large agricultural irrigation systems, not least of them the giant Central Arizona Project canal that runs all the way from the Colorado River to Tucson. Given such ambitious efforts to conjure up water, it's no surprise that at the University's very first graduation ceremony, on May 29, 1895, one of the commencement speakers gave a learned (and, by many accounts, overlong) speech titled "The Development of Irrigation Law."

To this day, dozens of University of Arizona scholars and researchers are involved in the study of water. Some, from the scholars of the critical zone to hydrological engineers, are concerned with the physical movement of water. Others are concerned with which way to make it move, the purview of economics and of water policy.

It is in this last field that Helen Ingram stands as one of the nation's most important water scholars. A policy specialist and former director of the Udall Center for Studies in Public Policy, she wrote fifteen books and hundreds of articles that examine and complicate a western truism: "water flows uphill toward money." It does just that in so many cases, thanks to the, now-lessening, political clout of developers and agriculturalists, but at a cost. "I noticed," Ingram wrote in an issue of *Journal of the Southwest* devoted to her work, "that there were consistent losers in the process: Native Americans and the environment." To bring these losers to the table, Ingram consistently and constantly advocated for factoring every member of the constituency of water, not least Native Americans and spokespeople for the voiceless environment, into the equation of how water is divided and used.

That Helen Ingram should have become so prominent was a fight against the odds, for, as she wrote, "I had to talk my way into the graduate program at Columbia University as an exceptional female worth the trouble." At her first academic job, she chose to study water resource policy, "a subject matter choice that any political science mentor would have vetoed." One of the only women in the field, she was often overlooked, often "generally underestimated." Even so, she forged on, building a strongly interdisciplinary program (because so few people in political science, her home discipline, were interested then in water) that included geographers, historians and ethnohistorians, engineers, and legal scholars. Through her efforts over many decades, the University of Arizona is now among the country's leading centers for water studies generally.

Helen Ingram, internationally renowned scholar of water policy. Photograph by Emlyn Oliver Agnew, courtesy of Helen Ingram.

Helen Ingram did not work in a vacuum. For one, a geographer of a more scientific bent, Connie Woodhouse, has long been working on a deep history of the Southwest's ancient climate, using paleoclimatology as a guide to the present use of water resources "not as an afterthought," as she writes, "but as part of the process of shaping a science agenda." A strong advocate of science and scientists taking a leading role in formulating public policy, Connie Woodhouse was named a Regents Professor in 2020, recognizing the importance of her work in understanding the limits of the Colorado River hydrological system.

Hydrologist Shlomo Neuman was inducted as a Regents Professor in the very first class in 1988, an indication of how important water is in the foundational curriculum of the University. Whereas amateurs might bring a divining rod in the hope of finding underground water, Neuman has written more than 360 scholarly articles on subsurface flow dynamics, mapping how water moves through aquifers and using geomorphology and the geology of what are called fractured rocks to predict where water will be found.

Still another Regents Professor, Hoshin Vijai Gupta, teaches and studies hydrology, atmospheric sciences, and public policy. A specialist in bringing algorithms and systems theory to the study of water formation, he teaches a four-course sequence that draws on his background in mathematics, civil engineering, geology, and hydrology. Gupta also directed the NSF-funded Sustainability of Semi-arid Hydrology and Riparian Areas initiative, which applied science to policy in order to arrive at best practices for the health of water resources in places where they are scarce.

Following Helen Ingram's example, University of Arizona scientists, researchers, and scholars are involved in water projects all over the state and the Southwest. Some policy experts are at work in formulating conservation measures for farmers in a time when allocated water from the Colorado River is in sharp decline. Some atmospheric scientists are studying water vapor in clouds to help predict events in which too much water is present— namely hurricanes and typhoons. Some public health specialists are improving techniques for measuring the presence of communicable diseases in water supplies, building on a project begun in 2020 that used wastewater as an index of the spread of COVID-19. All are helping us gain a greater understanding of—and, with luck, more wisdom concerning—that most precious of things in our arid home.

THE MARITIME DESERT

Oceanography and Marine Biology

T HE GULF of California, a large inlet of the eastern Pacific Ocean, extends more than seven hundred miles along the western coast of Mexico, nearly isolating the long peninsula called Baja California, or "lower California." Ecologists divide the Gulf, which is also called the Sea of Cortez, into two (and sometimes three) distinct parts. The northernmost part, which is less than four hours' drive from Tucson, is generally shallow, seldom attaining depths of more than six hundred feet. South of the large islands of Ángel de la Guarda and Tiburón, the Gulf deepens, with one deep-sea canyon system reaching ten thousand feet below the surface.

The Gulf of California is amazingly diverse in marine life, so much so that the famed oceanographer Jacques Cousteau once called it "the world's aquarium." Among the many marine mammals that come to the Gulf are whales of many species, including the blue whale—the largest animal that has ever existed—fin whale, humpback whale, gray whale, sperm whale, and orca, all of which breed there. The Gulf of California is so historically rich in fish and shellfish species that an extensive fishing industry has developed around it, an industry so active that much of the region's marine life is now under threat. International environmental organizations and University of Arizona scientists have worked with the government of Mexico to help develop conservation zones and other strategies to preserve sea life.

Although it may seem very distant and very different from the inland desert where we find ourselves, the Gulf of California is an important component of the desert ecosystem, affecting our climate and influencing the movement of plants, animals, and people across the land. For that reason, University of Arizona oceanographer Richard Brusca has termed the Sonoran Desert a "maritime desert," which well describes the interaction of the elements. The University has led the way in studies of the Gulf and its influences on the Sonoran Desert, with anthropologists, biologists, geologists, climatologists, and other specialists contributing to the vast store of knowledge that the University has helped amass about our region.

One University scientist, Katrina Mangin, teaches marine biology at the undergraduate level and does scientific outreach at local schools. During the semester, she takes her students on field trips to the Gulf of California, while in summer she ranges farther abroad, leading a field school in the Galápagos Islands of Ecuador. She has long conducted specialized research on one small denizen of the Gulf, a "zooid" called the samurai hydroid (*Samuraia tabularasa*), a miniature sea jelly (popularly called jellyfish) attached to a branching base by tentacles. The samurai is a relative newcomer to the Gulf of California, either an invader or a species that had been there all along but whose population exploded. Whatever the case, it became noticeable in the intertidal zone in 1984, and in that short time, it has made itself at home, clearing tidal rocks of barnacles and making room for algae, which in turn sustain populations of small sea snails called limpets. From a limpet's point of view, the arrival of the samurai hydroid has been a good thing, while the barnacles likely have a different opinion. Whatever the case, the samurai provides a highly useful example of environmental change and the consequences it can have on food chains and habitats—a matter increasingly important to know.

CLIMATE WARRIORS

University Scholars Lead the Fight

I**T'S EVIDENT** to anyone without a vested interest in saying otherwise that the climate is changing, rapidly and for the worse, thanks in large measure to the use of fossil fuels that shroud the planet in warming greenhouse gases. It's also evident, from dwindling water supplies, scorched crops, and ever-rising temperatures, that something needs to be done—and fast.

Here at the University of Arizona, some of the most prolific scholars of the sciences and policies surrounding climate change are women whose work might just save the planet one day. At the forefront is Jessica Tierney, an associate professor of geology who was honored with the NSF's $1 million Alan T. Waterman Award, the highest honor apart from the Nobel Prize that is available to scientists early in their careers. Tierney is a lead author on the United Nations' Intergovernmental Panel on Climate Change report *Climate Change 2021: The Physical Science Basis*, and in her own work, she examines biomarkers—fossil molecules, that is—locked inside rocks and layers of sediment. In the bargain, Tierney has created a discipline within the earth sciences that might be called "molecular paleoclimatology," enabling scientists to reconstruct past climates in the hope of gaining clues to the present and future.

Joellen Russell, now head of the world-class Department of Geosciences, grew up in a Native Alaskan village on the shores of the cold North Pacific Ocean, and the ocean has been her calling ever since. Trained as a geologist, but with joint appointments as a distinguished professor of lunar and planetary sciences, hydrology and atmospheric sciences, and mathematics, she studies flows and currents in the oceans (as well as the atmosphere of Titan, a moon of Saturn) to gain an understanding of how they relate to the overall oceanic environment, which in turn, of course, relates closely to Earth's climate. One of her research projects led to the creation of a new paradigm in climate science: warmer climates produce poleward intensified westerly winds, which in turn regulates the transfer of carbon dioxide from the atmosphere into the ocean and back again. In her current seaborne project, Russell says, "one thing we're looking at is the level of oxygen and how it changes with acidification, the addition of nitrates from agricultural runoff, and the like." To do so, she travels into the Southern Ocean surrounding Antarctica, launching and monitoring thousands of robotic floats called the Argo array, which measure water temperature, salinity, and current speed. "It's incredibly hard and dangerous work," Russell says, "but I wouldn't want to do anything else."

Joellen Russell, a scholar at home in deep space and in the depths of Earth's polar oceans. Photograph by Chris Richards, courtesy of Chris Richards and the University of Arizona.

Associated with the Climate Assessment for the Southwest (CLIMAS) project, the recipient of a 2022 grant of $6 million from the National Oceanic and Atmospheric Administration, associate professor of public health Heidi Brown is examining the role of climate in public health. The effects are many: with rising heat, for example, come rising levels of air pollution—to say nothing of the deleterious effects of too much heat to begin with. One important component of the CLIMAS project, which has many branches of research, is that it brings in members of Arizona's twenty-two Indigenous communities, helping them to identify short-term and long-term problems and participate in addressing them.

Diana Liverman, Regents Professor emerita in the School of Geography, Development & Environment, is a pioneering authority on the human dimensions of global climate change, with a particular interest, developed since the 1980s, in questions of climate justice—the unequal distribution, for example, of climate-related drought and famine in poor countries that lack the wherewithal to deal with such matters. Elected to both the National Academy of Sciences and the American Academy of Arts and Sciences in the United States and to the British Academy in the United Kingdom, Liverman is active in developing climate policy and studying adaptations to climate change, especially in the area of food security.

All four of these scholars amply illustrate the observation by Elizabeth "Betsy" Cantwell, then the University's senior vice president for research and innovation, that "the University of Arizona has a moonshot culture. That is, we have permission to think big, take risks, and courageously address the world's most complex problems."

SHAKE, RATTLE, AND ROLL

Vladimir E. Zakharov and the Physics of Turbulence

EVERY SEASONED air traveler has encountered turbulence at some point or another, and everyone has a war story about hitting a pocket of stomach-churning, skittering air that can make a plane behave as if it's slaloming down a roiling waterfall. Turbulence is natural, the inevitable outcome of the medium of the air following the laws of physics—more precisely, those of fluid dynamics. That doesn't make encountering a patch of it any less scary, but it's common—perhaps all too common, given the reportedly growing incidence of turbulence with a heating atmosphere and climate change.

We think of air as being, well, air. But air seems to think of itself as an especially thin form of water, for its flows are just about the same as those of liquid. Consider, as Leonardo da Vinci did, much fascinated, how a slow-moving stream flows, placidly and without surface disturbance, until it encounters a snagged tree or an underwater boulder, whereupon it ripples. An air analog might be the thermals that rise up from mountain ranges as the air warms over the desert, which anyone who's flown into Tucson in summer well knows.

One fluid-dynamics textbook calls turbulence the outcome of "nonlinearities and statistical imponderables." But Vladimir Zakharov (1939–2023), a physicist who was named a University of Arizona Regents Professor of mathematics in 2005, had been pondering the behavior of turbulence for decades. Born in the Soviet Union, he studied engineering, then moved on to nuclear physics, taking a doctorate in the field. In 1992, when the Soviet Union collapsed, Zakharov joined the faculty of the University of Arizona, working at the intersection of mathematics and physics. His work was astonishingly broad, with contributions to plasma theory and soliton theory, the latter concerning solitary waves that retain their shape and speed as they travel; his interest in nonlinear waves has borne expression in influential publications on topics such as the formation of wind-driven waves in the ocean and the mathematics of turbulence, the latter giving rise to formal mathematical modeling that correlates air-to-water density and wave size. The use of weak-turbulent theory, as Zakharov and his colleagues call it, has applications in optics, astronomy and astrophysics, plasma physics, and the study of gravity and superfluid movement, quite a suite of real-world uses for a tool described as belonging to theoretical physics.

As is true of so many members of the faculty, Zakharov was a person of parts, for along with his distinctive accomplishments in science, he was also a published poet in Russian. Still, it is as a scientist that he is best known, elected as a fellow in both the American Mathematical Society and the Optical Society of America (now Optica) in 2012. His work has proven of broad application in astrophysics and space science as well, for which reason he has also been honored by having an asteroid, 7153 Vladzakharov, named for him.

A VISIONARY PRESIDENT

Henry Koffler

B ORN IN Vienna, Austria, in 1922, Heinrich Koffler spoke no English when he arrived in the United States in 1939, shortly after the Third Reich had absorbed his homeland. His widowed mother joined him in New York two months later, and, under the spell of the German author of western novels Karl May, they moved to Prescott, Arizona. There Koffler attended high school and learned the new language in just a few months. In 1940, at the age of eighteen, he enrolled in the University of Arizona, earning a bachelor's degree in agricultural chemistry in only three years. He earned a master's degree in bacteriology in 1944 and a doctorate in microbiology and biochemistry in 1947, both from the University of Wisconsin, and embarked on a distinguished academic career, eventually serving as chancellor of the University of Massachusetts.

It was from that post that the Board of Regents lured Koffler back to his alma mater in 1982, the first graduate of the school to serve as its president. He insisted that the usual expensive inauguration be skipped so that the money could be spent for other purposes. Like his predecessor, chemist John Schaefer, Koffler was concerned with institution building. One of his acts, which involved no small amount of delicate negotiation, was to fold several independent colleges and departments into the College of Arts and Sciences, realizing many efficiencies in the bargain. He also saw to completion the massive Gould-Simpson Building, a new home for the chemistry and biology faculty, an addition to the Steward Observatory, the new University of Arizona Cancer Center, and a thoroughgoing renovation of what would be named Centennial Hall while moving the world-renowned Center for Creative Photography into its present home.

Henry Koffler was well known for being affable and even-tempered, though he had a retiring manner that some observers mistook for aloofness. He returned to the classroom from time to time and was popular with students, and he made undergraduate education and minority-student retention strong priorities while at the same time continuing to build the University into a major research institution. By the time he retired from the presidency in 1991, joining the chemistry faculty, the student body had grown to more than thirty thousand, the faculty and staff had expanded by seven hundred, and twenty-four new buildings graced the campus. What is more, external research funding brought in by grants and gifts grew by more than 300 percent, to $192 million (about $435 million today).

No sooner had he retired than, with his wife Phyllis Koffler, Henry Koffler developed Academy Village, a retirement community for academics, on the far eastern outskirts of Tucson. At its heart is a center for continuing education, Arizona Senior Academy, in which, it seems, everyone is both teacher and student at once. For his part, Henry Koffler revived a long-dormant interest in art, producing and exhibiting numerous abstract expressionist paintings that complemented a large collection that he had built over the years.

Henry Koffler, chemist and onetime University president. Photograph courtesy of the University of Arizona.

In 2000, the University of Arizona renamed the Chemistry-Biology Building the Henry Koffler Building. Henry Koffler died in Tucson in 2018, at the age of ninety-five.

GOING ORGANIC (AND INORGANIC)

The Department of Chemistry and Biochemistry

I N 1944, a delegation of U.S. Army Air Forces officers called on the University of Arizona chemistry department with two problems on their minds. The first was that two bombers had crashed on takeoff during training at nearby Davis-Monthan Air Field, and the officers were concerned that a saboteur might be at work. The second was that American planes sent to the Soviet Union were crashing as well, their landing gears having failed. The University chemists set to work, and they quickly determined that the bombers were using fuel of the wrong octane and the Soviet-bound planes needed a significant boost in antifreeze to keep the hydraulics from seizing up in the brutal winter.

Chemistry is an eminently practical discipline, even if, at its theoretical edges, it verges into the most intractable problems of physics, astronomy, mathematics, and biology. Many of those practical applications came at the hands of University chemist Carl Shipp Marvel (1894–1988), nicknamed Speed for his ability while a college student to study all night, sleep late, and still make it to breakfast before the dining hall closed. He proudly used the nickname in even the most formal correspondence, though he wasn't a terribly formal man, so popular among students that he mentored more than 325 students through to their doctorates and beyond. More, Marvel made important contributions to the development of polymer chemistry over a long career, which lasted from 1920 to 1978. During those years, among other things, Marvel developed synthetic rubber for the military, deprived of natural sources of rubber with the Japanese conquest of Southeast Asia during World War II. In the ensuing space race, Marvel synthesized a compound polymer called polybenzimidazole, which is resistant to temperatures as high as 1,100°F The material was first used in space suits and then became an important lifesaving component in firefighting clothing and in buildings, where it proved to be a safe substitute for asbestos.

So prolific was Speed Marvel that polymer chemists ever since have studied and built upon his work. It's entirely fitting, in that regard, that one of the largest conference rooms in the headquarters of the American Chemical Society in Washington, D.C., is called Marvel Hall. But, not content to stand still, chemists at the University of Arizona have since expanded on Marvel's polymer work to develop an even stronger and more heat-resistant material, polyetherimide (PEI), that has the added benefit of being lightweight, a boon for both firefighters and astronauts. Apart from shielding against heat, the material also protects against the harmful radiation that would be encountered in space and at high altitudes in Earth's atmosphere, and uses have been found for it in manufacturing components for buildings, automobiles and airplanes, and even medical devices.

The study of chemistry lends itself to similarly wide applications. Chemists at the University are involved in developing new energy sources, purifying water and remediating polluted soil, combating climate change, inventing pharmaceuticals and medical devices, and putting technologies for the future in place, among many other topics of research. The current Department of Chemistry and Biochemistry, highly ranked nationally, offers courses of study that include analytical, organic, inorganic, and physical chemistry as well as biochemistry and astrochemistry, along with numerous interdisciplinary graduate programs. One of them is headed by Regents Professor of Chemistry Lucy M. Ziurys, who has discovered new molecules in deep space, working at the intersection of chemistry, astronomy, biology, and physics. In 2019, the American Astronomical Society awarded her the Laboratory Astrophysics Prize, its highest honor.

On the analytical front, Galileo Professor of Chemistry M. Bonner Denton has been hard at work in the laboratory and classroom since arriving as an assistant professor in 1971. He holds a dozen patents on chemical instrumentation, spectroscopic particle detection, and other fields and has published more than two hundred peer-reviewed articles, but he has acquired extracurricular renown as a member of the National Commission on Forensic Science, a collaborative effort of the U.S. Department of Justice and the National Institute of Standards and Technology. In that role, Denton examines forensic methods for their scientific validity, noting with some impatience, "Your beautician has more required federal government regulation than most forensic laboratories do, and they testify in court." Among other things, he has improved the chemical analysis of bullet fragments and of homemade bombs, the latter of which has an important military application, for Denton has been working to develop a sensor capable of detecting a bomb at a thousand times the sensitivity of current sensors, which would enable soldiers to identify the presence of an explosive device long before they came near enough to it to be harmed.

Housed in a newly renovated building with a collaborative learning commons, the Chemistry and Biochemistry Department also emphasizes chemical education. One faculty member, Colleen Kelley, has written a series of comic books by which young readers can learn the fundamentals of chemistry, a project supported by the highly competitive NSF Innovation Corps. Expect to see a stream of inspired STEM students on campus in the coming years, thanks to Kelley's story-driven, entertaining approach to chemical problem-solving.

MYSTERIES OF THE MIND

Cognitive Science

S CHOLARS AT the University of Arizona explore many places that are essentially blanks on the map: the deepest reaches of the universe, the deepest recesses of the world's oceans, the deepest layers of the lithosphere and the critical zone. But perhaps the least completely understood places into which they're looking are far closer to home—namely the deep inner workings of the human mind.

That's where a field in which our school has long been a leader comes in: cognitive science. Like so many other new areas of inquiry, cognitive science involves many traditional disciplines: linguistics, neuroscience, psychology, computer science, philosophy, the list goes on. This is because cognitive science, born in the 1950s, asks questions that necessarily draw on the knowledge of many disciplines. What does it mean to think? How does the mind know? How do we make decisions? What is consciousness, and when did it develop? How do we learn, and how do we remember? How does the mind relate to the world, and does the world represent reality?

These are tough questions to unpack in the first place, much less to explore, and a philosopher might approach them in very different ways than an anthropologist or a computer programmer. So it is with cognitive science, which, unlike, say, physics, ventures numerous competing theories about such matters.

Among the leading University of Arizona cognitive sciences is Lynn Nadel. Trained as a psychologist, he began exploring neural mechanisms in the 1960s. After arriving at the University of Arizona in 1985, when cognitive science was coming into its own on campus, he served as the head of the Department of Psychology, overseeing the beginnings of its being a central component of the new School of Mind, Brain and Behavior within the College of Science. There psychology stands alongside neuroscience, communication, and speech and hearing sciences, with outreach to other units as diverse as the College of Medicine and the Eller College of Management. Among Nadel's many scholarly accomplishments, for which he has received many honors, is the discovery that the hippocampus of the brain is the site of a spatial mapping system that is responsible for accessing memory and is central to the representation of context. Nadel's research has important implications not simply for memory but also for the study of syndromes such as post-traumatic stress disorder, social anxiety disorder, and agoraphobia. Add to all that Nadel's popularity as a professor and mentor, and it's small wonder that he was named a Regents Professor of psychology in 2003.

Another internationally renowned scholar is John G. Hildebrand, also a Regents Professor. A neuroscientist, Hildebrand trained in biology and biochemistry but soon found himself interested in fields such as chemical ecology, which put him in close contact with the chemistry faculty; arthropods as vectors of disease pathogens, which allied him with entomologists and physicians; and olfaction, the mechanisms behind the sense of smell, which is squarely within the realm of neuroscience but has obvious connections to many fields. A truly interdisciplinary scholar, Hildebrand has pursued research that has led to a new understanding of how the nervous system operates in organisms from the tiniest insects to the largest whales.

Other cognitive scientists pursue avenues of research that similarly open onto larger matters of the mind. LouAnn Gerken, for example, studies language acquisition, while Massimo Piattelli-Palmarini studies learning and cognition. Janet Nicol, a linguist, is an expert on how the brain processes sentences, as well as on the formation of syntax. Vicky Tzuyin Lai studies that trickiest of things to untangle, namely the emotions. The list goes on, and each contribution leads to a whole that is greater than the sum of its parts.

Several paths of study are available to students at the undergraduate and graduate levels. An undergraduate major is available in neuroscience and cognitive science, with the former focus involving more science courses related to neurobiology and the latter requiring more grounding in psychology, linguistics, and philosophy as approaches to cognition. Both tracks are challenging—and both, we can be sure, will yield scholars who will unlock still more hidden rooms behind the doors of perception.

WORKING IN THE BUGS

Insect Science

A T HEART, *desert* means "devoid"—absent, that is, of life. In fact, our Sonoran Desert home swarms with life, and quite literally. Apart from its hundreds of bird, mammal, and reptile species, the Sonoran Desert harbors at least thirteen thousand species of insects, with new species being discovered all the time. Amazingly, there are at least a thousand species of native bees alone.

Everywhere you look on campus, you'll find insects. Under leaves and plant debris lurk centipedes and ants. On the desert sand are beetles and walking sticks. Around fountains and pools are dragonflies and butterflies, and in the omnipresent mesquite trees are giant mesquite bugs—which, though they bear a forbidding name, are quite gentle, unless you're a mesquite bean pod. Though we don't like to talk about them, there are cockroaches all around us too, for which we should be grateful rather than grossed out. After all, in defense of Blattodea, cockroaches are an important source of food, especially for birds, and pollinators of many kinds of plants. More important, they are recyclers par excellence without which our planet would look very different, for without them and other "opportunistic feeders," we would drown in corpses, poop, and decaying, stinking plants.

With so much insect life around us, it stands to reason that the University of Arizona should have built an extraordinary corps of scholars devoted to entomology, or the study of insects. Some work in agriculture, others in biology, still others in cognitive science. In the last category, for example, one might find a native of Germany, Wulfila Gronenberg, a University neuroscientist who has conducted extensive research on the brains of hymenopteran species: ants, wasps, and bees. He notes that many hymenopteran species communicate

A staff member gives food and water to an eager audience of cockroaches at the Flandrau Science Center & Planetarium. Photograph by Gregory McNamee

complex information such as the location of pollen-rich flowers and remember the location of burrows where they have laid eggs, both of which indicate that these insects are able to construct mental maps of their environments that can extend for flights of more than a mile. Gronenberg has learned that these behaviors are controlled by higher brain centers called "mushroom bodies." Brain size has often been used as an index of cognitive abilities, but, he says, the number of nerve cells in a brain is a better indicator. By this measure, small bees such as the metallic green *Augochlorella* that can be found on flowers all around Tucson have higher neuronal densities in their heads than we do!

Judith Becerra, an associate research professor, is both a leading authority on giant mesquite bugs and an authority on plant-insect interactions. She first became interested in those mesquite bugs when her daughter and some of her daughter's friends were collecting a swarm and found yellow stains on their hands and arms. Out of curiosity, Becerra took some of the liquid back to her lab to study. The stain was a toxin so potent that it can kill a tarantula, but, as the girls found when they were collecting the bugs, it causes only a temporary skin discoloration in humans. Becerra found that the giant mesquite bug's toxin is chemically very similar to the compounds found in the brains of people with Alzheimer's disease—a discovery with possible implications for future research.

On another front, scientists have long wondered how ants decide to divide up tasks. A deliberate division of labor is, after all, essential to the survival of a colony, as some workers gather food, others provide defense, and still others tend to the queen and her offspring. But who hands out the assignments? Anna Dornhaus, a professor of ecology and evolutionary biology, is interested in how social insects organize themselves, with collective behavior growing from individual actions and, interestingly, collective decisions growing from them as well. Such decisions hinge on efficiency, group size, and the tasks that need to be done—for example, assigning the optimum number of workers to forage for food and sending them out into the field. Such results require learning and a complex system of communication on the parts of the social insects, which includes bees and ants. Dornhaus's work has enabled

scientists to rethink earlier views on animal communication and intelligence, and she has received many honors for her research.

By the year 2050, it's estimated that there will be nine billion people on our planet. That's a major tipping point: there's just not enough food being grown today to feed a population so large, and scientists are scrambling to find solutions ahead of that looming deadline, among them the technological innovations of the TERRA project. Born in Israel, professor of entomology Goggy Davidowitz became interested in insects, as he puts it with a laugh, while skipping school to spend time outdoors. Many years later, as a distinguished scholar and researcher, he became interested in a more specific problem: how to use insects to help feed all those hungry humans. But the question, Davidowitz says, is not which insect to grow, but instead how to harness technologies that produce multiple food sources from multiple waste streams. For instance, one of his lab's recent patents concerns a nearly closed system that combines insects, fish, hydroponic plants, and mushrooms. The insects can be fed on food waste that's been dried by a solar tower he invented, and then the insects can feed the fish, which in turn fertilize the plants and mushrooms. But the chain can be turned around: fish, mushrooms, and plants can feed insects, and plants can feed mushrooms and insects, and so on. "The goal is to find the best insect for whatever kind of waste we have," Davidowitz says, noting that he and his students are working with a dozen species of insects to find the answer to that question.

(Asked which insects taste best, by the way, Davidowitz says that's in the taste buds of the beholder: "One insect that we grow tastes nutty to me, but it tastes bland to one of my students, and it tastes like green vegetables to another student." Come 2050, there'll be plenty of opportunities to find our favorite flavors.)

Nearly thirty professors and hundreds of students are involved in insect research on campus and out in the field, work that is necessarily interdisciplinary in nature. They're well served by one of the foremost research collections of any public university. While taking care of a collection of more than two million insect specimens and overseeing the Insect Diagnostics Clinic, W. Eugene Hall has been conducting research on the featherwings, becoming one of the world's foremost authorities on the smallest free-living nonparasitic insects known to science. He took a roundabout route to achieving that distinction, starting his first formal scientific studies as a high school student with the intention of becoming a herpetologist, planning to study the natural history of Sonoran Desert tree frogs. While still in high school, he worked at the University, studying fossilized pack rat middens, herpetology, and ichthyology. When he enrolled at the University, he did so as a studio art major, but along the way, he took undergraduate entomology classes, and that was all it took to hook him on the wild world of insects. "I was amazed by the sheer diversity of insects," Gene Hall says. "I still am."

TAKING A BITE

Justin Schmidt and the Pain Index

A S CURIOUS avenues of research go, Justin Schmidt's is one of the most remarkable, and it packs quite a punch. In the early 1980s, while working with colleagues on a scholarly paper, he realized that we had no reliably reproducible measurement of how much arthropod bites and stings hurt—nothing comparable to, say, the Scoville scale that scientists use to measure the "bite" of a chile pepper.

Schmidt (1947–2023), a University of Arizona entomologist, set out to create such an instrument. He constructed a simple scale that ran from 0 to 4, with 0 being the sensation of being stung or bitten outside your clothes to 4 being an intensely painful, long-lasting assault on the senses. Right in the middle is the ordinary sting of a bee, painful to be sure, but not painful for long.

To test and refine his scale, Schmidt tried out being stung and bitten by all kinds of crawling and flying critters for the next half dozen years. With the help of his battered nervous system, he learned all kinds of things. For one, he reckoned that a honeybee's sting is akin to your oven mitt's having "a hole in it when you pulled the cookies out of the oven," while a harvester ant digs in like a power drill on an ingrown toenail—nothing anyone would ever really want to experience, in other words.

We have it easy here in Arizona, at least comparatively. Schmidt reported that the worst pain he experienced is the sting of *Pogonomyrmex badius*, the Florida harvester ant, which he likened to having your muscles shredded. Just a bit less painful is the Pepsis wasp, which we do have here in the Sonoran Desert. If you get stung by one, Schmidt counseled, perhaps the best thing to do is lie down and scream. As he put it, memorably, that level 4 pain is "blindingly fierce, shockingly electric. A running hair dryer has just been dropped into your bubble bath." A carpenter ant ranks a touch lower on the scale, but that diligent worker earned the Schmidt pain index a mention in the 2015 movie *Ant-Man*, just at the moment when the hero is bitten by one.

Most pain, Schmidt emphasized, is not permanently damaging, nor is it meant to be. Inflicting it is mostly a warning sign from an animal that you need to behave differently—to get away from a hive, say, or a valued food source. Schmidt himself reached this understanding through excruciating trial and error: it's been estimated that he was stung or bitten by more than six dozen kinds of venomous insects. That's surely a world record, and a selfless gift to science and knowledge.

A CURIOUS GLOW

The Nuclear Reactor

IT WAS 1958. The space age was being born, and the Cold War was steadily heating up to uncomfortable levels. In a couple of dozen select universities across the United States, the federal government was ramping up a program to train nuclear engineers for the work of making weaponry—but, as important, for an ambitious plan to seed the country with nuclear power facilities as part of President Dwight D. Eisenhower's Atoms for Peace initiative.

So it was that, quietly, a small building next door to the Student Union that housed the Electrical Engineering Department came to host a small nuclear reactor, located in a basement laboratory that measured only fifteen by twenty feet and was some fourteen feet below ground level. Sunk beneath twenty feet of recirculating water in a stainless steel tank only a tenth of an inch thick and a little more than four feet high, the nuclear core contained small slugs of uranium that, according to departmental dissertation records, were provided by the Atomic Energy Commission after having been "rejected for not meeting certain rigid specifications."

That might have raised eyebrows, but the nuclear reactor operated safely once it went

The little-known nuclear reactor, once housed near the Student Union Memorial Center. Photograph courtesy of the University of Arizona.

online in December 1958—and, scientists noted, the facility was always "subcritical," meaning that the core was not subject to melting down, while the water system was not connected to the University's, so contamination of the water supply was impossible. Indeed, for many years, training generations of nuclear scientists, the reactor was one of the campus's best-kept secrets. I knew about it only because I had a class—in ancient Greek, of all things—that met in a classroom directly above the contraption. Said a retired professor of nuclear engineering, "Very few realized there was a nuclear reactor there. We liked it that way. We didn't want to attract attention."

The reactor was modified in 1972 and again in 1973, receiving fresh fuel and control upgrades. Even so, as one administrator remarked, the electrical power generated by the reactor was exceedingly small—enough only to operate a hundred or so hotel-room hair dryers. In time, however, the Cold War wound down, and nuclear power was no longer an attractive option. In 1996, the College of Engineering disbanded the nuclear engineering program and abolished its undergraduate and graduate degrees. In 2009, the University decided to close the facility. It took several months to shut the reactor down, not just because of the problem of disposing of the radioactive fuel but also because the laboratory contained both asbestos and lead paint. The fuel rods, technically the property of the U.S. Department of Energy, were removed in December 2010. After being decontaminated, the facility was finally decommissioned and disassembled in April 2012. The space the reactor once occupied is now used for other College of Engineering laboratories.

BASKING IN SUNSHINE

The Solar Energy Research Laboratory

A RIZONA MAY lack a few things—water, notably—but it has one commodity in such abundance that we've eschewed daylight savings time ever since it was introduced. That abundant commodity is sunshine, of course, and the University of Arizona has long been a leader in discovering ways to make efficient use of it as a source of energy.

Although there were forerunners in solar energy research dating back to the 1920s, our story really begins in 1957, when the Institute of Atmospheric Physics requested a building for a new Solar Energy Research Laboratory. Once the request had made its way through channels, the Board of Regents approved it, authorizing $15,000 (about $163,000 today) for a building to be constructed near the site of the present Medical Center. The rub was that while the institute raise the required matching funds, when the building as designed by director Raymond Bliss, with its then-futuristic solar heating and cooling system, was costed out, it came to nearly four times the original allocation. A much-simplified building was put up instead, and its workers did such research as they could under comparatively primitive conditions until the lab was folded into the Environmental Research Laboratory in 1967, then eventually folded entirely.

Solar energy research had its ups and downs for the next couple of decades, even as University energy economist Helmut J. Frank strongly advocated for solar as part of Arizona's future energy mix and a scattering of physicists and engineers worked on developing ever more affordable solar systems. The University did its part by making use of solar resources in new constructions whenever possible—just look at the rooftops as you stroll through campus, and you'll see abundant evidence of this. Look especially at the Applied Research Building, opened in the spring of 2023, which makes use of both solar and wind energy.

Now fast-forward from 1957 half a century, to 2007, when Erin Ratcliff arrived on campus to do postdoctoral research. Guided by Neal R. Armstrong, who was named a Regents Professor of Chemistry in 2013, she became a research scientist in a unit he created, the Center for Interface Science: Solar Electronic Materials. Now an associate professor of chemistry and chemical engineering, Ratcliff adapted Armstrong's interdisciplinary model to what is now one of the nation's leading Energy Frontier Research Centers, a network coordinated by the U.S. Department of Energy. In 2023, her Center for Soft PhotoElectroChemical Systems began working on a project to use semiconductors to harvest sunlight and produce electrical energy that would in turn create materials called solar fuels, such as solar-generated hydrogen.

The new center leverages talents from scholars, researchers, and students from all over campus, as well as other institutions nationally and internationally. Among its most recent initiatives is the development of organic polymers—another area in which the University has long been a leader, thanks to the pioneering chemist Carl Shipp Marvel—to respond quickly to chemical reactions along many possible pathways. These new polymers are both durable and adaptable, and in combination with advances in semiconductor science, they point the way toward fulfilling the national goal of net-zero carbon emissions by the year 2050.

Ratcliff's research is not an outlier. Many other University scientists and technologists are working on such initiatives as AzRISE, a laboratory for developing ever more efficient means of generating electricity from the sun. The College of Optical Sciences has been developing a hybrid solar converter that uses the full extent of the solar spectrum, allowing utilities to harness energy even on days when the sun is not shining. Another project of the college involves the development of "solar glass" to harvest solar radiation and bring it to colonies of algae to accelerate photosynthesis, addressing both energy and food production.

Getting to that renewable energy future of long-ago dreams will require the efforts of the academy, government, and business. Recognizing that, the University has taken the lead in establishing certification programs for solar technicians and engineers, for it is expected that by 2035, at least seven hundred thousand new jobs will be created in the solar industry field. There will be plenty of opportunities, in other words, for Wildcats to make proverbial hay while the sun shines in a future that's just around the corner.

INNOVATION AND INVENTION

The UA Tech Park

IN THE mid-1970s, Ed Roberts, the owner of a little technology company in Albuquerque, New Mexico, that had been badly beaten up by a sudden downturn in the market for the high-end calculators he was making, decided to switch gears. He had a risky idea: he would retool his company to make a personal computer, which he called Altair. For a time, one of his employees was a young man named Bill Gates, who founded a technology company that he eventually called Microsoft.

Meanwhile, in California, a young engineer named Steve Wozniak showed his boss a computer he had cobbled together out of leftover parts. That boss, another engineer named Bill Hewlett, passed on Wozniak's proposal that his company, Hewlett-Packard, manufacture the thing, so Wozniak and his friend Steve Jobs built the Apple I personal computer in a Bay Area garage.

At about the same time, a Yale University graduate named Frederick W. Smith hit on the idea to integrate airmail service with tightly managed high-tech information systems organized around an innovative hub-and-spoke system of routes. Hoping to land a contract as the exclusive carrier for the Federal Reserve Bank, he named his fledgling company Federal Express. Smith never did land that Federal Reserve contract, but FedEx went on to earn untold billions of dollars.

These are success stories of bootstrapping, ones that rely on no little amount of luck as well as pluck. There are many more stories of failure, in part because we have often come up a little short, nationally, in the work of channeling the energies of innovators to successful ends. Government funding of academic science and engineering research and development has long been in decline relative to GDP, while corporate research-and-development investments have also fallen dramatically, leaving it to universities to take up the work of innovation and invention.

Enter the University of Arizona Science and Technology Park, a well-kept secret—secret only because it's located far from the main campus. Founded in 1994 on property acquired from IBM, well before many of the dozens of research parks around the country, the UA Tech Park joins the efforts of corporations, start-ups, laboratories, and science and technology incubators with funding through federal grants, tax incentives, private funds, and other instruments. The successes of the Tech Park immediately demonstrate the effectiveness of consolidating research, industry, education, and investment in a single cluster, a single place, where innovators and inventors can meet over coffee, hash out problems, cook up collaborations, and share ideas. Good things happen, in short, when people meet and work side by side, and the clustering inherent in what is called an innovation zone cannot but yield—well, innovation.

Located on Tucson's far southeast side, with nearly two million square feet of leasable space, and with another sixty-five-acre facility closer to the city center and a laboratory in Oro Valley, the Tech Park has made its mark in many and varied ways. On its main campus, for example, world-leading authorities on solar energy are developing ever more efficient means of harvesting and distributing the power of the sun and providing consumers with the fruits of their research to date, providing 25 megawatts of power by means of 223 acres of solar panels, enough to power the park itself twice over or to provide electricity for some 4,600 homes.

Pharmacologists work there to create non-opioid painkilling medicines, of critical importance in a time of epidemic opioid addiction and abuse. Agricultural scientists are developing an industry around the use of the native plant called guayule as a sustainable source of rubber. A laboratory is producing a "terahertz transistor" that, it is hoped, will speed up computing via superconducting. Tools for laparoscopic surgery, a new test for Down syndrome, advances in 3-D printing, a camera that monitors brain pathways in anesthetized patients, more efficient sunscreen lotions, an underwater tent to provide safety (from sharks, among other possibilities) to oceanographic researchers, an autonomous firefighting aircraft—these and many more things have emerged from the park, with the University of Arizona ranked twenty-eighth in the nation in the number of patents granted for inventions.

The University of Arizona Tech Park contributes nearly $2.5 billion annually to Pima County's economy, as well as nearly $53 million in tax revenues. It is one of the region's largest employment centers, with more than six thousand workers. It houses more than seventy-five technology companies and business organizations, Fortune 500 companies (Microsoft among them), and start-ups alike.

University research parks are economic engines responsible for job creation, research, and innovation, for new and better ways of doing things. It may be a well-kept secret, but the UA Tech Park is moving us into the future in countless ways.

The John P. Schaefer Center for Creative Photography, one of the University's most renowned artistic gems. Photograph by David Olsen.

WORDS, IMAGES, AND MUSIC

Just as the humanities teach us to understand what it means to be human—and, with luck, how to do a better job of that role—the arts teach us how to appreciate the beauty of the world, of creation, and of our aesthetic responses to it. At the forefront of the University of Arizona's arts complex, located in the northwestern quadrant of the old campus, is the internationally renowned John P. Schaefer Center for Creative Photography, its name honoring the visionary president who brought that repository into being. Across the way is an extraordinarily comprehensive art museum, as well as classrooms, studios, and performance spaces devoted to the visual arts, acting and filmmaking, musical performance and composition, playwriting, and other artistic pursuits, while just next door is the constantly busy—and constantly surprising—College of Architecture, Planning and Landscape Architecture, where art and science meet to produce the spaces in which we live, work, play, and study.

REVENGE OF THE NERDS

A Campus Classic

T'S MOVE-IN day, a steamy, muggy, hot exercise toward the end of southern Arizona's monsoon season. At a redbrick dorm, a cluster of young men, pocket protectors stuffed full of pens and mechanical pencils, stands in bewilderment, away from home for the first time and at a bit of a loss. Their collective brainpower could fuel an entire city, the last generation of math whizzes who understand how to use both a computer and a slide rule. And they're sitting ducks for the college football crew, who poach their housing when their own dorm catches fire.

Thus the opening of *Revenge of the Nerds*, a lighthearted and decidedly fun comedy filmed at the University of Arizona in 1983 and released in 1984. Campus watchers will recognize settings across the campus, from an interior shot of Bear Down Gym to several dorms and, late in the film, an extended sequence on the Mall. Old Main figured prominently, as did the dorms on the western end of the campus, and hundreds of students earned a few dollars as extras. (If you don't blink for a second, you'll see me flitting across the screen on a bicycle, at considerable distance from the action, since I didn't know a scene was shooting across the way.) Best of all, the film, studded with rising talents such as Robert Carradine, Michelle Meyrink, Timothy Busfield, and Anthony Edwards—and let's not forget a young and little-known John Goodman—showed the University of Arizona off to best advantage, a beautiful, sun-splashed campus of palm trees, handsome buildings, and endless possibilities for hijinks. Irreverent and just a little raunchy, the film was a lot of fun, and it launched a franchise that, while it didn't alter cinematic history, saw sequels over the following decade.

A few other films have been shot on the University campus. *Glory Road* (2006), following the fortunes of the first interracial women's basketball team in the 1960s, was partly shot at Bear Down Gym. *Bodies, Rest & Motion*, a 1993 romantic comedy, featured a little-known British actor named Tim Roth as well as Tucson's own Jon Proudstar, who has gone on to star in the beloved Native American series *Reservation Dogs*. Even the 1963 pilot for the television series *The Fugitive* occasionally captured a campus building or two, as did the 1974–76 crime drama *Petrocelli*. But no film embraced and celebrated our school as much as *Revenge of the Nerds*, a silly comedy that holds up well to this day.

WILDCAT DAYS

Making the Student Newspaper

IT WAS November 22, 1963, a Friday. Mort Rosenblum was working away in his sophomore newswriting class in the journalism department when Brewster Campbell, a former news editor famed for his gigantic white walrus mustache and habit of dressing, no matter what the weather, in a three-piece suit and tie, burst into the class and announced that President John F. Kennedy had been shot. "We all ran to the Model 15 AP printer in the closet and watched the bulletins tap out at sixty words a minute," Rosenblum recalls. "The *Wildcat* staff raced around the campus for reaction and edited AP stories into a wrap-up. We flooded the campus with a special edition in boxes and delivered to frat/sorority houses within about five hours—hot type flat press rushed out by our regular commercial printshop up the road."

The technology hadn't changed much a dozen-odd years later, when David Fitzsimmons took up a post as the *Arizona Daily Wildcat*'s editorial cartoonist. Says Fitzsimmons, "I loved it so much that I'd go into the newsroom even when I didn't have to produce a cartoon. There was always something going on. I moved my desk so that it would be close to the AP wire so that I could be the first to read the news."

Affectionately known as Fitz, David Fitzsimmons went on to enjoy a long career as the prizewinning editorial cartoonist for the *Arizona Daily Star*, a place where many *Wildcat* alumni cut their teeth as professional journalists. Mort Rosenblum was one of them too. With a long-standing interest in international events, he worked his way into a job with AP—the Associated Press, that is—and in time became one of a handful of special correspondents who were at liberty to hop on a plane and go anywhere in the world to cover a

Edsel

An *Arizona Daily Wildcat* political cartoon by David Fitzsimmons from 1976, reproduced courtesy of the artist.

story. Today, sixty years later, he's still working away, the author of a dozen books and thousands of articles and for many years a visiting professor in the Department of Journalism.

The *Wildcat* has been in continuous publication since 1899, its creation encouraged by President Millard M. Parker. It was originally called *Sage Green and Silver*, after the school's colors at the time, and was published only monthly. It was prosaically renamed the *University of Arizona Monthly Magazine* the following year. In 1908, when it moved to a semimonthly schedule, it was renamed again, to *University Life*. The magazine became a weekly in 1912, and in 1915 it became a newspaper bearing the name the *Arizona Wildcat*. With a staff numbering no more than a dozen, the paper—free and without a fixed office—did what it could to cover every aspect of student life (and more than a little gossip about the faculty and administration).

In the decades that followed, the *Wildcat* moved from place to place—for a time a corner of the Agriculture Building, then in the basement of the football stadium, and finally the Student Union. After World War II, when returning veterans enrolled in the university and asked for coverage beyond campus, the paper expanded its horizons, acquiring that storied AP newswire. On April 21, 1965, with an expanded staff of twenty-one and a robust ad-sales department, the *Arizona Wildcat* added *Daily* to its name, becoming one of just a few dozen student newspapers to publish every weekday.

The editor of that first iteration of the daily student paper was a Tucsonan named Frank Sotomayor, who went on, as a writer for the *Los Angeles Times*, to win a Pulitzer Prize. Another Pulitzer winner alum was Douglas D. Martin, who earned the prize while working as the managing editor of the *Detroit Free Press*. He became a much-liked professor of journalism, advisor to the paper, and author of the first history of the University, *The Lamp in the Desert* (1960). Edith Auslander, a distinguished alumna, was an editor at the *Arizona Daily Star* for many years and served on the Board of Regents, while alumnus Scott Carter took his talents as a film reviewer to Hollywood, where he has worked as the executive producer of *Real Time with Bill Maher* for many years.

Merl Reagle became one of the country's best-known crossword puzzle creators, while Tim Fuller, photo editor during the early 1970s, is an internationally renowned photographer. Fuller's boss, editor Jay Parker, moved on from journalism to become a professor of international relations at the U.S. Military Academy at West Point. Prolific writer Mary Alice Kellogg, who covered local news and politics, went on to work as an editor and contributor at CBS, the *New York Times*, *GQ*, and dozens of other publications, while Sheila McNulty, editor-in-chief in 1988–89, has published thousands of articles in business and economics for papers such as the *Wall Street Journal* and *Financial Times*. She recalls having taken considerable heat for an editorial suggesting that basketball coach Lute Olson's staggeringly high salary be put to uses that better served the student community. It wouldn't be the first time a *Wildcat* staffer would court controversy. Fitz, for instance, recalls some unhappy talk from across Speedway when he satirized some of the vigorous—well, let's just say academic— politics that were going on in the College of Medicine in the mid-1970s.

The *Arizona Daily Wildcat* uses much different technology from the newswires and hot type of yore, publishing online as well as print editions. But, as has been true since 1899, there are plenty of stories out in the world that have to be chased down and told—and capable, talented writers to do that necessary work.

JULIA REBEIL AND THE ART OF THE PIANO

The School of Music

BORN IN 1891, Julia Marie Rebeil came from Tucson aristocracy, her mother born into the Redondo family, *norteño* Mexicans who had prosperous cattle ranches and farms in southwestern Arizona, her father a French immigrant who became a bank president in his new hometown. She showed strong aptitude for music at an early age, and after graduating from high school, where she studied music alongside members of the Ronstadt family, she earned a bachelor's and master's degree in Chicago and did postgraduate work at the Fontainebleau music conservatory near Paris, France, where her performances were lauded.

Rebeil gained early fame as a concert pianist, touring internationally, but she was also an accomplished violinist. While performing, she helped budding musicians studying both instruments. One of her assignments was to perform for and teach American soldiers in France at the end of World War I, after which she returned to Tucson.

Almost immediately on her homecoming, Rebeil was recruited to teach at the University, a then-rare woman faculty member. Her cause was helped by the fact that, at the time, there was a widely held view that musical appreciation should be a part of every well-rounded person's education, with social dancing to live musical accompaniment a core part of the women's physical education curriculum. In all events, Rebeil taught both violin and piano and headed the piano program from 1926 to 1953, having been promoted to full professor in 1930. Among her students were the Tucson-born African American progressive classical composer Ulysses Kay, who went on to teach music at the City University of New York, and

Constance Knox Carroll, another Arizona native and one of the most renowned interpreters of classical piano works of her day.

Thanks to Julia Rebeil, then, students did not have to leave Tucson in order to acquire a musical education, as she, Luisa Espinel, Manuel Montijo, and other Tucsonans had had to do before her. She retired from teaching at the University in 1969 and died at her home on North Sixth Avenue in 1973. A memorial scholarship was established in her name soon afterward, and the School of Music, now called the Fred Fox School of Music, has continued to attract outstanding faculty members and to produce distinguished graduates who have collectively mastered an orchestra's worth of instruments. First among equals, perhaps, was Paula Fan (1952–2023), who became the primary professor of piano after earning her bachelor's degree in music at the University in 1973. Fan, who passed away while on tour in Australia, was a world-renowned performer who recorded twenty albums, performed on five continents, and, to our city's great benefit, was the principal pianist for the Tucson Symphony Orchestra for thirty-one years. Among other distinguished graduates are Marcela Molina, now executive director of the Tucson Girls Chorus and a well-known choral conductor; percussion teacher Arthur Vint, who has revitalized the Tucson jazz scene since returning to his hometown after a decade of playing and recording in New York; and Brian Lopez, a classical guitarist who has gone on to wed flamenco and border music to rock 'n' roll, creating a unique Sonoran Desert fusion.

POP MUSIC TAKES THE STAGE

Talking Heads, Fleetwood Mac, and Other Memorable Acts

D**AVID BYRNE** has put his stamp on rock, the visual arts, literature, the theater, Broad-way, and world music, collaborating with such eccentric greats as Tom Zé, Laurie Anderson, and Brian Eno. You would not have known that any of that was in the cards, though, when he took the stage in the old Student Union Ballroom on September 21, 1979. Nervous to the point of a twitchy kind of panic, dressed like an anticipatory extra from *Revenge of the Nerds*, he looked distinctly out of place when he strode into the middle of the ballroom's wooden floor, ringed by students in plastic stools, and began to strum the ringing opening chords to "Psycho Killer" on a twelve-string acoustic guitar. One by one, his three bandmates in Talking Heads came out and joined in, and soon the floors of the ballroom were shaking as if under attack by a category 5 hurricane instead of a couple of thousand bouncing Wildcats. The floor took a harder hit still a couple of months later, when the hyperactive New York band the Ramones came to campus and converted a huge crowd to the gabba-gabba-hey way of life.

"Nervous" was an understatement when it came to a band that played on September 14, 1982, in the same venue. Opening for the British punk band Gang of Four, the quartet was out of tune, out of time, off key, and visibly miserable. I turned to a friend and confidently predicted that they would go nowhere. They were R.E.M., and they went somewhere.

The Student Union, Crowder Hall, the old University Auditorium and its rebirth as Centennial Hall: all have offered crowd-pleasing if not life-transforming music over the years. Centennial Hall was one of the first places to book the Cuban artists assembled by guitar master Ry Cooder as the Buena Vista Social Club, for instance, and the place where Tucsonans first saw the musical *Rent*. Wilco, noted purveyors of edgy Americana, played a sold-out show on June 18, 2009, that Tucson fans are still talking about. Frank Zappa, the Police, and Tom Petty and the Heartbreakers all trod the pre-renovation Centennial's boards in 1980, sixteen years before Bob Dylan transfixed the room, twenty-one years before John Prine, the Black Crowes, and Los Lobos took the stage on various dates.

McKale Memorial Center got into the music business for a few gigs, hosting the likes of Van Halen before someone decided, speaking of floors, that a basketball court and the pounding of shoes, mic stands, amplifiers, and drums weren't the best mix. The same held for the football stadium, which saw what is believed to be the largest concert crowd ever assembled in Tucson when Fleetwood Mac played it on August 27, 1977. Backed by the

Johnny Ramone of the Ramones, one of the most famous rock bands to perform at the Student Union Ballroom. Photograph © Cliff Green, courtesy of the photographer.

Marshall Tucker Band and Kenny Loggins and at the pinnacle of their fame, Mac drew an audience of some seventy thousand ticket buyers, most of them students—and because the stadium wasn't fully enclosed, a few thousand other listeners wandered in as well without benefit of tickets. (I confess.) The crowd did a thorough job of trashing the stadium grass at the very beginning of the football season, which may explain why the stadium didn't see another concert until April 2009, when Kelly Clarkson, Jay-Z, Third Eye Blind, and the Veronicas thrilled a far smaller but still enthusiastic crowd.

The Ramones, incidentally, were backed by a Tucson band called the Pedestrians, most of its players not yet of college age. Pen Pendleton, drummer for another Tucson punk band, Jonny Sevin, did go to college—the University of Arizona, that is, where he landed the job of booking acts for the Associated Students of the University of Arizona by way of the Student Union Activities Board. Through his good offices, a little corner of the Student Union basement called, appropriately enough, the Cellar began to host performances by local bands, some of which would become internationally famous: Giant Sandworms, now Giant Sand, then featuring a guitarist named

Rainer Ptacek, whom Led Zeppelin singer Robert Plant traveled halfway across the world to record with; the Pills, which became Gentlemen Afterdark, a neo-glam band produced by the famed Arizona shock rocker Alice Cooper; the Serfers, later to become Green on Red, who beat Wilco to the punch in essentially inventing the alt-country genre; and many another act.

Remembers University alum Terry Owen, whose nom de rock is Fish Karma, "I played at Eat to the Beat, which was held in the Cellar. Every Tucson band played there, along with plenty of out-of-state bands. (I opened for Jane's Addiction in the Cellar.) The Cellar also hosted Comedy Corner, a show that ejected many participants into the entertainment world, such as Pete Murrieta, who created the TV series *Greetings from Tucson*."

It's easy to be golden-age nostalgic, but the beat goes on. Through Arizona Arts Live and other organizations, the University still stages plenty of musical events, sponsoring shows such as the annual Hotel Congress extravaganza that often reunites those Eat to the Beat–era bands, the Tucson Meet Yourself food-and-music celebration founded by Big Jim Griffith, and portions of the annual Tucson Jazz Festival, as well as performances by artists who bring mariachi, blues, classical, rock, country, and just about every other flavor of music to Tucson audiences.

WORLDS OF ART

*Willem de Kooning, Rancho Linda Vista,
and the College of Fine Arts*

A S ART thefts go, it was an oddly amateurish effort. The day after Thanksgiving in 1985, a man and a woman entered the University of Arizona Museum of Art (UAMA), nearly empty on that holiday weekend. There was nothing particularly unusual about them, described to the police as a woman in her midfifties with strawberry blonde hair and a man of apparently much younger age with a mustache and, like the woman, thick glasses. While the woman distracted the security guard and museum staffer on duty by producing a campus map and asking for directions, the man raced upstairs to a gallery that housed abstract expressionist Willem de Kooning's 1955 painting *Woman-Ochre*, sliced it out of its frame with a box cutter, rolled it up and tucked it inside his coat, and, with the woman, left the building and drove off in a rust-colored car.

The suspects disappeared into thin air, and while bulletins went out throughout the art world to keep an eye out for someone trying to sell *Woman-Ochre*, the painting vanished too.

Fast-forward to 2017, and an odd resolution presented itself. An antiques shop in Silver City, New Mexico, had acquired, part and parcel, the estate of a woman who lived in the countryside a few miles away. Behind a bedroom door was a painting, hung casually, that the owners of the shop put on display for sale. A customer remarked that it looked like a de Kooning, a highly collectible item. The shop owners took to their search engines and happened on a story in the *Arizona Republic* commemorating the thirtieth anniversary of the heist. They called UAMA director Olivia Miller and emailed photographs of the piece—by then reckoned as being worth as much as $100 million—to her. A day later, Miller and several staffers were on their way to Silver City, where they recovered the painting and returned it to Tucson.

Once it was authenticated, the job of assessing the damage to the painting was next. The painting had been cut, in the first place, and torn from its backing, then restretched and fitted into a new frame. Some of the paint had chipped and flaked, and there were tears here and there. It took restorers at the Getty Museum in Los Angeles three years to repair all the damage, whereupon a party of University police officers and U.S. Department of Homeland Security agents escorted *Woman-Ochre* back to Tucson in a heavily guarded eighteen-wheeler.

The de Kooning painting is now proudly on display in a much more secure museum, alongside paintings by Mark Rothko, Jackson Pollock, Georgia O'Keeffe, and other modern masters. But questions remain that will occupy art historians and crime writers for years to come. Why did the thieves—both retired schoolteachers from New York City—do what they did? Why did they tuck *Woman-Ochre* away for all those years without trying to cash in on their crime? For the time being, we can only guess.

One of nine museums on campus, the UAMA isn't exactly a well-kept secret, though more visitors are always welcome. The same has been true of the arts faculty since the College of Fine Arts was created in 1934: many of its faculty have been renowned in the art world, but few have engaged in what a musician friend of mine calls "tireless self-promotion."

Soft-spoken and studious, Robert Colescott (1925–2009), to name one faculty member, was one of the best-known painters of his generation, working with themes from Black history in often parodic works. His *Wreckage of the Medusa*, for instance, plays with Théodore Géricault's famed painting *The Raft of the Medusa* by inserting Black figures into the action: where in Géricault's original, the single Black figure appears to be dead, in Colescott's work, the three Black figures of the five survivors are very much alive, even if the self-portrait of the artist looks a bit puzzled about the pandemonium following the sinking of the ship on which he's booked passage. Colescott had just joined the University of Arizona art faculty when he became the first Black artist to be featured on the cover of the flagship journal *Artforum*, and he was the first Black artist to represent the United States at the Venice Biennale. To cap it off, in 1990, Robert Colescott was the first member of the art department to be named a Regents Professor, honoring both his original work and his status as a beloved teacher.

The many students who passed through the workshops and classes led by Bruce McGrew (1937–99) held him in similarly high esteem. Said one to art historian Paul Gold, "I found him fascinating—he spoke in parables and riddles, like a poet, and in his speech, there was always something between the lines, and it just tuned me in." Born in Kansas, McGrew was drawn to both the desert and the sea, and after earning an MFA at the University in 1964, he stayed on, painting luminous landscapes, ever so slightly abstract, and exhibiting widely. With several other members of the art faculty, McGrew formed Rancho Linda Vista, a cross between commune and artists' colony in Oracle, which has figured prominently in the creative history of Tucson for nearly half a century. (Biosphere 2 is just a few miles down the road.) One of McGrew's students, incidentally, was the Luiseño sculptor Fritz Scholder (1937–2005), the first Native American to receive an MFA in fine arts and a founding faculty member of the Institute of American Indian Arts in Santa Fe, New Mexico.

Aurore Chabot, who has been on the arts faculty since 1988, is a well-known and highly collected ceramicist who works in clay and mixed media and who has been featured in more than one hundred exhibits around the world. Some of her pieces are small and subtle, while other large ceramic mosaics are sweeping bursts of color and form. Influenced by folk art from around the world, she has crafted everything from large masklike objects to playful pieces such as the brightly tiled and intriguingly titled *If You Cracked a Football Open While Sleeping*. Chabot's work enshrines her lifelong interest in archaeology, anthropology, and history, and she has trained hundreds of students over the years.

Perhaps the most convivial ambassador for the fine arts not just at the University but also in the wider community was Maurice Grossman (1927–2010), a ceramicist and painter who joined the University faculty in 1955. Born in Detroit and raised in poverty, Maurice decided early on that he was going to approach life with a smile on his face. Evenhanded and encouraging, he taught art to generations of students while also serving as an advocate for gay rights, civil rights, and Buddhist meditation. After he died following complications from heart surgery, a memorial was held in the largest plaza in downtown Tucson. Even it wasn't large enough to accommodate the thousands of people who came to pay their respects.

A TREASURE HOUSE OF IMAGES

The Center for Creative Photography

ANSEL ADAMS (1902–84) was both an artist and a technician, a master of the enlarger and the darkroom, one of the greatest and most productive photographers in the history of art. Other photographers, looking at iconic images such as *Monolith, the Face of Half Dome* (1927) and *Moonrise, Hernandez, New Mexico* (1944), immediately recognize that they are in the presence of a master, and generations of gallery- and museumgoers have agreed. On the occasion of an illuminating 2018 exhibit at the University of Arizona's Center for Creative Photography, *Ansel Adams: Performing the Print*, timed to coincide with Adams's 116th birthday, the noted photojournalist David Kennerly said, reverently, "When you have seen a completed print, you have seen God."

It was Ansel Adams who brought the internationally famed Center for Creative Photography (CCP) into being. Or rather, it was John Schaefer, then the president of the University, who engineered what turned out to be a great occasion in the art world, for which reason CCP now bears Schaefer's name. It began when he invited Adams to stage a solo exhibit at the UAMA in 1974. As Schaefer recalls, "I asked him ten minutes into the show if he would like to give his archives to the University of Arizona, which was a reflection of my inexperience and naivete about how long you should be courting someone like this before you ask a question. He was a bit surprised, but after about five minutes he said, 'You know, Berkeley thinks they're getting my archive, but all they're going to do is bury it in the basement of the Bancroft Library, and no one will ever see it. If you'd like to talk about photography in a broader sense, I'd like to spend some time with you.' So he invited me up to his home, I spent three or four days with him, and out of that came the Center for Creative Photography."

Visitors at the John P. Schaefer Center for Creative Photography view a suite of photographs by musician and artist Linda McCartney, a noted University alumna. Photograph by Gregory McNamee.

The acquisition was not without controversy, for it also came with a price tag of $300,000 for the archive (about $1.9 million today). As Schaefer recounts, even though the funds came from sources other than the state, members of the legislature were quick to pounce on what they perceived to be a staggeringly high cost. Clarke Bean, then president of the Arizona Bank, went before the doubters and convinced them that, as Schaefer says, "it was a tremendous coup for Arizona." Considering spending by tourists and visitors, licensing fees, and other revenue it has generated, the archive also turned out to be a phenomenal bargain.

With Ansel Adams in Arizona's camp, other photographers followed: Aaron Siskind, Harry Callahan, Imogen Cunningham, Lola Álvarez Bravo, Wynn Bullock, Edward Weston, Garry Winogrand, Richard Avedon, W. Eugene Smith, the list goes on and on. Schaefer appointed Harold Jones, a photographer and professor of art, to head the photographic archive. Beginning in 1975, the archive was first housed in an old bank west of the Main Gate and then, in time, moved to the extraordinary fifty-five-thousand-square-foot building it now occupies, which was opened in 1989 and is part of the University's Fine Arts Complex in the northwest quadrant of campus.

"What does it mean to make a picture that speaks to someone?" asks curator Rebecca Senf. It's a question that lies at the core of the center's mission. The CCP may have begun,

in effect, as a repository for the work of Adams, but it has since grown to become one of the world's premier photographic archives, housing more than five million objects and representing more than two thousand photographers. Adds Senf, "One of the things that a curator thinks about is what their institution can do that no other can." The answer is that no other photographic institution connected to a university is both an archive and a museum, a place open to scholars for research, to artists for the preservation of their works, and to the public to appreciate the play of light—and the capturing of lightning in a bottle—that makes that picture of which Rebecca Senf speaks. In myriad ways, many unique, the Center for Creative Photography offers a profound education for anyone interested in the photographer's art.

BUILDING THE WORLD

The School of Architecture

YOU COULD hear her coming down the hall from a long way off, alternately muttering and hacking a bone-dry smoker's cough, back in the days when people smoked—and, worse, smoked in offices, public spaces, even classrooms. She could be brittle and intimidating, especially in charette sessions devoted to critiquing student designs. "I was terrified," says Mitchell Freedman, who graduated with a bachelor's degree in architecture in 1980. "Judith Chafee could take months of work apart in a couple of minutes. But even when she did, I learned a lot from her."

Chafee (1932–98) was an architect with a long résumé of practice that included a partnership with the famed Walter Gropius. Born in Chicago, she had come to live in Tucson as a young child and moved back and forth between the two cities to attend school. There's no better city for architecture than Chicago, of course, and she took some strong ideas about how buildings should be built from that city's example. But she was also in love with the desert, and when she moved permanently to Tucson in 1970, she built numerous houses that are among the Old Pueblo's most memorable structures.

It wasn't quite the Marine Corps, but what is now called the College of Architecture, Planning and Landscape Architecture (CAPLA) offered perhaps the toughest curriculum of any on campus, with students regularly pulling all-nighters to fulfill their demanding coursework and piles of assignments. In return, those students got some of the best architectural education in the country, with a faculty strong on working architects with ample experience, including, today, Teresa Rosano, Robert Vint, and Courtney Crosson, all of whom have won awards for their designs and their teaching as well.

The same was true of retired professor John Messina, who used historic buildings in Tucson as a teaching laboratory and helped develop the University of Arizona's master design plan, which assures a subtle unity between what's been called the Red Campus and the modernist—and even postmodernist—buildings that have gone up in recent decades, such as the Applied Research Building and a trio of nearby dormitories. And on campus and off, University Distinguished Professor of Architecture Mary Hardin has worked with students for many years to build low-cost, energy-efficient housing, combining teaching and practical work and in the process winning numerous awards, including seven to date from the prestigious American Institute of Architects.

The earliest architect to teach at the University was MIT-trained Annie Graham Rockfellow (1866–1954), one of the handful of women licensed to practice in the entire country in her day. Rockfellow taught for only two years, from 1895 to 1897, and then only drafting (as well as English, geography, and history), before being lured away by Henry O. Jaastad's thriving architectural firm as its chief designer. There she designed Tucson's El Conquistador Hotel and Safford School, two of the city's most prominent buildings. She went on to design many homes and churches, though among her best-known surviving structures are the old buildings that once comprised the Desert Sanatorium, a clinic that has since been enveloped by the campus of the Tucson Medical Center.

CAPLA's students number several famed architects. Rick Joy, in practice in Tucson since 1993, is a strong advocate of building using locally available materials such as adobe bricks and rammed earth. Joy has earned many awards for his work, including the American Academy of Arts and Letters Award in Architecture (2002) and the National Design Award from the Cooper Hewitt, Smithsonian Design Museum (2004), and he frequently lectures at universities and museums around the world, including right here at home. Teresa Rosano, a graduate and now faculty member, and her partner, Luis Ibarra, have won national awards and coverage for their "desert modernist" design work. And Mitchell Freedman, having learned so much from Judith Chafee and other architects, operated one of the most successful large-building architectural firms on the East Coast, working from offices near Washington, D.C., often on projects commissioned by the federal government. In gratitude for the education he received, Mitch funds a scholarship that sends three CAPLA students to architecturally interesting places of their choice anywhere in North America.

The building in which CAPLA is housed went up in 1965. Part of the Red Campus in the Fine Arts Complex, it looks nondescript from a distance. Get closer, though, and you'll see that there are dozens of experiments going on inside and out, with innovations in such things as solar energy–powered electricity and building materials from recycled plastics that might otherwise end up in the ocean. A laboratory for a better future, something is always going on there—and that something is always fascinating.

TREADING THE BOARDS

Playwright Elaine Romero

WHEN SHE was very young, Elaine Romero discovered that she had a talent for telling stories. In college, Romero continued to tell stories, mostly writing poems while studying literature. "The head of the theater department there came up to me and said, 'I notice that you attend all the plays we put on—twice,'" she recalls. "It was true. I was going to all the performances I could, experiencing the plays in three dimensions after reading them on the page—learning that language lives in a room, and not just on a page."

Soon Romero was working on plays of her own, without formal background but with a sense of the possibilities of telling her stories in many voices, with a lyricism and rhythmic energy that came from those years of reading and writing poetry. She has indeed been busy ever since, writing dozens of plays, some short, concentrated moments of monologue that last only a few minutes, some full length. Ambitiously, she wrote a five-play series about war, beginning with *Graveyard of Empires*, which was staged in Chicago in 2012. It depicts a software engineer who has designed a drone that, years later, kills his son in a friendly-fire incident. The bloodspilling comes as a result of a tiny error of programming, the kind that makes our cell phones hiccup and refrigerators click. "He's brilliant, but still he makes an error." That's the very definition of tragedy as the ancient Greeks would have understood it, and altogether modern as well.

Armed with a master's degree in playwriting, Romero came to Tucson in the early 1990s and began to teach playwriting as an adjunct at the University. After a time, however, she decided to leave teaching, saying, "I was always interested in teaching, but I still had plenty to learn myself."

And so she devoted herself to writing full time, building an extensive body of work that has been staged in venues around the world. Many of her plays, such as *Barrio Hollywood*, commissioned by the San Diego Repertory Theatre in 1999, and *The Fat-Free Chicana and the Snow Cap Queen*, are set in the U.S.-Mexico borderlands with themes that touch on issues of Latina/o culture. In the former, a young Mexican American boxer braves the ring in order to lift his family from poverty, a dream that is soon complicated. Staged by Borderlands Theater in Tucson, that family-based drama was inspired by a sign Romero saw on Tucson's west side advertising a long-gone boxing gym. In the latter, similarly inspired by real life, generations clash over how to prepare traditional food with an eye to current concerns for health, whence the evocation of *manteca* (lard) in the title. Is there a way to balance that tradition—and that lard—with jogging, eating disorders, and other emanations of modern life? Romero's comic play digs deep into questions of identity.

Romero rejoined the faculty of the University in 2014, teaching writing in the School of Theatre, Film & Television. Awarded tenure in 2018, she is now an associate professor—and a magnet for playwriting students from all over. The department is growing, and with it the theater community in Tucson. "We're seeing much bigger national recognition for the work we do here," she says, "and Tucson is its own place, with its own sound, just like Chicago has its own sound. We're tuning the keys, and what we're hearing is the voice of the community."

BROADCASTING ARIZONA

KUAT and The Desert Speaks

T ELEVISION CAME to Arizona, as it did to most places in the country, in the early
1950s. By the time the decade was drawing to a close, it had become clear that the
medium wasn't going to disappear anytime soon and that there were jobs to be had
in the new field in front of and behind the camera. The University of Arizona responded
in two ways: creating a radio-television major within the College of Liberal Arts but first
establishing a station of its own, bearing the transparent name KUAT, or UA TV.

The oldest public television station in Arizona, KUAT went online on March 8, 1959, fully
seven years after it was given federal clearance to air on channel 6. The station's studios were
first located in Herring Hall, the old gym/auditorium near Old Main, with programming
restricted to a couple of hours each weeknight, and with that programming mainly taking
the form of rather static lectures by University faculty members on subjects such as chemistry, Spanish, and Native American cultures of the Southwest. Programming expanded to
include a few national offerings when KUAT joined the National Educational Television
network, which would be succeeded by the Public Broadcasting Service in 1970.

In the mid-1960s, the University proposed to move its transmission tower from behind
Herring Hall to Tumamoc Hill, above the Desert Laboratory. Instead, because the tower
would have stood in the Tucson International Airport flight path, it was relocated to Mount
Bigelow, in the Santa Catalina Mountains, where Tucson's other television stations had tow-
ers. When the new Modern Languages Building was completed in 1967, KUAT moved to
basement offices there, and the following year the University began to operate a radio station

as well, at first dubbed KFIF-AM and then KUAT-AM, with an FM channel devoted to news and classical music, inaugurated in 1975.

On the television side, KUAT aired a few locally produced programs. One, called *The Living Desert*, featured staff members of the Arizona-Sonora Desert Museum exhibiting animals from the collection in a studio setting. A forerunner of the popular local show *Arizona Illustrated* did a segment on University researcher David Yetman, trained as a philosopher but fluent in the natural and human history of the Sonoran Desert, who was doing field research among the Seri and Mayo peoples of Mexico. When it proved that Yetman was a natural on camera, he became a regular guest. In 2000, he went to work for KUAT as host of a program called *The Desert Speaks*, which, taking the place of *The Living Desert*, highlighted the plants, animals, places, and peoples of our region. All along, Yetman, a former member of the Pima County Board of Supervisors who had worked to preserve numerous natural venues as parks and protected areas, was writing books, traveling, and building on his already encyclopedic knowledge of our corner of the world.

The Desert Speaks wrapped in 2009, in part a victim of the Great Recession. With producer/director Daniel Duncan, Yetman, long on the Southwest Center faculty, crafted a show with a still larger vision. *In the Americas* debuted in 2011 and found him traveling to every corner of the two continents. The show is notable for being largely unscripted, or, as Yetman says, "in the field and impromptu." The eleventh season of the nationally aired show found Yetman and Duncan headed for the southernmost reaches of South America, far from the relatively mild climes of the Sonoran Desert, building on and adding to a lifetime of experience as a scholar and broadcaster. "It's a tough job," says Yetman with a smile, "but someone's got to do it."

A HOBBY FOR EVERY HOBBYIST

Faculty Pastimes

O NE OF the great joys of belonging as a student to an intellectual community of learners, teachers, and doers is that you can always find someone who can share and extend your interests in, say, microbiology or archaeology, Sanskrit or AI. The same is true of interests that aren't strictly academic, for there are student groups everywhere devoted to all sorts of extracurricular pursuits, from politics to spelunking, flying experimental aircraft, hiking in the Santa Catalina Mountains, and playing Dungeons & Dragons.

Faculty and staff members have fewer such groups, at least formally organized, available to them on campus, but they've still found ways to have fun in their off hours. Many do so through music. Kevin Gosner, professor of history, for example, enjoys playing old-fashioned mountain music on the dulcimer, and when summer rolls around, he attends a gathering of like-minded musicians in Appalachia. Beverly Seckinger, a professor of film, plays bass in numerous local bands, and philosophy professor Laura Howard likes nothing better than to wail away on an electric guitar. Elizabeth Shaw, founding editor of UA Press in 1959, organized and ran an opera company in her spare time, and Michael Kotutwa Johnson, who teaches traditional Hopi methods of dryland farming, sings opera at a professional level. Thomas Fleming, a professor of astronomy and popular presenter at the Flandrau Science Center, sings in the Arizona Repertory Singers choral group, while dean of libraries Shan Sutton is a renowned scholar of the famed rock band the Grateful Dead—and, when he's not writing about the group, he's attending concerts by its various surviving offshoots all over the country.

Film studies professor Beverly Seckinger plays bass and guitar for the Wayback Machine and other groups in her off hours. Photograph © Bill Moeller, courtesy of the photographer.

Steve Reff, as popular an economics lecturer as Gerry Swanson, was a monster in the hockey rink in his day, coaching the University's team for decades in his free time. The late Doug Canfield, seemingly a mild-mannered professor of English, was a devoted martial artist with numerous degrees of black belt prowess behind him. Regents Professor of English Edgar A. Dryden is a whiz on the basketball court and, when I was a student, took great joy in pulverizing anyone who dared challenge him, with mean three-point shots and expert lay-ups. Tom Sheridan, author of the canonical book *Arizona: A History* and a distinguished ethnohistorian, is a master of show-jumping horses. Allan Hamilton, a neurosurgeon and robotics expert in the College of Medicine, raises Lippizan horses at his ranch on the outskirts of Tucson. Pia F. Cuneo, professor of art history, loves riding horses so much that she has become a world authority on the iconography of horses in medieval and Renaissance art, writing, "Although to some the topic of early modern horsemanship may seem like nothing more than an eccentric professor's 'pet' project, it actually provides the cultural historian with a gold mine of information."

It may seem eccentric indeed, but classics professor and renowned archaeologist David Soren is also an authority on early horror movies, the product of a youth spent in movie theaters hiding from the likes of Frankenstein's monster and the Wolf Man. He's published several books on horror in the movies. His fellow classicist Richard C. Jensen prowled antique shops across the land, becoming a noted dealer in early American furniture with a vast trove of knowledge on the subject.

Bonner Denton, a professor of chemistry, was the first person on earth to take a race car beyond three hundred miles per hour—a car that he, beg pardon, Frankensteined from a 1959 vintage British sedan. "What you want to do is build a car that will not fly," he explained when he accomplished the feat in 2008. "We hope not to fly, but quite frankly, I never intended this car to go much over 300 mph." Charles M. Falco, a professor of optical sciences, collects motorcycles—and art about motorcycles, so much so that he curated an exhibit on the subject at the famed Guggenheim Museum. And Michael B. Schiffer, a professor of anthropology and a founder of what is called processual archaeology, is a world authority on electric cars, whose history, surprisingly, goes back more than a hundred years. That's not his only hobby: he collects stamps, pocket radios with vacuum tubes, and handheld calculators.

When he's not teaching mathematics, Alexander Badyaev is searching out rare wildlife and photographing animals in their natural habitat, winning international awards for his work. When she's not uncovering the secrets of hydrogen, astronomy professor Erika Hamden is cooking up a storm, putting her diploma from Paris's famed Le Cordon Bleu culinary school to work.

That's just a tiny sampling, but what's clear is that the excellence these teachers exhibit in play as well as work speaks to our thriving, diverse intellectual community, one that welcomes experimentation and self-development. And whatever the interest, there's someone here who stands ready to help. There's that old saying about all work and no play . . . so play on!

Arizona Stadium, soon to be packed with Wildcat football fans. "A" Mountain can be seen in the distance. Photograph by David Olsen.

TAKING THE FIELD

The growth of athletics at the University of Arizona parallels that of scholarship, research, and academics: from small and humble beginnings has come a longtime tradition of excellence. This holds for a broad range of sports, from swimming and diving to softball, football, men's and women's basketball, and many other athletic pursuits. Legendary coaches such as Ina Giddings, Fred Snowden, and Lute Olson have left enduring marks on Wildcat sports, but our school's successes on the playing field have been a definitive team effort—a team made up not just of generations of players but also of spirit squad members, marching band musicians, mascots, tutors, administrators, front-office interns, thousands on thousands of devoted fans from both town and gown, and—well, the list goes on, as it is sure to do far into the future. Bear Down, Cats!

BEARING DOWN

Pop McKale and Wildcat Football

H**E WAS** only twenty-four when he arrived in Tucson in 1911, but students at Tucson High School soon took to calling James Fred McKale "Pop" (1887–1967). Hired to teach history, Pop McKale also coached the school's sports teams so effectively that they regularly beat University of Arizona squads just across the way, playing them as a necessity given that there was no other school within five hundred miles that could field collegiate-level teams. The solution to ending these embarrassing defeats, although President Arthur Wilde opposed the stratagem and had to be overruled by the Board of Regents, was to bring McKale to the University, and so McKale was hired to be the school's athletic director in 1914 at a salary of $1,700 (about $50,600 today).

Pop McKale immediately set about toughening up the student players, deepening the benches, sorting the players into squads, and assigning them numbers. Football had long been established on campus, with the University fielding its first true team in 1897. (Intramural play had begun in 1889.) On Thanksgiving Day that year, the team faced off against Tempe Normal School, which would become Arizona State Teacher's College, Arizona State College, and then, in 1958, Arizona State University. The Tucson team lost 11–2. It wouldn't be for another forty years, in 1937, that the two schools' rivalry was set in stone over, it's said, a recruiting violation that found Arizona State poaching three would-be players who had already committed to the Wildcats. Spirited competition aside, collegiality ruled: when a team from the Phoenix Indian School arrived short a player in 1908, one Arizona football player joined the opposing team to even the roster for the duration of the game.

Said McKale to his 1914 squad, "We are on the eve of a winning football season, so boost, but don't boast. Remember, there are no quitters in the University." The team responded well, playing hard against numerous better-funded California schools and, again on Thanksgiving, beating Pomona College 7–6 before a hometown crowd of 1,500 spectators, the largest audience to date. So energetically did they play, in fact, that a *Los Angeles Times* reporter admiringly wrote that "the Arizona men showed the fight of wildcats," a name the team instantly adopted. Some of that toughness, one might hazard to say, came from the fact that the team played on bare desert dirt until 1917, when someone thought to plant grass on the athletic field.

The Cats would fight just as hard in succeeding seasons, with dropkicker Harold McClellan leading the nation in scoring in 1921, even as McKale lobbied to build a stadium and gymnasium to take the place of the athletic field that stood to the south of Old Main on the site of the present Forbes Building. He got the gymnasium first, its name taken from the last words of a football player, John "Button" Salmon, who, dying after an automobile accident, urged McKale to tell his teammates to "bear down." Bear Down Gym opened a few months later, on January 21, 1927, when an audience of about three thousand students, townspeople, and visitors watched the men's basketball team defeat Arizona State 29–18.

James Fred "Pop" McKale, the University's athletic director and head coach, in about 1920

A stadium for the football squad followed in 1929, located where the present stadium now stands, though with only one set of bleachers. Funds for the construction came from a campaign mounted by a former football player who served as a consultant to copper mining companies, which readily paid three-quarters of the $100,000 construction cost (about $1.7 million today), the remainder coming from donations by faculty, students, and alumni. A second funding campaign in 1937 extended facing sets of concrete bleachers at a cost of $80,000 (about $1.4 million today), paid for by the Associated Students. In 1946, the south end of the stadium was enclosed, this time paid for by ticket sales from the football games themselves, with dormitories built under the seats on the south and west sides.

In what is rapidly approaching the century that has followed its first version, the football stadium has been made and remade many times, and, like the neighboring McKale Memorial Center, Arizona Stadium is now a state-of-the-art facility. Meanwhile, it has seen some extraordinary coaches and players over the years. One was halfback Art Luppino, dubbed the Cactus Comet, who in 1954 and 1955 earned the nation's highest scores in rushing. In Luppino's first year on the team, the Cats took the occasion of the first television broadcast of a home game by beating Arizona State College by a humiliating 35–0. Linebacker Ricky Hunley, the University's first College Football Hall of Fame inductee, and placekicker Max Zendejas were two of the seven All-American players during the tenure of Larry Smith (1980–86), with twenty of his players winning starting positions on NFL teams. Coach Dick Tomey (1987–2000) chalked up ninety-five wins during his years, the most of any Wildcats coach, and took the team to seven bowl games. And Wildcat players such as Glenn Parker, John Fina, Rob Gronkowski, Tedy Bruschi, Nick Foles, Brad William Henke, Lance Briggs, and Chris McAlister are legendary names among NFL fans.

Asked what he considered the three very best Wildcats football seasons, longtime *Arizona Daily Star* sports reporter and columnist Greg Hansen lost no time in naming first 1986, when, on November 22, the Wildcats trounced a Rose Bowl–bound ASU 34–17. To add insult to injury, Hansen told me, "Chuck Cecil clinched the game with a 106-yard interception return, perhaps the greatest play in UA football history." (Cecil, who played and coached pro ball, returned to Tucson to join the University's coaching staff in 2017.)

Hansen's second choice is 2014, when the Cats beat ASU once more. The Cats, he noted, hadn't won a championship since the 1930s, but on November 28 they took down ASU, which was ranked number 13 nationally, by a score of 42 to 35. The victory clinched the Pac-12 South championship for the Cats, as well as the number 8 slot nationally.

Third, and greatest of all, was 1998, when, after beating the University of Nebraska 23–20 on December 20 at the Holiday Bowl in San Diego, the Cats closed their season with an all-time high record of 12–1 and the number 4 slot nationally, also a school record. Dick Tomey's "desert swarm" defense and All-American cornerback Chris McAlister, by Hansen's reckoning, were the magic ingredients. But there was more, as Hansen wrote in the *Star*: "The 1998 Wildcats were no fluke. They had perhaps the top offensive line in school history: Edwin Mulitalo, Steven Grace, Bruce Wiggins, Yusuf Scott and Manu Save didn't miss a start. They created a space for Pac-12 rushing leader Trung Canidate, who set a modern school record with 1,220 rushing yards." Sadly, he reminded me, the Cats didn't make it to the Rose Bowl that year, thanks to that single loss. But, he concluded, "they were clearly the best team in school history."

Bear Down!

THE BIRTH OF A MASCOT

Wilbur and Wilma Wildcat

THERE WAS a time when the University of Arizona football team was accompanied by an actual living, breathing wildcat—more accurately a bobcat, *Lynx rufus*, but Wildcats the team has been named from very early on, and so a wildcat it was and is. In 1915, the first such live cat, then called Rufus Arizona in honor of President Rufus von KleinSmid, appeared on the gridiron after having been purchased from an army blacksmith for a little less than $10 (about $300 today). Live bobcats appeared with the football squad until 1959. That year, two undergraduate students, Richard Heller and John Paquette, created a costume with the help of a $100 grant (about $1,025 today) from the Associated Students, and the human Wilbur, portrayed by another undergraduate named Ed Stuckenhoff, debuted at a game against Texas Tech University on November 7, 1959. The original costume, it has to be said, was a bit on the cartoonish side, but Wilbur was an instant hit, the person inside—his identity a closely guarded secret—a master of mugging, cheerleading, and taunting the opposing team.

Wilbur underwent a makeover in 1976, his round-eyed, smiling, cloth visage replaced by a plastic head bearing a fierce look and topped off with a cowboy hat. For a few years, Wilbur packed a six-shooter as part of his "rhinestone cowboy" look, but the weapon was retired with the rise of real-life gun violence. In 1977, for the first time, a woman won the role of Wilbur, and in 1986, a second mascot named Wilma Wildcat bowed in and, in an odd moment of anthropomorphic traditionalism, married Wilbur in a ceremony on November 21 of that year before a football game against ASU. Wilbur—formally, Wilbur T. Wildcat, the "T" standing for "the"—and Wilma T. Wildcat now appear at athletic events other than football, and as part of the University's Spirit Program, they often attend alumni gatherings, the Rodeo Day parade, children's festivals, and similar venues. Two male and two female students portray Wilbur and Wilma, respectively, and receive a small stipend for their work.

SEEKING A LEVEL PLAYING FIELD

Ina Gittings

NA ESTELLE Gittings—pronounce her first name *Ee-na*—was born in 1885 and grew up in a hamlet on the Nebraska frontier, where there weren't enough children to field a team of any sort unless it was made up of both boys and girls. She thus played baseball, football, and basketball, swimming in local creeks in summertime and sledding and snowshoeing in winter. Gittings had a keen sense of equity, and when she took her first teaching job on a university campus, she was quick to complain that only a handful of the school's dozens of bathrooms were available for women to use. After unsuccessfully lobbying for the creation of a woman's building with those bathrooms, as well as athletic facilities and other amenities, she left, entering the army as a medical therapist during World War I and later helping resettle Armenian victims of the Turkish genocide.

In 1920, Gittings received an offer from University of Arizona president Rufus von Klein-Smid to head the women's physical education program—then called "physical culture"—for a salary of $2,000 a year (about $31,400 today), less room and board at $60 a month. She accepted the position, arriving at a campus where the stated goal of women's athletic training was to develop good posture, poise, and grace, with courses that gave pride of place to calisthenics and "pageantry," as well as gymnastics and folk dancing. Underlying that goal was the eugenic supposition that healthy women would give birth to healthy babies, quite apart from using physical education to train them to become "ladies." In any event, the inequalities abounded so that, for instance, the University pool was available to women only with the proviso that they wear floor-to-ceiling robes to shield their bodies from view outside the water. President von KleinSmid later abandoned this rule with the sensible observation that the women's swimming suits of the time already extended to below the knee.

When Ina Gittings arrived in Tucson, she immediately set about reforming women's physical education, adding tennis and basketball to the mix of sports available to women students. She just as quickly ran afoul of athletic director Pop McKale, who, on learning that an intramural women's game was scheduled for Old Herring Gym, ordered a football player to flood the floor with a fire hose the night before. Gittings returned the favor, demanding greater funding and better facilities for women's athletics from both McKale and University president Homer Shanz, sometimes sending delegations of women students to deliver arguments for fairer treatment, sometimes bursting into offices to deliver a list of requirements.

Ina Estelle Gittings, head of women's athletics, in about 1925. University of Arizona Photograph Collection, courtesy of Special Collections, The University of Arizona Libraries.

It took fully twenty years for those requirements to take shape on campus, but the physical plant began to change. In 1920, when Gittings came to the University, there were 158 women students on campus, while by 1940 there were more than 1,000. Formerly confined to a single room in Old Main, the women's athletic program gained ever more ground, with Gittings sometimes appropriating the men's practice fields and again clashing with McKale. In the end, a women's field was built on the site of the University vegetable garden after women students protested with signs that read, "Better Co-eds or Better Onions?" Soon women were playing field hockey, basketball, badminton, and volleyball, practicing archery, and holding track events.

Gittings was somewhat slower to toss out the initial goals of physical culture, with a 1932 newspaper article noting that "the secret of the co-eds' great physical advantage is the instruction they are receiving from Miss Ina Gittings on how to be lovely, how to be beautiful, and how to be charming." Still, Gittings insisted that these things derived from "health, strength, and grace" and argued that her students could carry what they had learned throughout life: "To learn some form of recreation and develop a lasting interest in such sports as tennis, swimming, horseback riding, golf or baseball adds a wholesome touch to one's entire life and a sense of youth that can never be lost." The horseback riding component was an important part of Gittings's program, and she developed an equitation regime that trained women to ride according to the exacting, demanding standards of the U.S. Cavalry.

In time, Gittings expanded the women's athletic roster to include more than twenty separate activities. In 1936, too, Gittings scored a coup by winning that long-desired women's building, one that occupied the site where the Gallagher Theater later stood next to the Administration Building. The Gallagher went into service in the remodeled space in 1970, after another building was built for women's sports on the easternmost end of the Mall, completed in 1964 and named Physical Education for Women. Although Gittings died in 1966 at the age of eighty-one, it was not until 1985, thirty years after her retirement, that the building—with numerous restrooms, as she had demanded so many years earlier—was named in her honor. She was also an early entry in the always evolving Women's Plaza of Honor alongside Centennial Hall.

The inequalities were slower to go away. In 1970, women's athletics programs nationwide received only 2 percent of college athletic funding. It took years, decades, for the numbers to begin to even out, and even now the discrepancy is great. It took years, too, for Gittings to convince University officials that women athletes deserved to wear letter jackets, as male athletes did; the University relented by allowing letter sweaters, but with the letter "A" circled to distinguish it from the men's badge. And in 1951, after thirty-one years of heading the women's physical education department, Gittings's salary was $5,688 (about $66,400 today), in terms of buying power only a little more than half again her initial salary of 1920, and a little more than half of what Pop McKale was being paid. Even so, Gittings was a careful investor. With deep connections to Tucson's business and civic organizations, she may have had the last laugh: she became rich after buying and selling 480 acres of land in the western foothills of the Santa Catalina Mountains, running alongside the thoroughfare that bears her name—albeit now locally pronounced *Eye-na*.

A LONG HISTORY OF COURT APPEARANCES

Men's Basketball

NVENTED IN 1891 by a Canadian immigrant to the United States named James Naismith, the game of basketball proved so immediately popular that by October 1896, the *Arizona Daily Star* reported at the time, it "has been introduced to the campus and the boys are playing often." It took another eight years for the game to evolve from an intramural activity to a formally established team sport, the players assembling on the court outside the newly built gymnasium at Herring Hall.

Given the difficulties of travel in those early years, the basketball team generally played squads close to home, including local high schools as well as the colleges that would become Arizona State University and Northern Arizona University, first going up against the former in 1913. When Bear Down Gym opened in 1927, indoor play became the norm, but the competition still tended to come from nearby schools, with occasional jousts with California and New Mexico squads. It wasn't until after World War II that the team began to emerge as a regional powerhouse, winning the Border Conference title in 1946 and, in 1951, gaining national ranking under coach Fred Enke (1897–1985) as the eleventh-best team in the country. Enke, a former Wildcat football player, was the longest-serving head coach in the school's history, his tenure extending for thirty-six years, from 1925 to 1961. Between 1945 and 1951, the Cats won eighty-one consecutive home games, an astonishing record that would not be approached again until 1987–92, with a run of seventy-one consecutive home games.

Things were up and down in the years after Enke. In 1971, for example, the Wildcats record was 6–20, dismal enough that the coaching staff was let go. A young former player named Fred Snowden (1936–94), the first Black head coach at a major university in the United States, stepped in in 1972, and in his first year the count rose to 16–10. In 1976, the Cats won the Western Athletic Conference championship and made it to the elite eight at the NCAA national championships, amounting to the best season in the school's history to date. Alas, Snowden's last season was star-crossed, and on closing the 1981–82 season with a 9–18 showing, he retired. He was inducted into the University Hall of Fame in 1988.

Snowden's retirement opened the way to a new era in men's basketball with the arrival of Lute Olson, who transformed the Arizona squad over a tenure that lasted a quarter century. He had come to Arizona after a distinguished career at the University of Iowa, whose basketball arena was locally known as the "house that Lute built." That didn't stop Lute from bringing the Wildcats to his old home court in 1987 to face off against a team rated third in the country. On the fateful night of December 12, the Cats beat the Hawkeyes 66–59, one of many high points in a season that ended in national championship competition featuring some of the best players in the school's history, including Steve Kerr, who went on to serve as head coach of the NBA Golden State Warriors; Sean Elliott, later a player for the 1999 NBA champions the San Antonio Spurs; Kenny Lofton, who traded basketball for baseball after trying out for the Cats squad on a whim and immediately getting swept up in the 1988 MLB draft; and Harvey Mason, who became one of the most influential music producers in Hollywood, later heading the Recording Academy, the home of the Grammy Awards. So meaningful was that episode in Wildcat basketball history that in the 2021–22 season, the Wildcats revived the uniform of that era, marked by a saguaro logo, a large block "A" on one leg of the shorts, and the word "CATS" on the other side.

Lute, as he was universally known, was a genial but determined and hard-driving coach, and under his leadership a reinvigorated Arizona appeared in an unprecedented twenty-four consecutive games at the NCAA tournament, taking the national championship in 1997. As the noted *Arizona Daily Star* sportswriter Greg Hansen exalts of one run-up to that extraordinary victory, "Arizona 85, Kansas, 82, March 21, 1997 in Birmingham, Alabama. The Jayhawks were 35–1 and a clear favorite to win the national championship. When Arizona pulled off an almost unimaginable upset, it made possible a trip to the Final Four and follow-up victories over No. 1 seeds North Carolina and Kentucky, the first time any team had ever defeated three No. 1 seeds in the Big Dance. Beating Kansas made it all possible."

But let Grant Hill, the legendary Duke University shooter, tell the story of a doomed date with the Cats in 1991. As he writes in his 2022 memoir *Game*, "We traveled to Arizona to play a Wildcat team whose entire roster was seemingly seven feet. We clawed to force the game into one overtime and then another. The game was so tense, the air so dry, that the gum I grinded on dissolved into paste by the time the second overtime opened. We dropped the

The Wildcat men's basketball squad takes the court against the University of Wisconsin Badgers on December 9, 2023. The Cats won, 98–73, retaining their number 1 ranking in the Associated Press Top 25 poll. Photograph by David Olsen.

game, knowing that we could and should have beaten them." To which a local fan might have replied, nah, not a chance: in that 1991 double-overtime game, the Cats took Duke 103–96, a monumental victory considering Duke's reputation as one of the best basketball schools in the country. It would take a full decade before Duke got its revenge, beating the Cats 82–72 at the 2001 NCAA tournament.

Lute Olson was inducted into the Naismith Memorial Basketball Hall of Fame in 2002, two years after suffering a debilitating stroke. After two season-long leaves of absence, he reluctantly retired in 2008 with an extraordinary record of 589–188. When he left, he had put into place an organization that no team in the country dared take anything but seriously and had established the University of Arizona as a basketball powerhouse. Named National Coach of the Year five times, Lute passed away in 2020. The following year, Tommy Lloyd was lured away from Gonzaga University to become head coach. Over the first fifty games of his first season, Lloyd led the Wildcats to a 45–5 record, the second-best record in NCAA history.

At forty years old, Bear Down Gym was in a state of some disrepair in the late 1960s, small, and without much of a maintenance budget. One former athletic director, Dick Clausen, told Greg Hansen that he had begun agitating for a new gym almost as soon as he was hired in 1958, but he met indifference in the administration and sometimes hostility from penny-pinching legislators, especially those whose districts were in Arizona State University territory. Finally, after brainstorming with the politically astute University vice president Marvin "Swede" Johnson, Clausen figured out how to overcome their objections: name the new gym for Pop McKale, who was well respected around the state. The ploy worked, and in 1973, the Wildcat basketball squad and the athletic administration relocated to a new home at the McKale Memorial Center on the southeast edge of the campus, the street before it fittingly called Fred Enke Drive.

The facilities were a vast improvement over the old Bear Down Gym, with seating for 14,750 fans and a state-of-the-art synthetic floor that promised superior performance—but that, within a couple of years, developed so many air bubbles and cracks that it was pulled up and replaced with a traditional maple floor. That fix having been made, the McKale Memorial Center is considered one of the preeminent collegiate sports arenas in the United States. The basketball court is named in honor of Lute Olson and his wife, Bobbi Olson, whose contributions to the University of Arizona are inestimable.

BUILDING A WINNING TEAM

Women's Basketball

I **N 1912,** the year Arizona became a state, a group of women students approached President Arthur Wilde and requested permission to organize a basketball squad. Wilde, it's said, brushed aside the request, pointing out that they had a nice patch of grass outside their dormitory on which to play the far more fitting game of croquet. Undeterred, a few years later, the women students began to organize intramural games, using the hoops at Herring Hall when they were free, first playing class against class (the juniors won against the seniors in 1922) and then organizing a varsity squad that played a terribly limited schedule—intramural games, mostly, with occasional bouts against Tucson High School and, farther afield, what would one day become Arizona State University.

Only in 1971, half a century after those first organized games, did the University join the Association of Intercollegiate Athletics for Women, fielding a women's basketball team for the first time. The following year, the Lady Wildcats, as they were known, closed their inaugural season with an 8–4 record. A decade later, in 1981, the team joined the NCAA, becoming part of the new Pac-10 Conference in 1986 and the Pac-12 Conference in 2011. During that time, the team won slots in the annual NCAA tournament eight times, going all the way to the Final Four in 2021 and then losing the championship game to Stanford only by a point, a heartbreaking 53–54.

Seven of those championship runs were under the helm of Joan Bonvicini, the winningest coach in University of Arizona women's basketball history, with 287 victories in her tenure between 1991 and 2008. Bonvicini arrived with the diplomatic remark that she was "starting from scratch," five of the six coaches who preceded her having amassed what can only charitably be described as a dismal record (37–100 between 1980 and 1985, to name one particularly sad era).

It was head coach Adia Barnes who took the women's team farthest up the championship ladder. Arriving in 2016, she had played for Bonvicini over four sparkling seasons between 1995 and 1999, racking up twenty-two individual records while she was at it and becoming the first University women's player to be drafted into the WNBA, where she played for a succession of teams before moving on to play internationally in Italy, Israel, and Ukraine. Bonvicini offered a coaching spot to Barnes in 2010, but she was still enjoying a strong career as a player and declined. A few more years would pass before Barnes returned to Tucson, and a few more before her team, with players from all over the United States and Europe and captained by the extraordinary Aari McDonald, reached its pinnacle in 2021—its pinnacle to date, that is. Go Cats!

FIGHT, WILDCATS, FIGHT

The Pride of Arizona

IN **1929**, a chemistry major and future state legislator named Douglas Stanley "Doug" Holsclaw, a former "yell leader" at University of Arizona athletic events, composed a fight song that he called "Fight! Wildcats! Fight!" For some reason, the sheet music was scored for ukulele, banjo, and guitar, hardly the brass and drums that a good scrum calls for. After it was first played at the 1930 homecoming game, it fell into the hands of the popular singer Rudy Vallee, who performed the song nationally with his big band on NBC Radio a few weeks later.

Holsclaw's composition enjoyed a good run, serving as the school's official pep anthem until, in 1952, a band director named Jack K. Lee flew over the University on his way to interview for the job here and saw "Bear Down" written on the roof of the gym. Inspired, he wrote a fittingly titled song, "Bear Down, Arizona":

> *Bear Down, Arizona*
> *Bear Down, Red and Blue*
> *Bear Down, Arizona*
> *Hit 'em hard, let 'em know who's who;*
> *Bear Down, Arizona*
> *Bear Down, Red and Blue*
> *Go, go, Wildcats, go;*
> *Arizona, Bear Down*

Bear Down Gym, as seen from the air in 1929.

Both Holsclaw and Lee had superb marching bands to perform their tunes at athletic events. That tradition dates to 1902, when the ROTC fielded a twelve-member band. The ROTC band lasted until 1920, when the University recruited forty student musicians for a full-strength band, offering a unit of credit for their service. The assembled band first performed at the opening of the 1922 football season and was hailed as the best marching band in the West, a distinction awarded many times over the next decades. So popular was the band that it performed at the halftime show for the inaugural Super Bowl in Los Angeles, and it marched in the parade at the inauguration of President Jimmy Carter. In 2009 and again in 2015, it was ranked as one of the ten best marching bands in the country by a conference of college band directors.

The Pride of Arizona, as the marching band is now called, has more than 250 members today—musicians, a drum line, baton twirlers, a cheer section, and a color guard. Go to any Wildcats game, and you'll find that it's as much fun to watch them in action as what's happening on the court or field. Now under the direction of Allison Howard, the students are clearly having fun too, and they're a great source of Wildcat pride indeed.

MAKING THE PITCH

Wildcat Softball

THE FIRST softball game in the world was played in 1887, and women were playing softball on the University of Arizona campus not long afterward. It seems strange, then, that it was only in 1974 that the Arizona Wildcats formally inaugurated a fast-pitch squad—but once that happened, the Wildcats were off and running, entering pennant races and winning championships in conferences around the country.

The very first Wildcat team, coached by Judy Spray, chalked up an inaugural season record of 11–3 and went to the Women's College World Series. Squads went to the series again in 1975, 1977, and 1979. The Cats moved out of the Intermountain Conference to the Western Collegiate Athletic Association in 1981, remaining with the conference after it became the Pac-10, and returned to NCAA postseason play in 1987.

It's no coincidence that 1987 was the first full year that a powerhouse of a coach, Mike Candrea, headed the team. Candrea stayed with the Cats from 1986 to 2021, retiring with the distinction of having the most wins in collegiate softball history: 1,674 of them, to be exact, including eight national titles. Each year from 1988 to 2003, the Wildcats appeared in every Women's College World Series, winning their first national championship in 1991 and repeating the victory in 1993, 1994, 1996, 1997, 2001, 2006, and 2007. All told, the Cats made twenty-five World Series appearances in the thirty-four years between 1988 and 2022.

It wasn't Candrea who won those games, of course, but instead class after class of phenomenal players out on the field. One was Jennie Lynn Finch, who played from 1999 to 2002 and pitched her way to the national championship in 2001. Ranked the second-greatest player in women's collegiate softball history, she went on to pitch for the gold medal–winning U.S. team in the 2004 Athens Summer Olympics. She returned to the Olympics in 2008, helping the American team win the silver medal in Beijing, and played professional softball until retiring in 2010.

A winning pitcher needs a winning catcher. One of the best was Dejah Mulipola, who played from 2017 to 2021, Candrea's last year. Ranking as the team's second-best fielding catcher in its history, Mulipola smacked out her fiftieth home run in her redshirt senior year, ending her collegiate career at the 2021 Women's College World Series. The previous year, she played for the silver award–winning U.S. team at the Tokyo Olympics, and she went on to play pro ball.

Jenny Dalton played second base from 1993 to 1996. She also racked up fifty home runs, as well as an .800 hitting percentage and two hundred RBIs, a conference record, and was named Pac-10 player of the year in her final season. Lovieanne Jung transferred to Arizona in her third year, playing shortstop and, with Jennie Finch, she served on the U.S. Olympic teams of 2004 and 2008; she earned the Pac-10 top five record for batting percentage at .838. At third base, Jenae Leles, another fifty-homer hitter, was on the national championship Wildcat teams of 2006 and 2007. Leah Braatz, Nancy Evans, Leticia Pineda, Amy Chellevold—the list of top-ranked players goes on, and it will surely grow as new players step up to the plate.

Playing at home in the Rita Hillenbrand Memorial Stadium, the women's softball team is now coached by Caitlin Lowe, a former player who was on the championship 2006 and 2007 squads and just one of six players to date to be named an All-American every year she played. Look for many more championship seasons for the team to come.

A footnote: Mike Candrea was with the softball Cats for a long stretch. So, too, was Dave Rubio, who coached women's volleyball for thirty-one years until retiring in 2023. Along with Candrea, he was one of just six Wildcats coaches to be named National Coach of the Year, and his list of All-American players—including Kim Glass, Jennifer Abernathy, Kendra Dahlke, and Madi Kingdon—will be familiar to every collegiate volleyball fan. With his teams, Rubio won 570 games, a Pac-12 record, and led the Wildcats to twenty NCAA tournament appearances.

AN OASIS IN THE DESERT

Arizona Swimming

IT MAKES good sense that a school located in a perennially hot environment would consider a swimming pool to be a good thing. It does not necessarily follow that such a school would build a world-class swimming facility and develop into a powerhouse of competitive swimming, but that's just what has happened at the University of Arizona over the years.

Swimming has long been a favorite recreation at the University. The first pool went in near the Engineering Building in 1916—though, perhaps in order to minimize the luxurious nature of the structure, it was labeled a reservoir for irrigation and firefighting that just happened to be lined with concrete and whose water recirculated to prevent the buildup of algae. A couple of other pools followed, one reserved for men behind Bear Down Gym, another built at the rear of the new Student Union in the 1950s and available to all students. The swimming pool completed in 1973 as part of the new McKale Athletic Center was coed as well. The McKale Pool was renamed the William G. and Dolores D. Hillenbrand Aquatic Center in May 1989, following a generous gift from that family, and completely remade into an Olympic-level facility devoted to training for the men's and women's swimming and diving programs. It received a $15 million renovation in 2018–19 with the addition of the 25 × 33-meter Kasser Family Pool. Today, with twenty-two lanes and a diving pool depth of seventeen feet, the Hillenbrand Aquatic Center is considered one of the nation's premier outdoor competitive aquatic facilities.

Throughout its history, the University has fielded competitive swimming and diving teams, though it was in the 1970s that its squads were consistently strong. First represented in the 1960 Olympics, Wildcat athletes had taken thirty-seven gold, twenty-seven silver, and

The women's swimming team in 1931.

fifteen bronze medals as of the 2020 Tokyo Olympics; the first medalist, in fact, was swimmer Patty Kempner, who won a gold at the Rome Olympics in 1960 as part of the women's 400-meter medley team. Swimming and diving have continued to represent an outsize portion of these wins, with, for example, current women's diving coach Michele Mitchell earning silver medals in 1984 and 1988 and two of her students, Claire Febvay and Angelique Rodriguez, making three Olympic appearances apiece.

No Wildcat has earned more Olympic medals to date than Amanda Beard, who won two gold, four silver, and one bronze medal in long-form breaststroke and intermediate medley events between 1996 and 2004. A world record holder, Beard went on to enjoy a career in advertising and modeling before becoming a sportscaster. Amy Van Dyken earned an astounding six gold medals in the 1996 and 2000 Olympics in events including the 100-meter butterfly, 50-meter freestyle, and 400-meter medley.

Now on the coaching staff, Lara Jackson was a nine-time NCAA champion during her years as a Wildcat and, in 2009, won national titles in the relay, medley, and freestyle events. And no one will be surprised if Delaney Schnell, named Pac-12 Scholar Athlete of the Year in 2023, adds to her medal count in diving—including a silver at the Tokyo Olympics in the 10-meter synchronized event—over a long and promising career to come.

The men's side has seen many victories as well. One recent Wildcat, Brooks Fail, holds four of ten top times in swimming events and tore up the water in his favorite event, the 500-meter freestyle. Nick Thoman won silver and gold medals in the 2012 Olympics, the first for the 400-meter backstroke and the second for the 4 × 200-meter medley. Swimming for South Africa in three Olympics, Ryk Neethling took gold in the 400-meter freestyle relay in 2004. Simon Burnett, another triple Olympian, swam for Great Britain in 2012, six years after being named the University's outstanding male athlete. And two Olympians, Nathan Adrian and Matt Grevers, are now volunteer coaches at Hillenbrand, working with veteran Wildcat swimmer and head coach August Busch to hone cohorts of victors to come.

Among other notable accomplishments, the University of Arizona is the home of the first-ever collegiate para swimming program. Founded in 2021 under coach Laura Utsch, the initial squad was made up of already enrolled students, but as of 2023 the team is reaching out to recruit adaptive swimmers from all over the country. The growing team now participates in Paralympic events and other national competitions.

The University seal greets the sunset, with "A" Mountain in the distance. Photograph courtesy of the University of Arizona.

WILDCATS FOREVER

Some Notable Alumni

COUNTLESS PEOPLE—STUDENTS, faculty, and staff—have passed through the volcanic gates of the University of Arizona since it was founded in 1885. Many of those Wildcats have become well known, representing just about every pursuit, as the following list, a very brief one at that, suggests.

Joseph M. Acaba (1967–), hydrogeologist, astronaut

Richard W. Aldrich (1953–), neuroscientist

Hector Avalos (1958–2021), biblical scholar, anthropologist, professor

Lew Ayres (1908–96), actor, musician

Marianne Banes (1957–), chef

Ron Barber (1945–), politician, business owner

Carla Blackwell (1957–), urban planner

Daniel W. Bradley (1941–), physician, virologist, codiscoverer of the hepatitis C virus

Brian Bromberg (1960–), musician, producer

Jerry Bruckheimer (1943–), television and film producer

Eduardo Cadava (1954–), literary critic and historian, professor

Richard H. Carmona (1949–), physician, former U.S. Surgeon General

John P. Carpenter (1957–), archaeologist

Edison Cassadore (1962–), Native American literature scholar, professor

Robert Cauthorn (1956–), journalist and technologist

Anna Maria Chávez (1968–), attorney, inspirational speaker, former Girl Scouts of the USA CEO

Jessica Cox (1983–), pilot, martial artist, motivational speaker

Max Cutler (1990–), entrepreneur, producer

Ettore "Ted" DeGrazia (1909–1982), sculptor, artist

Autumn DiGaetano-Fedoruk (1983–), humanities scholar, business leader

Jay Anthony Dobyns (1961–), undercover law enforcement officer, author, actor, football coach

Travis Edmonson (1932–2009), songwriter, musician

Sherman Fairchild (1896–1971), business leader, inventor

Mitchell Freedman (1957–), architect

Jim Furyk (1970–), professional golfer and Olympian

José Galvez (1949–), photographer, journalist

Brian Garfield (1939–2018), novelist, screenwriter

Paul Giblin (1966–), Pulitzer Prize–winning journalist

Conrad F. Goeringer (1949–2012), publisher, bookseller, political activist

M. Andre Goodfriend (1957–), U.S. diplomat, humanities scholar

Andrew M. Greeley (1928–2013), Catholic priest, novelist, sociologist

Savannah Guthrie (1971–), sportscaster, journalist, attorney

Brad William Henke (1966–2022), professional football player, actor

Zeb Hogan (1973–), biologist, television personality

John Hughes (1950–2009), writer, film director

Robert Wood Johnson IV (1947–), business leader, diplomat, sports team owner

Kourtney Kardashian (1979–), media personality, entrepreneur

Jane Kay (1939–), journalist, environmentalist

Jefferson Keenan (1957–), musician, attorney

R. Alexandra Keith (1968–), business leader, entrepreneur

Steve Kerr (1965–), basketball player and coach, sports commentator

Barbara Kingsolver (1955–), author

Greg Kinnear (1963–), actor

Susan M. Knight (1956–), journalist

Aline Kominsky-Crumb (1948–2022), underground cartoonist

Jerry Livingston (1909–87), songwriter, musician

Lorna Lockwood (1903–77), attorney, Arizona Supreme Court justice

Terry J. Lundgren (1952–), business leader and Macy's chief executive officer

Thomas Keith Marshall (1870–1931), miner, editor, politician, business leader

Linda Eastman McCartney (1941–98), photographer, musician, author

James McMurtry (1962–), musician, actor

Dipti Mehta (1986–), dancer, actor, microbiologist

Andreas Gerasimos Michalitsianos (1947–97), astronomer, astrophysicist

Arturo Moreno (1946–), business leader, sports team owner

Craig T. Nelson (1944–), actor, automobile racer

Ai Ogawa (Florence Anthony) (1947–2010), poet, professor, scholar of Japanese literature

Donald R. Pettit (1955–), chemical engineer, astronaut

Jane Rigby (1978–), astrophysicist, Presidential Medal of Freedom awardee

John M. Roll (1947–2011), attorney, judge, law professor

Regina Romero (1974–), environmental activist, mayor of Tucson

Linda Ronstadt (1946–), singer, author

Richard Russo (1949–), novelist, screenwriter, professor

Rico Saccani (1952–), symphony conductor

Brian Schmidt (1967–), astronomer, Nobel Prize–winning astrophysicist

Francis Richard "Dick" Scobee (1939–86), aviator, astronaut

Emory Sekaquaptewa (1928–2007), attorney, judge, Hopi tribal leader

Garry Shandling (1949–2016), comedian, television personality and producer

Ron Shelton (1945–), novelist, screenwriter, filmmaker

Roger Smith (1932–2017), actor, screenwriter, producer

Frank Sotomayor (1944–), Pulitzer Prize–winning journalist

Stephen Spinella (1956–), actor

David Stern (1956–), musician

Clifford Stoll (1950–), computer scientist, author

Nora Sun (1937–2011), entrepreneur, diplomat

Vicki Lewis Thompson (1950–), novelist

Ayọ Tometi (1984–), communicator, political activist, cofounder of Black Lives Matter

Jonathan Van Ness (1987–), stylist, television personality

David Foster Wallace (1962–2008), novelist, essayist, professor

Kate Walsh (1967–), model, actor, entrepreneur

Paul Francis Wehrle (1921–2004), pediatrician, microbiologist, immunologist

Kristen Wiig (1973–), comedian, actor, screenwriter

Gordon Willey (1913–2002), archaeologist, professor

Timothy F. Winters (1953–), classicist, professor

The westernmost portion of the University Mall, flanked by the Administration Building, Student Union, and Old Main. The Joseph Wood Krutch Garden bisects the Mall in the middle distance. Photograph by Gregory McNamee.

ACKNOWLEDGMENTS

T IS early in the morning on an already blistering late August day in 1975, the monsoon clouds beginning to billow overhead, the cicadas studiously chirring away. Having chosen Harvard as a safety school but having had the good fortune to be admitted to the University of Arizona, I am waiting in a long line of first-year students to secure a punch card—if that term doesn't mean anything to you, never mind—that will allow me to gain admittance to a desired class. I fall into conversation with a fellow longhair who will become a lifelong friend, the renowned archaeologist John Carpenter. Another line, another punch card, six lines in all for six cards to secure a full course load. Along the way, I meet several other young men and women with whom I am still in touch, while some of those first-year courses will change the course of my life (turning me from a major in government, as political science was once called here, to anthropology, for one) and introduce me to a wealth of knowledge.

In five years as an undergraduate and graduate student at the University, I accrued countless intellectual debts to teachers, staff members, and fellow students. Most are mentioned by name in the text of this book, and while I'll risk leaving someone out inadvertently, I want to thank in particular Kathleen M. Sands, who gave me a D on my first freshman comp assignment and made me realize immediately that going to college was a far different matter from floating through high school; Lee Fischler, a spectacularly foulmouthed master of close reading; Rodney Peffer, Bess Strauss, Steve Strauss, and George Wood, who took me through the equivalent of graduate school in philosophy without my ever attending a single class in the field; Scott Mahler, my brother by another mother, and his fellow Michigander Mitch Freedman; my Virginia homies Scott Leysath and Joe Wooten, who came here to study the year before I did; Sterling Vinson, Thomas Worthen, Marie Bahr-Volk, and Richard Jensen, whose collective brilliance caused me to become, finally, a classics major, and fellow classics students David Stern, Kristy Kogianes, Timothy Winters, Todd Cooper, and Andre Goodfriend; Ellen Basso, Ray Thompson, Richard Diebold, and Timothy J. Finan, mentors in anthropology, and Thomas E. Sheridan, one of the finest anthropologists the University has ever produced; and William Christie, Paul Turner, Mary Jane Cook, and Sigmund Eisner, with whom I studied linguistics and the history of the English language in graduate school. All set examples that I hold close to my heart to this day.

After I earned my master's degree, I worked in Mexico for half a year but, suffering from a terrible illness, returned to Tucson to recover. It was my good luck, in that year of recession, to meet Elizabeth Shaw, then the assistant director of UA Press, who hired me as a proofreader early in 1981. By the time I left the press nearly ten years later to try my hand at full-time freelance writing and editing, I had worked my way up to the position of editor-in-chief. The authors I worked with—Nancy Mairs, Chuck Bowden, David Sapir, Joy Harjo, Edward Abbey, N. Scott Momaday, Tiana Bighorse, Richard Shelton, and Ofelia Zepeda, among scores of others—were a dream team whose writing remains influential decades on. I've managed to live without adult supervision since going freelance in 1990, but generations of staff members later, I think of the press as an extended family. I am particularly grateful to Kristen Buckles, the present editor-in-chief, and director Kathryn Conrad for inviting me to write this book. I am grateful as well to former University president John Schaefer, whom we have met on many pages here, and to Shan Sutton, dean of libraries, for their guidance, support, and encouragement. With his vast trove of institutional knowledge, Victor Baker, Regents Professor of hydrology and atmospheric sciences, geosciences, and planetary sciences, helped me avoid some entirely avoidable misinterpretations and errors. I take full responsibility for any that remain, to say nothing of any hallucinations masking themselves as memories.

Further thanks go to Jim Martin, who hired me as a student worker at the University bookstore for a couple of years in the late 1970s; Charles Davis, who lured me away from the bookstore with a graduate teaching fellowship in the English Department; Michelle Piontek, John Drabicki, Alex Sugiyama, Price Fishback, David Pingry, Mark Stegeman, Keisuke Hirano, Tom Dalton, and especially Mark Walker, of the Department of Economics in the Eller College of Management, where I taught an upper-level writing course for fourteen years; and William Plant, Kellee Campbell, Shiloe Fontes, and Shipherd Reed, who for many years have been kind enough to invite me to join them in creating exhibits at the Flandrau Science Center & Planetarium.

I owe thanks to dozens of staff members and faculty across the campus who helped answer my many questions, and particularly Jason Ground of the Office of University

Communications. (As for those who didn't help, well, please start responding to your email.) Tyler Meier and Sarah Kortemeier of the Poetry Center went above and beyond the call. My friend and University alum David Olsen's wonderful photographs grace many of these pages, and I'm honored to have them. Greg Hansen, sportswriter extraordinaire for the *Arizona Daily Star*, was generous in his reminiscences of Wildcat glories. The answers to many other questions came from two books: Phyllis Ball's self-published *Photographic History of the University of Arizona* and Douglas D. Martin's *The Lamp in the Desert: The Story of the University of Arizona* (UA Press), the former of which takes University's history from 1885 to 1985 and the latter from 1885 to 1960. John Schaefer generously shared with me his unpublished memoir of his time as president. As to quoted matter, in instances where living contemporaries are speaking, it is almost always in conversation with me as I researched this book, if not over coffee or enchiladas years ago. (There's a reason I keep extensive notes.) In a few instances, quotations from contemporaries are taken from University news stories, press releases, and web sites.

I dedicate this book to the memories of Conrad Goeringer, Phil Gerard, Rich Handler, Jane Hill, Scott Douglas McNamee, Paul Rosenblatt, Paul Simon, Emory Sekaquaptewa, Paul Smith, Donna Swaim, and other friends who have crossed the horizon, and I raise a glass to Wildcats past, present, and future for making the University of Arizona a place of wonder.

INDEX

ABOUT THE AUTHOR

Gregory McNamee (BA 1978, MA 1980) is a longtime Tucsonan transplanted from Virginia. He is the author of more than forty-five books and more than ten thousand periodical pieces. He is a contributing writer to *Kirkus Reviews* and a contributing editor and consultant in world geography to *Encyclopaedia Britannica*. Please visit his web page at www .gregorymcnamee.com and drop a note to him there or at mcnamee@arizona.edu.